THE ILLUSTRATED HISTORY OF THE
FIRST CRUSADES

THE ILLUSTRATED HISTORY OF THE
FIRST CRUSADES

AN EXPERT ACCOUNT OF THE FIRST, SECOND AND THIRD CAMPAIGNS TO
TAKE JERUSALEM, ILLUSTRATED WITH OVER 300 FINE ART PAINTINGS

CHARLES PHILLIPS

southwater

This edition is published by Southwater,
an imprint of Anness Publishing Ltd,
Blaby Road, Wigston,
Leicestershire LE18 4SE;
info@anness.com
www.southwaterbooks.com;
www.annesspublishing.com

Anness Publishing has a picture agency outlet
for images for publishing, promotions or
advertising. For more information, please visit
www.practicalpictures.com

Publisher: Joanna Lorenz
Editorial Director: Helen Sudell
Executive Editor: Joanne Rippin
Copy Editor: Jay Thundercliffe
Designer: Nigel Partridge
Jacket Design: Adelle Morris
Production Controller: Bessie Bai

ETHICAL TRADING POLICY
At Anness Publishing we believe that business
should be conducted in an ethical and
ecologically sustainable way, with respect for
the environment and a proper regard to
the replacement of the natural resources
we employ.

As a publisher, we use a lot of wood pulp in
high-quality paper for printing, and that wood
commonly comes from spruce trees. We are
therefore currently growing more than
750,000 trees in three Scottish forest planta-
tions. The forests we manage contain more
than 3.5 times the number of trees employed
each year in making paper for the books
we manufacture. Because of this ongoing eco-
logical investment programme, you, as our

customer, can have the pleasure and reassur-
ance of knowing that a tree is being cultivated
on your behalf to naturally replace the materials used to make the book you are holding.
For further information about this scheme, go
to www.annesspublishing.com/trees

Previously published as part of a larger
volume, *An Illlustrated History of The Crusades
and the Crusader Knights*

PUBLISHER'S NOTE
Although the information in this book is
believed to be accurate and true at the time
of going to press, neither the authors nor the
publisher can accept any legal responsibility
or liability for any errors or omissions that
may have been made in this book.

PICTURE ACKNOWLEDGEMENTS
ART ARCHIVE, pp7, 21t, 22t, 23t, 23b, 27t,
27b, 28t, 28br, 29, 40t, 32b, 35, 38br, 41b,
42b, 42b, 42t, 43tr, 44b, 45b 50, 51b, 54b,
54t, 57t, 68, 71t, 73t, 84, 94b, 95tr, 95b
254b, 115, 123t, 128, 129, 133, 136b, 137t,
137b, 139b, 141t, 158b.

BRIDGEMAN ART LIBRARY: pp1, 3, 7b, 9b,
12t, 20b, 21b, 24t, 25t, 25b, 26t, 26b, 28bl,
30t, 31t, 31b, 32t, 33, 34t, 34b, 36, 38t, 39t,
39b, 40b, 41t, 43tl, 44t, 45b, 46b, 46b, 47t,
48, 49, 51tl, 51tr, 53, 54b, 55t, 56b, 56t, 59t,
60, 61t, 62t, 62b, 63b, 64, 66, 67t, 67b, 69t,
69b, 70t, 70b, 71b, 74t, 75b, 76, 77t, 79b, 80,
81bl, 82b, 82t, 86b, 89t, 89b, 90, 91t, 92b,
93, 95tr, 96t, 96b, 97t, 97b, 98, 100, 101t,
103b, 104b, 105t, 106, 107tl, 107b, 107tr,
108t, 109t, 109b, 111t, 111b, 112t, 112b,
116t, 117t, 119t, 119r, 120b, 121b, 122t,
124b, 127, 132, 134, 135t, 135b, 140b, 141b,
142t, 142b, 143b, 145t, 146, 147b, 148b,
149t, 149b, 150, 151b, 152b, 153t, 153b,
154, 155t, 159t.

AKG pp2, 3tl, 3bm, 3br, 4tl, 4bl, 6t, 6b, 7t,
8b, 9t, 10b, 11t, 15b, 18, 30b, 38br, 52t, 57b,
58, 72t, 73b, 75t, 79t, 81t, 83br, 83, 88, 93t,
99, 103tr, 108b, 110, 113t, 114, 116b, 117b,
118b, 120t, 122b, 123b, 124t, 125l, 125t,
138b, 138t, 139t, 143t, 144, 145b, 147t,
151t, 158t.

ANCIENT ART AND ARCHITECTURE: 14t,
52b, 61b, 94t, 140t.

CONTENTS

INTRODUCTION

On 7 June 1099 the Christian armies of the First Crusade came within sight of Jerusalem, the city they passionately desired to liberate from its Muslim rulers, the Fatimids of Cairo. The crusaders' journey from Europe to Jerusalem had taken no less than three years, and involved great suffering and the loss of thousands of lives. Now, on the hillside celebrated as Mountjoie ('Mount Joy') by pilgrims, crusaders fell to their knees, many in tears and kissing the ground, praying for God's help to set free the city in which Jesus Christ had, according to their beliefs, taught, suffered, died and risen again.

The armies had been mobilized by a dramatic sermon delivered by Pope Urban II at Clermont, France, on 27 November 1095. He had called a holy war to drive what he called the 'vile race' of 'Turks and Arabs' from the Holy Land, and had personified the city of Jerusalem – 'from you,' he said, addressing the knights, soldiers,

▼ *Peter the Hermit, the monk who managed to mobilize the People's Crusade, preaches to the pilgrims.*

▲ *The Crusader army catches its first sight of the city of Jerusalem, 7 June 1099.*

churchmen and others in his audience, 'She asks for help!' Urban's sermon in fact inspired two expeditions to Jerusalem: first, a popular movement of pilgrims and soldiers known as the People's Crusade left in April 1096; second, the Princes' Crusade – a group of five armies commanded by nobles and minor members of European royalty – departed in stages from mid-summer 1096 onwards. After many desperate setbacks, the remnants of the People's Crusade, led by Peter the Hermit, united with the princes' armies on the march on Jerusalem.

MUSLIMS IN THE EAST

Pope Urban made his declaration at Clermont in response to a plea from Alexius I Comnenus, ruler of the Christian Byzantine empire of Constantinople, for aid from the Christians of Europe in fighting Islamic forces in the eastern Mediterranean. In particular, Alexius wanted reinforcements to combat the Seljuk Turks who had defeated one of his predecessors as emperor, Romanos IV Diogenes, at the Battle of Manzikert on 26

August 1071; in the wake of this victory the Seljuks had captured a great deal of territory from the Byzantines, but by the 1090s Seljuk power appeared to be on the wane after decades of expansion and Alexius saw an opportunity to fight back. The Seljuks were only the latest in a long line of formidable Islamic forces that opposed the Byzantines and other Christians in the eastern Mediterranean. The faith of Islam had been established in Arabia around 500 years earlier by the Prophet Muhammad (c.570-632). Its followers, Muslims, had spread at stunning speed northwards and eastwards from the Arabian peninsula – winning remarkable victories against the powerful Byzantine and Persian empires, in the course of which they captured Damascus in Syria in 635, the Persian capital Ctesiphon in 637 and Jerusalem in 638. They then moved far beyond towards India and China. They had also headed westwards, capturing Alexandria in Egypt from the Byzantines in 643, then taking lands across northern Africa and into Spain. Their attempts to invade France were turned back at the celebrated Battle of Tours of 732 by the King of the Franks, Charles Martel.

By this date the rulers of the Islamic empire, the Umayyad caliphs, had control of a territory greater than that held by the Roman empire at its height. The Umayyads governed from Damascus, but they were ousted in 750 by their cousins the Abbasids, who moved their capital to Baghdad in Iraq; a separate dynasty, the Fatimids, was established in Egypt. By the time of the First Crusade another Muslim force, the Seljuk Turks – tribesmen from central Asia who had converted to Islam – had control of Baghdad and had captured much of Palestine from the Fatimids. The Seljuks were a particular problem for the Byzantine empire in Anatolia. (When the crusade armies reached Jerusalem in 1099, the city was held once again by the

▲ *In the encounters between Christian crusaders and their Muslim enemies, both sides called on God to support their cause.*

Fatimids, who had recaptured it from the Seljuks in 1098.)

In March 1095 Alexius sent ambassadors to appeal to Pope Urban II at the Council of Piacenza in northern Italy. His message made much of the threat to Christian holy places posed by the Turks. Probably in this communication, and certainly in a surviving earlier letter to Count Robert II of Flanders, Alexius sought to stir up the anger of European warriors by alleging that the Seljuks were terrorizing Christians in the east, performing forced circumcision of boys and raping women; these accusations were repeated by Urban in his speech at Clermont. Alexius was hoping to mobilize an army of disciplined, well armed knights, but got more than he bargained for when Urban's speech inspired the creation of the vast, impassioned but largely ill-equipped forces of the People's Crusade.

PILGRIMS, SOLDIERS, CRUSADERS

The crusaders embarked on the great journey to the Holy Land for a variety of reasons. Most were driven by religious fervour. In his speech at Clermont, Pope Urban explicitly called on his listeners to go to the Holy Land as a form of pilgrimage and of penance. He decreed that undertaking this dangerous mission effectively guaranteed an individual's salvation, declaring – according to the account of his speech by Robert the Monk, a 12th-century chronicler of the crusade – 'Take on this journey for the remission of sins, in confidence of the undying glory of God's kingdom.' There was an established tradition of pilgrimages by European Christians to visit the scenes of Christ's life in the Holy Land and Jerusalem, particularly the

▼ *The religious element of the crusades is perfectly illustrated by the rise of the orders of warrior monks.*

Church of the Holy Sepulchre, said to contain Christ's burial place, and every member of the crusade armies made a vow to go to Jerusalem and offer prayers in this church.

Many of the knights in the army were also seeking honour and glory. Knights were mounted warriors, usually landholders providing military service to their lord in return for the right to hold land as a fiefdom under the feudal system that structured medieval society. According to the chivalric code that governed knightly behaviour at the time, a knight was expected to seek opportunities to develop and demonstrate his prowess in battle and prove himself worthy of knighthood.

A few participants must also have been excited by the adventure, and the opportunity to enrich themselves through the spoils of battle: at Clermont Pope Urban emphasized the great wealth in the lands of the East and told his listeners, 'the possessions of the enemy will be yours … since you will make their treasures your spoils.' However, it should also be noted that it was extremely expensive for a knight to mount, dress and equip himself to go on crusade and many crusaders had to mortgage their property or sell their land to afford the expedition.

The knights, soldiers and others who embarked for Jerusalem did not call their venture a crusade or themselves crusaders. Above all they saw their enterprise as a pilgrimage. On the dramatic day of Urban's sermon at Clermont the many men who poured forward to pledge themselves to the task reportedly began to mark their clothes with a cross, in devout reference to the Cross on which Christ died, and the pilgrim-soldiers in the armies became known as crucesignati ('those bearing the mark of the Cross'). The word 'crusade' did not come into general use until the 12th or 13th century, and entered English by way of Old French crozada and Spanish cruzada and more modern French croisade.

JERUSALEM CAPTURED

In June 1099 the Christian army began a siege of Jerusalem. Its Fatimid governor, Iftikhar al-Daula, had strengthened the fortifications, expelled the Christian inhabitants of the city so none could admit their compatriots and sent for a relief army from the Fatimid capital of Cairo. The crusaders set to work building wooden siege towers and on 15 July, after they had made a penitential procession around the city walls, they captured Jerusalem.

Then for two days they ran riot, looting and slaughtering the inhabitants of the city, both Jews and Muslims. Arabs called the crusaders Franj ('Franks') and chronicler ibn al-Athir wrote of the terrible attack in mid-July, 'the Franj spent a week slaying Muslims … Jews had gathered in their synagogue and the Franj burned them alive. They also attacked the saints' monuments and the tomb of Abraham, may peace be upon him.' According to the Gesta Francorum ('The Deeds of the Franks'), an anonymous chronicle of the crusade written in 1100–1101, the attackers pursued the fleeing defenders

▼ *At Nicaea, Antioch and Jerusalem, the armies of the First Crusade used siege equipment against the city fortifications.*

ruthlessly, killing and dismembering them all the way to the Temple of Solomon where 'there was so much killing that the blood came up to our ankles.' Many took the opportunity to enrich themselves – according to the same account, 'the crusaders seized silver and gold, mules and horses, and buildings full of all manner of riches.'

In the aftermath the crusaders elected European nobleman Godfrey of Bouillon, who had been a leading figure in the crusade and one of the first men to scale the walls, as their ruler. He refused to be named king in the city in which Christ had died and took the title 'Defender of the Holy Sepulchre'. Then they defeated a Fatimid relief army of around 50,000 troops led by vizier (administrator) al-Afdal Shahanshah at Ascalon, 35 miles (55km) east of Jerusalem.

Thereafter the majority of the crusaders departed for home, having achieved – against all odds - the task they had set out to do. However, a core group of perhaps no more than 300 knights and 2,000 foot soldiers remained to defend the territories they had captured.

OUTREMER, THE LAND OVERSEAS

In the course of the crusade and its aftermath the crusaders established four Christian territories in the Holy Land. These were together known as Outremer (from French for 'the land overseas', so called because the territories lay on the eastern shore of the Mediterranean). The first was the County of Edessa, established by Baldwin of Boulogne and based on the city of Edessa (modern Urfa, Turkey) in 1098; the second was the Principality of Antioch, based on the Syrian city of that name and established by Bohemond of Taranto in the same year.

The third territory was the Kingdom of Jerusalem, created in 1100 in the aftermath of the city's capture. Following the death of Godfrey of Bouillon, his brother Baldwin of Boulogne (now known as Baldwin of Edessa) was crowned King of Jerusalem – unlike his brother, he had no qualms about accepting the royal title. A fourth territory was the County of Tripoli, established in 1109 and ruled initially by Bertrand, an illegitimate son of crusader lord Raymond of Toulouse who had died in 1105. The territories of Outremer survived in one form or another until 1291 when the last European Christians in the Holy Land were driven out by another Muslim force, the Mamluks of Egypt.

WARRIOR MONKS AND CASTLES

The defence of Christian territories in Outremer was in part the responsibility of groups of warrior monks created with papal blessing in the aftermath of the First Crusade. The Knights Hospitaller of St John of Jerusalem had its origins in a group running and defending a hospice (guest dwelling) or hospital for pilgrims to Jerusalem; the brotherhood was recognized by Pope Paschal II in 1113.

The Poor Knights of Christ and the Temple of Solomon began as a body of knights formed to protect pilgrims to Jerusalem: they were recognized by the Church at the Council of Troyes in 1129 and confirmed by Pope Innocent II in 1139. The brotherhood was later known as the Knights Templar. Other brotherhoods included the Teutonic Knights, the Knights of St Lazarus and the Knights of St Thomas Acon.

The warrior monks had a reputation for waging war with ferocity and great brav-

▼ The ruins of Castle Belvoir still stand in Lower Galilee, Israel.

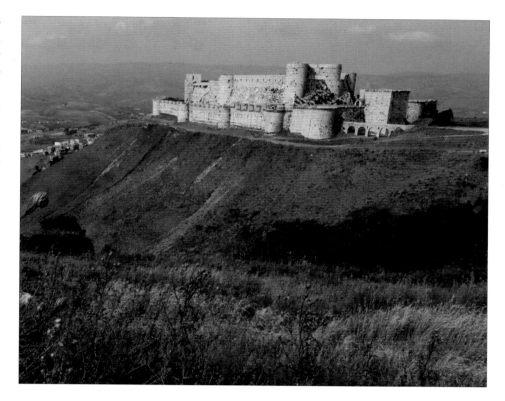

ery. They built and garrisoned a number of castles in the territories of Outremer, including Krak des Chevaliers ('Castle of the Knights') at Qal'at al-Hisn in Syria, which was held by the Knights Hospitaller, Belvoir (also held by the Hospitallers) 12 miles (20km) south of the Sea of Galilee in Jordan and Chastel Blanc, a Templar fortress in northwestern Syria.

A SECOND CRUSADE

Muslim powers in the Middle East regrouped and fought back against the Christian lords of Outremer. On Christmas Eve 1144 Imad ed-Din Zengi, the ruler of Aleppo and Mosul, stunned

▲ The still impressive crusader castle, Krak des Chevaliers, was one of the many fortresses built by the Templars.

the Christian world by recapturing the crusader-held city of Edessa. Pope Eugenius III called a second crusade in a bull issued on 1 December 1145 and again on 1 March 1146.

French churchman Abbot Bernard of Clairvaux, a brilliant orator, preached the crusade and inspired many of the great rulers of Europe to take the cross. These included Kings Louis VII of France and Conrad III of Germany, as well as Frederick, Duke of Swabia (subsequently the Emperor Frederick I Barbarossa). However, the campaign was a humiliating failure that included a terrible defeat at Dorylaeum at the hands of the Seljuk Turks and ended in an unsuccessful siege of Damascus.

A THIRD CRUSADE

Meanwhile the Muslims in the eastern Mediterranean increasingly overcame past divisions to pursue a jihad or holy war against those they saw as European invaders. Syria was reunited under Imad ed-Zengi's son Nur ed-Din after he took power in Damascus in 1154. He embarked on a series of efforts to oust the Fatimids in Egypt and in 1169 his general Asad ed-Din Shirkuh bin Shadhi and Shirkuh's nephew Salah ed-Din Yusuf (later called Saladin) took power in Cairo. After Shirkuh died just three months later, Saladin himself became vizier of Egypt. He was determined to create a new Islamic empire by uniting Egypt and Syria. He also moved against the Christians in the Holy Land, inflicting a heavy defeat on them at the Battle of the Horns of Hattin on 4 July 1187, during which he captured the treasured Relic of the True Cross (reputedly a piece of the cross on which Christ was crucified). He recaptured Jerusalem on 2 October that year.

Defeat in the Battle of the Horns of Hattin and the loss of the relic of the True Cross caused consternation in Europe and Pope Gregory VII had issued a bull calling for a new crusade in October 1187 before news of the fall of Jerusalem had even reached Italy. In 1188 Kings Philip II of France and Henry II of England and Emperor Frederick I of Germany all committed themselves to the venture. Before Henry II could depart he died at Chinon, France, in 1189 but his son Richard I did

▲ German Emperor, Frederick, was one of the European leaders to respond to Pope Gregory VII's call for a Second Crusade.

embark. In September 1191 Richard won a notable victory over Saladin at the Battle of Arsuf, but he did not proceed to besiege and retake Jerusalem, probably because he realized that although he was well placed to capture the city he did not have sufficient manpower to hold it against an

inevitable response from Saladin. The crusade ended in a negotiated settlement at the Treaty of Jaffa.

NUMBERING THE CRUSADES

The armies who fought to recapture Jerusalem in 1096-99 did not imagine they were taking part in the first of a series of holy wars, for they believed they had embarked on a divinely inspired mission to establish Christian rule in the Holy Land. Moreover, as we have seen, the word 'crusade' was not used by contemporaries. Later historians labelled and numbered the crusades and agreed a list of nine crusades, including the three – First (1095-99), Second (1147-49) and Third (1189-92) – covered in this volume, and then also the Fourth (1202-04), Fifth (1217-21), Sixth (1228-29), Seventh (1248-54), Eighth (1270) and Ninth 1271-72) described in this book's companion volume.

Modern historians have had disagreements over this list, for there were several smaller crusades between the ones listed above (including some covered in this book, in 1101 and 1107-08) and there

◄ Saladin and Richard I fight at the Battle of Arsuf, during the Third Crusade.

were other crusades in Europe (for example, against Islamic Moors in Spain and groups such as the Cathars of southern France, declared heretics by the Roman Catholic Church) that are not included in the traditional list. In this book and its companion volume, for reasons of clarity and to make it easier to compare this account with other published sources, we have followed the traditional numbering and refer to other crusades by name (generally its leader or destination) or date.

THE CRUSADES AND THE CULT OF CHIVALRY

The events described in this book left a deeply troublesome historical legacy that is still being worked through today. As a result, the crusades have a fierce modern relevance, for study of the causes and events of these wars of faith remains profoundly relevant at a time when political and religious leaders still seek to summon the memory of the crusades and of jihad in their attempts to mobilize followers.

Moreover, beginning in the very years in which the crusades took place, chivalric literature played a key part in the development in the institution of knighthood; the great deeds of knights were presented in poems, songs and chronicles as a source of inspiration to new chivalric acts. Godfrey of Bouillon was the subject of a cycle of chansons de geste (songs celebrating the deeds of knights) in the 11th century. The cycle included the Chanson d'Antioche ('Song of Antioch') of c.1180,

▲ *Godfrey of Bouillon, French knight and crusader hero of many* chansons de geste, *is pictured here conquering Jerusalem.*

reputedly based on an earlier poem written during the First Crusade by Richard le Pélerin ('Richard the Pilgrim'), who is said to have travelled on the crusade and begun the poem during the Siege of Antioch. Richard I, the English king celebrated as Coeur de Lion ('Lion-hearted') on account of his great courage, was the subject of an Anglo-Norman romance 'Richard Coeur de Lion' just 50 years after his death (1199), and this was reworked in an English romance of the late 13th century. These and later works made

much of Richard's rivalry and encounters with Saladin. Clashes between the two were the subject of surviving illustrations, including a celebrated image of the pair jousting in the English Luttrell psalter of c.1340. In the medieval period – and, subsequently, for more modern audiences – chivalric literature, while it often amplified the deeds and reputation of the figures involved, created an enduring image of the knight as an embodiment of noble virtues, of bravery, simplicity of spirit, undaunted religious faith and strength of character.

▼ *A noble crusader knight spears a Saracen in an illustration from the Luttrell psalter.*

THE KINGDOMS OF PALESTINE

To understand the movements of the great crusading armies, and appreciate the drama of their adventures, it is helpful to know the routes they took and the boundaries they crossed.

Tracing the long and dangerous journey made on the First Crusade underlines the enterprise's vast ambition and daring (shown on the map below). From central and northern Europe, some from as far north as England, or from southern France, by a variety of routes – across the Holy Roman Empire and Hungary, or through Italy and by sea across the southern Adriatic – the great armies marched under the banner of the cross to Constantinople, capital of the Byzantine empire, then on across Anatolia and down the Mediterranean coast towards their glittering goal, the Holy City of Jerusalem.

Across these thousands of miles trailed many, many thousand men (and some women), first the somewhat ragged forces of the People's Crusade – according to Byzantine princess Anna Comnena, to see them was 'like looking at rivers flooding together from all directions' – then no fewer than five princely armies. The routes of the four main princely armies are detailed on the map. Faith and the inspirational words of Urban II and the crusade preachers drove them on and helped them keep their nerve: this was a great adventure but also a daunting and frequently terrifying challenge. In taking the cross many had cried 'God wills it!' and the belief that they were destined to achieve their goal bore the core of the crusaders onward in the face of hardship, defeats and the deaths of comrades. More than

three years elapsed between the departure of the first elements of the People's Crusade in April 1096 and the bloody capture of Jerusalem in July 1099.

JERUSALEM

With the Holy City in Christian hands for the first time since AD638, the crusaders began building. They erected a palace beside the al-Aqsa Mosque, in the place

▼ *The first of the main princely armies to depart was that of Godfrey of Bouillon, who left Lorraine in August 1096. Bohemond of Taranto set sail from Bari in October 1096. At the same time Raymond of Toulouse left southern France and Robert of Flanders set out from the north. Their combined forces took Nicaea in June 1097 and marched across the Sultanate of Rum.*

The Routes of the First Crusade
→ Raymond of Toulouse
→ Robert of Flanders
→ Godfrey of Bouillon
→ Bohemond of Taranto
→ Combined forces

400 km
400 miles

The City of Jerusalem during the First and Second Crusades

N

St. Stephen's Gate

Church of St. Mary Magdalen

Church of St. Anne

Jehoshaphat's Gate

Jehoshaphat Street

Pool of Bethesda

PATRIARCH'S QUARTER

Via Dolorosa

Tancred's Tower

Golden Gate

TEMPLE AREA

Church of the Holy Sepulchre

Hospital of St. John

Church of St. John the Baptist

Pool of the Patriarchs

David Street

Temple Street

David's Gate

The Tower of David

St Mary's Hospital

Royal Palace

Church of St. Martin

Hospital of the Knights Templar

Tanner's Gate

Church of St. James the Great

Church of St. Peter in Chains

Zion Gate

▲ *Pilgrims entered the city by David's Gate in the west and went directly to the Church of the Holy Sepulchre. Christ reputedly entered the city on Palm Sunday through the Golden Gate, beside the Temple Area.*

believed to be the site of the ancient Temple. Later this became the headquarters of the Knights Templar, and a new palace was built in the west of the city at the Tower of David, by David's Gate. In this place King David had reputedly written the Book of Psalms in the 11th-10th century BC. Under the Muslims, bells had been banned from churches, but now they were restored and rang out over the capital of a Christian kingdom in the Holy Land, a city perceived as the centre of the world.

In the course of 50 years to c.1150 the crusaders built the great Romanesque Church of the Holy Sepulchre, containing the rock of Calvary on which Christ was

crucified, and the site of his tomb. Pilgrims visiting Jerusalem could follow the 'Way of the Cross' from the site of Pontius Pilate's palace on Jehoshaphat Street to the site of Christ's crucifixion and burial.

THE CONQUESTS OF SALADIN

Less then a century later, beginning in July 1187, Muslim leader Saladin won a series of victories that brought the Christian Kingdom of Jerusalem close to extinction (shown in the map right). Crossing the River Jordan from the east with an army of around 30,000 on 30 June 1187, Saladin defeated Guy of Lusignan, King of Jerusalem, and a 20,000-strong army in the Battle of the Horns of Hattin on 4 July. Jerusalem was an easy target after this victory, in which the crusaders famously lost their treasured relic of the 'True Cross' on which Christ died, for the Kingdom's military force was all but wiped out.

Saladin and his troops captured Acre and other strongholds along the Mediterranean coast: from Acre he headed north and took Sidon and Beirut, then marched south and took Jaffa and Ascalon before moving inland to capture Jerusalem on 2 October 1187. He campaigned again in 1188, in the north, and won several further victories, including the capture of the fortress of Saone. But he did not take Tyre, and this would be an invaluable foothold for a Christian revival in the Holy Land.

▼ *Saladin campaigned at great speed, determined not to allow the Christians to regroup. He took Acre just four days after the victory at the Horns of Hattin, then captured Ascalon, during a solar eclipse, exactly two months after Hattin. By 20 September he had marched inland to begin the siege of Jerusalem.*

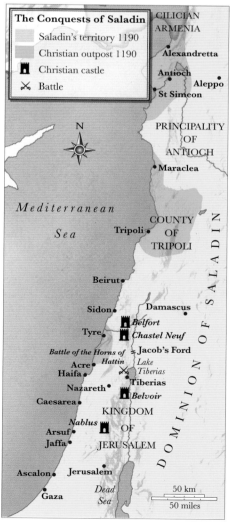

The Conquests of Saladin

Saladin's territory 1190

Christian outpost 1190

Christian castle

Battle

CILICIAN ARMENIA

Alexandretta

Antioch

Aleppo

St Simeon

PRINCIPALITY OF ANTIOCH

Maraclea

N

Mediterranean Sea

Tripoli

COUNTY OF TRIPOLI

Beirut

Sidon

Damascus

Belfort

Tyre

Chastel Neuf

Battle of the Horns of Hattin

Jacob's Ford

Acre

Hattin

Lake Tiberias

Haifa

Nazareth

Tiberias

Caesarea

Belvoir

KINGDOM OF JERUSALEM

Nablus

Arsuf

Jaffa

DOMINION OF SALADIN

Ascalon

Jerusalem

Gaza

Dead Sea

50 km

50 miles

TIMELINE

▲ *Moors besiege a Christian castle in Spain.*

March 1095 Byzantine Emperor Alexius Comnenus I sends envoys asking Pope Urban II for help against the Seljuk Turks.
27 November 1095 At Clermont, Pope Urban II launches the First Crusade.
April 1096 The first two waves of the People's Crusade, one led by Walter Sans Avoir and one by Peter the Hermit, depart for the Holy Land.
May 1096 Crusaders under Count Emicho of Leisingen carry out attacks on Jewish communities in the Rhineland.
1 August 1096 The armies of the People's Crusade arrive in Constantinople.
21 October 1096 The People's Crusade is routed by Seljuk Turks in Anatolia.
November 1096–May 1097 Crusade armies led by Hugh of Vermandois, Godfrey of Bouillon, Bohemond of Taranto, Raymond of Toulouse and Robert of Normandy arrive in Constantinople.
6 May 1097 Crusaders begin siege of Nicaea, capital of the sultanate of Rum.
19 June 1097 Nicaea surrenders to Byzantine emperor Alexius Comnenus I.
1 July 1097 Crusaders defeat Seljuk Turks at the Battle of Dorylaeum.
21 October 1097 Crusaders begin the siege of Antioch.
December 1097 Bohemond of Taranto and Robert of Flanders defeat a Turkish army under Sultan Duqaq of Damascus.
January 1098 Morale is low among the crusaders, who suffer severe famine; many, including Peter the Hermit, desert.
9 February 1098 Bohemond of Taranto defeats a relief army under Radwan, Seljuk ruler of Aleppo at Harenc, 25 miles (40km) from Antioch.
10 March 1098 Baldwin of Boulogne creates crusader state: the County of Edessa.
April 1098 Embassy from Fatimid Egypt arrives at Antioch, offering crusaders possession of Syria if they agree not to attack Jerusalem. The crusaders decline the offer.
2 June 1098 Stephen of Blois begins march north to Constantinople.

3 June 1098 Crusaders capture Antioch. The citadel remains in Turkish hands.
6 June 1098 Relief army led by Sultan Kerbogha of Mosul arrives at Antioch and begins siege of crusaders within city.
14 June 1098 Peter Bartholomew claims to discover the Holy Lance in Antioch.
28 June 1098 Crusaders defeat Sultan Kerbogha in battle outside Antioch. The citadel surrenders.
December 1098 Crusaders from Antioch capture nearby Maarrat an-Numan.
January 1099 Raymond of Toulouse leads the crusade army south from Antioch, bound for Jerusalem.
January 1099 Bohemond of Taranto establishes the second crusader state, the Principality of Antioch.
8 April 1099 Peter Bartholomew undergoes 'Ordeal By Fire' in an attempt to prove that his claimed discovery of the Holy Lance in Antioch was genuine. He is severely injured and dies on 20 April.
May 1099 Crusaders capture Tortosa and march down the coast as far as Arsuf.
5-6 June 1099 Tancred of Hautveille and Baldwin of Le Bourg capture Bethlehem.
7 June 1099 Crusaders begin the siege of the city of Jerusalem.
13 June 1099 The Crusade army fails in its assault on Jerusalem.
7–9 July 1099 Crusaders hold a three-day penitential fast before renewing their assault on the city.

15 July 1099 The crusaders capture Jerusalem. For two days, 15–16 July, they run amok, killing and looting.
22 July 1099 Godfrey of Bouillon is elected Defender of the Holy Sepulchre.
1 August 1099 Arnulf of Choques is elected Patriarch of Jerusalem.
5 August 1099 Patriarch Arnulf announces he has found a piece of the cross on which Christ was crucified.
12 August 1099 Godfrey of Bouillon consolidates the victory in Jerusalem by winning the Battle of Ascalon.
1100 Pope Paschal II calls a new crusade in response to calls from crusader lords for reinforcements.
18 July 1100 Godfrey of Bouillon dies; his brother Baldwin of Edessa is elected to be his replacement.
September 1100 Crusader troops are mobilized in response to Pope Paschal's call to arms depart from Italy.
25 December 1100 Baldwin of Edessa is crowned King of Jerusalem.
1100 Patriarch Arnulf is replaced by Dagobert of Pisa, the new papal legate. Arnulf becomes Archdeacon of Jerusalem.
June 1101 The Italian crusaders, fighting alongside Byzantine troops commanded by Raymond of Toulouse and a French–Burgundian–German force under Stephen of Blois, are routed by Seljuks.
1101 The Kingdom of Jerusalem captures Caesarea and Arsuf.
May 1104 The Kingdom is further expanded with the capture of Acre.
1107 King Sigurd I of Norway embarks on crusade.
12 July 1109 After a long siege Tripoli surrenders to crusaders. Bertrand, illegitimate son of Raymond of Toulouse, becomes ruler of the fourth crusader state, the County of Tripoli.
May 1110 The Kingdom of Jerusalem captures Beirut.
4 December 1110 King Baldwin I and King Sigurd I of Norway capture Sidon.

1110 Tancred of Hauteville, veteran of the First Crusade and regent of Antioch, captures the castle of Krak des Chevaliers.

1113 Paschal II recognizes the Equestrian order of the Holy Sepulchre of Jerusalem.

1114 In Spain Count Berenguer of Barcelona leads a crusade against the Muslim-held Balearic islands.

1118 Pope Gelasius II declares a crusade against the Moors in Spain.

2 April 1118 King Baldwin I of Jerusalem dies and is succeeded by his cousin Baldwin of Le Bourg as Baldwin II.

19 December 1118 Crusaders in Spain capture the city of Saragossa.

28 June 1119 Artuqid Turkish ruler Ilghazi inflicts crushing defeat on Christian army in the Battle of the Field of Blood.

1122 Pope Calixtus II calls crusades to the Holy Land and Spain. A large fleet sails for Jerusalem from Venice.

*c.*1123 The brotherhood of the Order of St Lazarus of Jerusalem is established.

1124 With the help of Venetian crusaders, the Kingdom of Jerusalem captures Tyre.

January 1128 Knights Templar recognized at the Council of Troyes.

21 August 1131 King Baldwin II of Jerusalem dies and is succeeded by his daughter Melisende and her husband Fulk of Anjou.

13 Nov 1143 King Fulk of Jerusalem dies and is succeeded by his wife Melisende, co-ruling with their son Baldwin III.

24 December 1144 Turkish general Imad ed-Din Zengi captures the capital of the crusader state of Edessa.

1 December 1145 Pope Eugenius III calls the Second Crusade.

1 March 1146 Bernard of Clairvaux is commanded to preach the crusade.

Easter Day 1146 Bernard preaches the crusade at Vezelay in central France. King Louis VII takes the cross.

25 December 1146 Conrad II of Germany takes the cross.

1146 As the crusade is preached, violence breaks out against Jews in the Rhineland.

13 April 1147 Pope Eugenius III guarantees full crusading privileges to those fighting pagan Wends in the Baltic.

May–June 1147 Armies of the Second Crusade set out for the Holy Land.

mid-September 1147 German crusade army arrives at Constantinople.

24 October 1147 Crusaders aid in the capture of Lisbon from the Moors.

25 October 1147 In Anatolia German crusaders are defeated by Seljuk Turks.

8 January 1148 French crusaders are defeated by Seljuk Turks in Turkey.

19 March 1148 King Louis VII of France arrives in Antioch.

24 June 1148 The Council of Acre decides to attack Damascus.

23 July 1148 Crusader armies arrive at Damascus and lay siege to the city.

28 July 1148 After the arrival of a relief army under Nur ed-Din, crusaders abandon the siege of Damascus. This marks the end of the Second Crusade.

29 June 1149 Nur ed-Din defeats and kills Raymond, Prince of Antioch.

1153 Baldwin III takes power in his own right as King of Jerusalem.

1154 Nur ed-Din captures Damascus.

10 February 1162 King Baldwin III of Jerusalem is succeeded by King Amalric I.

26 September 1164 Pope Alexander III recognizes the Spanish military brotherhood of the Order of Calatrava.

▼ *Kurdish general Saladin the Great.*

1164–69 A power struggle in Egypt ends in March 1169 with Salah ed-Din Yusuf (later called Saladin) as vizier of Egypt.

*c.*1170 The Spanish military brotherhood of the Order of Santiago is established.

11 July 1174 King Amalric I of Jerusalem is succeeded by his son Baldwin IV.

October 1174 Saladin takes Damascus.

25 November 1177 Baldwin IV defeats Saladin at the Battle of Montgisard.

1185 Baldwin IV dies and is succeeded by his nephew Baldwin V with Raymond of Tripoli as regent.

1186 Baldwin V dies and is succeeded by his mother Sibylla. She rules as Queen with Guy of Lusignan as her consort.

4 July 1187 Saladin wins a decisive victory in the Battle of the Horns of Hattin.

8 July 1187 Acre surrenders to Saladin.

4 September 1187 Saladin takes Ascalon.

2 October 1187 Saladin succeeds in recapturing Jerusalem.

29 October 1187 Pope Gregory VIII calls the Third Crusade.

January 1188 Kings Philip II of France and Henry II of England take the cross.

March 1188 Frederick I of Germany takes the cross.

11 May 1189 German crusaders depart.

6 July 1189 Henry II of England dies; his successor is Richard I.

27 August 1189 King Guy of Jerusalem begins siege of Acre.

17 May 1190 German crusaders defeat the Seljuks and capture Iconium.

10 June 1190 Frederick I drowns.

25 July 1190 Queen Sibylla of Jerusalem dies, sparking succession dispute.

20 April 1191 Philip II arrives at Acre.

8 June 1191 Richard I arrives at Acre.

12 July 1191 Acre surrenders.

7 September 1191 Richard I defeats Saladin in the Battle of Arsuf.

April 1192 Sibylla's sister Isabella and her husband Count Henry II of Champagne take power in Jerusalem.

5 August 1192 King Richard I defeats Saladin at Jaffa.

2 September 1192 A treaty between Richard I and Saladin brings an end to the Third Crusade.

THE FIRST CRUSADE

When Pope Urban II finished the great speech at Clermont in 1095 in which he called knights to the First Crusade, those who rushed to obey his summons at once began to adorn their clothing with the sign of the cross – and the cross was soon established as the sign beneath which the crusader knights rode into battle. In its original biblical context the cross was a symbol of Christ's intense physical suffering, and of his refusal to foment violence and take up arms. Through the centuries it became an emblem of the power of God and of Christianity – and was worn by pilgrims, but in the hands of the crusade preachers and the knights they inspired, the cross turned into a symbol of dedication and military vigour – an icon that inspired faith, a badge of honour to be worn by those who signed up for the perilous journey to the Holy Land and a sign of the salvation they were seeking. It symbolised the faith and obedience embodied in the cry 'God wills it' that arose following Urban II's speech, the shout that became the battle cry of the crusader knights on campaign.

▲ *Muslim horsemen often pretended to flee. Crusaders lost many a battle by charging recklessly in pursuit of a feigned retreat.*

▶ *The knights who responded to Urban's call to arms were inspired by tales of the religious campaigns of Charlemagne and his knights, seen here beseiging the walls of Pamplona in AD778.*

HOLY WAR

Knights such as Godfrey of Bouillon and Robert of Flanders won enduring fame on the First Crusade of 1096–99, their exploits quickly embroidered in legends. Yet for every knight such as Godfrey or Robert there were many other crusaders who died uncelebrated and in wretched circumstances – of starvation, of disease, in battle or ambush – many having brought financial ruin on themselves after borrowing very heavily to make the trip. It can be difficult at a distance of several centuries to see why so many men (and women) were moved to risk so much on such a venture. A key explanation is that they were inspired to view the enterprise as a holy war – they saw themselves as the latterday counterparts of the Israelites, whose struggles against enemies of their faith were an inspirational prototype of the crusades. The biblical warrior Judas Maccabeus is said, according to the Second Book of Maccabees, to have gone into battle with a golden sword given to him in a vision by the prophet Jeremiah with words that could happily have given service as a blessing for medieval knights: 'Take this holy sword, a gift from God, wherewith thou shalt overthrow the adversaries of my people Israel'. Judas's soldiers followed him into battle in a manner that was equally suited as inspiration for the crusaders' assault on Jerusalem: 'Thus being exhorted with the words of Judas, which were very good, and proper to stir up the courage, and strengthen the hearts of the young men, they resolved to fight, and set upon them manfully; that valour might decide the matter, because the Holy City and the temple were in danger.'

▲ *The pope had the spiritual authority to judge even royal sinners.*

◄ *The army of Bohemond of Taranto comes under attack while trying to cross the River Vardar en route to fight in the First Crusade. The journey was long and arduous.*

FIGHTING A HOLY WAR
THEORIES OF JUST AND SACRED WARS

The Benedictine historian Guibert, Abbot of Nogent-sous-Coucy, author in the early 12th century of a chronicle of the First Crusade, declared that 'God has instituted in these days sacred wars, so that the body of knights ... can find a means of winning their salvation'. Guibert may have suggested that holy wars were created in his era by a watchful God, but in truth the idea of fighting a just and divinely sanctioned war had its origins centuries earlier, and had roots as far back as the biblical era.

THE EXAMPLE OF THE OLD TESTAMENT

There are many examples in the Old Testament of the Bible of warfare waged on God's instructions or in his name. The God celebrated in the Old Testament appeared to use warfare to achieve his ends; he himself dealt in death. According to the Book of Exodus (Chapter 15), after

▼ *The anger of Israel's warlike God brought ruin on the Egyptians when the Red Sea closed over them, allowing the Israelites to travel on towards the Promised Land.*

escaping from captivity in Egypt the Israelites sang a hymn of praise in which they joyously celebrated their miraculous escape, the parting of the Red Sea and the death of their enemies in its waters: 'The Lord is a man of war: the Lord is his name ... Pharaoh's chariots and his host hath he cast into the sea ... the depths have covered them: they sank into the bottom as a stone. Thy right hand, O Lord, is become glorious in power: thy right hand, O Lord, hath dashed in pieces the enemy.'

The Old Testament God did call on his people to kill on his behalf – for example, when he instructed King Saul (David's predecessor as the king of Israel): 'Thus saith the Lord of hosts, I remember that which Amalek did to Israel, how he laid wait for him in the way, when he came up from Egypt. Now go and smite Amalek, utterly destroy all that they have, and spare them not; but slay both man and woman, infant and suckling, ox, sheep, camel and ass' (1 Samuel 15: verses 2–3).

A gallery of Israelite warriors, including David, Gideon and Joshua, were venerated as proponents of righteous warfare, even as exemplars of the knightly

▲ *'And I beheld when He had opened the sixth seal, and, lo, there was a great earthquake ...' Martial language, such as this quote from the Book of Revelation encouraged Christians to believe that God sanctioned the use of violence.*

code of chivalry; chief among them and celebrated alongside David and Joshua among the 'Nine Worthies' of the biblical, classical and chivalric worlds was Judas Maccabeus, guerrilla fighter against Seleucid overlords of Jerusalem in the 2nd century BC.

Judas Maccabeus was said to have led his warriors into battle 'fighting with their hands, but praying to the Lord with their hearts' and in battle 'they slew no less than five and thirty thousand'; in the midst of this carnage they were 'greatly cheered with the presence of God'. This quotation is from Chapter 15 of the Second Book of Maccabees, part of the Old Testament for Roman Catholics and Eastern Orthodox Christians but in modern times usually considered by Protestant Christians to be in the Apocrypha, a selection of texts that is associated with the Bible but not seen as part of it.

St Augustine, kneeling, was inspired by the preaching of St Ambrose, right, the Bishop of Milan. Both men were great intellectuals and rhetoricians who developed theories of a just use of violence.

VIOLENCE OF THE LAST DAYS

In the New Testament, Christian knights and their clerical supporters drew on the warlike imagery of descriptions of the Day of Judgement in the Book of Revelation, in which celestial armies gave expression to the righteous anger of God, which was likened to a winepress. Many of the knights, clerics and ordinary people who travelled to the Holy Land on the First Crusade had a strong sense that they were living in the last days before the Second Coming of Christ, which gave a great sense of urgency to the need to achieve remission of sins. Moreover a key

incentive for travelling to Jerusalem was that the events of the Last Judgement were expected to be played out in the city where Christ died and was buried.

JUSTIFICATION OF HOLY WAR

Theoretical justifications of holy war drew on 4th- and 5th-century AD Christian writers, such as St Ambrose, Bishop of Milan, and his pupil St Augustine, Bishop of Hippo. These theologians drew on classical philosophy: in particular those of the 4th-century BC ancient Greek philosopher Aristotle, who developed the notion of a 'just war' waged for the purpose of maintaining peace; ancient Roman ideas that wars could justly be fought to defend oneself, to recover seized territory or property, or to inflict punishment on a wrongdoer as long as the war was fought with proper authority (of the state); and the theory of

the 1st-century BC Roman statesman Cicero, who argued that a just war had to be fought using just means or in the right way – for example, with bravery. As developed by St Augustine, the Christian theory of a just or holy war required that it be fought in self-defence or to recover a seized territory or possession, on proper authority, and with the right intentions and means by all involved. Augustine added that wars fought on God's authority did not breach the commandment forbidding killing.

These ideas of sanctioned violence, of just and sacred war, applied to public bodies, such as State or Church. Individuals were required to be obedient to these public bodies, and to fight if commanded to do so. But in their individual lives violence was not sanctioned, and here Christ's troubling commands to love thy neighbour and to show forgiveness applied. Here was the distinction between sanctioned violence carried out in defence of the Church under vows to maintain the peace of God, and private wars, the secular clashes between knights that were condemned by the Church.

▼ Augustine urged Christians to focus on a mystical heavenly Jerusalem in his work The City of God, *written shortly after 410.*

DEFENDERS OF THE FAITH

CHRISTIAN WARRIORS IN A HOLY WAR

The great Norman crusader lord Tancred of Hauteville was filled with energy, according to his biographer Radulph of Caen, by Pope Urban II's call to the First Crusade. Before departing on crusade, Radulph writes, Tancred was disturbed by the disjunction between on the one hand the demands of life as a feudal knight, which required him to wage war, and on the other the teaching of Christ to turn the other cheek and act with generosity to the needy. The new idea of crusading, in which waging war against pagans was presented as a form of devotional penance for Christian knights, was tailor-made to address such a difficulty, and Tancred responded with enthusiasm: in Radulph's words, 'as if he had previously been asleep, he came awake, his energy was aroused, his strength increased, his seeing grew sharper and his bravery was born'.

In the context of energizing knights to fight for the Church in distant lands, Pope Urban's conflation of waging war and doing penance was a stroke of genius, and a new departure. But the idea of fighting a holy war – and of being a holy warrior – was not a new one: Radulph may well have been overstating Tancred's sense of discomfort at the disjunction between his life as a knight and his life as a devout Christian. For the knights who travelled

on the First Crusade were descendants of Germanic tribes whose warrior-band philosophy, incorporating celebration of the military lord and of feats of martial vigour, had had a profound effect on thinking and writing about the Christian faith in the centuries since they had been converted in the 5th and 6th centuries AD.

▲ *In the 5th century, King Clovis of the Salian Franks began his people's long association with the Catholic Church when he converted to Christianity in order to marry Princess Clotilde. The faith became increasingly militarized.*

Figures such as Clovis I, the first Frankish king to convert to Christianity, and his successor, Charlemagne, were viewed as warrior heroes as much as they were Christian kings. Christian language and thought became infused with Germanic warrior imagery. For example, in the masterful 8th-century Anglo-Saxon poem *The Dream of the Rood*, the poet uses very military language in describing his dream of seeing Christ on the cross, calling Christ the 'young hero', 'the warrior', 'the Prince' and 'the Lord of Victories', and envisages Christ's actions on the cross as those of a fearless warrior.

HOLY WAR AND DIPLOMACY

One key divide between the westerners, or 'Latins', who travelled on crusade and the easterners, or 'Greeks', they went to help, derived from a distinctly different outlook on life, particularly when it came to diplomacy and war.

The Latins had a developed theory of the just, or holy, war and of the righteousness of combat, but the Greeks viewed conflict only as a last resort and preferred to settle disagreements through diplomacy and compromise. Many of the Latins were only a few generations separated from forebears among the Viking raiders, and the Greeks saw them as uncultured barbarians; for their part, the Latins viewed the Greeks as untrustworthy – particularly in their willingness to negotiate and sign treaties with Muslim powers.

FIGHTING TO PROMOTE CHRISTIANITY

Battle imagery invaded Christian thought, and Christian practices found a place on the battlefield. King Alfred of Wessex prayed with his commanders before battle and his warriors had Christian images on their weapons; in chronicles his wars were always presented as being for Christianity against pagans. Likewise, Charlemagne's battles against pagan enemies such as the Saxons were presented as holy wars. For the 'pagans', the price of defeat by Alfred or by Charlemagne was forcible conversion to Christianity. Such a war was self-evidently a holy one, fought in order to spread the faith. The empire that Charlemagne built was an explicitly Christian one.

FIGHTING TO DEFEND CHRISTIANITY AND THE CHURCH

From c.850 onwards when Charlemagne's empire began to fall apart, the chief foes were marauding pagans – Vikings, 'Saracens' (Muslim Arabs and Berbers) and Magyars. Fighting against these raiders

▲ *Christian Emperor Charlemagne leads his army at the walls of Pamplona, Spain, 778, from a 14th-century manuscript.*

was a defence of Christianity and the idea of 'Christendom' began to inform debate. The community of European peoples who had once been united under the Frankish empire were now bound by their common Christian faith and their opposition to non-Christian, pagan enemies.

In the 9th and 10th centuries, moreover, in increasingly lawless times, church authorities began to promote the theory that armed warriors had a responsibility to protect the weak, and particularly the Church. The churchmen promoted the Peace of God, under which warriors would swear to protect those who were not equipped to protect themselves – principally clergy and monks. In this context, fighting was a form of piety.

This initiative did more than condemn attacks on church property, going as far as to encourage violence in the interests of preventing lawless attacks. As with Urban's call to arms at Clermont, in the Peace of God initiative the Church was not simply giving its blessing to violence, it was rather bringing violence into being.

Throughout the period there were also those churchmen who resisted the glorification of violence, who continued to promote the monastic or clerical life as the ideal Christian one. Killing remained officially a sin. The Norman soldiers who fought at Hastings under William the Conqueror were required to do penance for the blood they had spilled, despite the fact that they were fighting under a papal banner (with the pope's backing) and the explicit approval of their clergy.

▼ *At Hastings in 1066 Christian Normans fought Christian Anglo-Saxons. Duke William's men were supported by the pope.*

MUSLIM EMPIRES

THE SPREAD OF ISLAM

In the late 11th century, prior to the First Crusade, control of the eastern Mediterranean was divided between the Christian Byzantine Empire based in Constantinople, the Sunni Muslim Seljuk Turks nominally ruled from Baghdad, rival Seljuk groups in Anatolia with a capital at Nicaea, and Shi'ite Muslim Fatimids from northern Africa. In eastern Anatolia the Muslim Turkish Danishmends were also a force to be reckoned with.

THE ISLAMIC EXPANSION

The great expansion of Islam began from the Arabian Peninsula in the 7th century AD. In the hundred years following the death of the Prophet Muhammad – founder of the faith – in 632, Muslim warriors created a vast empire stretching from Spain in the west to parts of China and India in the east, and encompassing Palestine, Syria and Mesopotamia.

▼ *Islamic warriors spread north, taking on the Persian and Byzantine empires, then eastwards across Africa to Spain by 711.*

THE PROPHET AND HIS TEACHING

The Prophet Muhammad was born in *c*.570 in the caravan city of Mecca, Arabia, a member of the Quaraish tribe. He began to preach in around 613 and established the new faith of Islam in exile from Mecca at Yathrib (later known as Medina, the City of the Prophet) in 620–30, before returning to Mecca from 630 until his death two years later.

Muhammad taught that there was one God, named Allah, Creator of all that existed, who demanded honour and submission from humans – the word *Islam* means 'surrender' (that is, to the will of Allah), while *Muslims* are so called from the Arabic for 'those who submit'. *Allah* was another name for the 'God of the Christians and the Jews'. Muhammad's teachings were gathered in the Koran, which his followers said completed and superseded the Christian and Jewish books; Muhammad was the final prophet in a sequence that also included Noah, Abraham and Jesus.

▲ *Angels Gabriel, Michael, Israfil and Azrail attend on the Prophet as he travels to Mecca. One of a set of 16th-century Ottoman illustrations on Muhammad's life.*

THE FIRST ISLAMIC LEADERS

Following the death of Muhammad in Mecca in 632, one of his followers, named Abu Bakr, a merchant and member of a minor clan in the Prophet's Quaraish tribe,

Expansion of Islam

- Islamic conquests at Muhammad's death
- Islamic conquests 632–661
- Islamic conquests 661–750
- → Direction of conquest

ATLANTIC OCEAN

FRANKS

SLAVS

LOMBARDS

Corsica • Rome

• Cordoba

Sardinia

Tunis • Sicily

Mediterranean Sea

Crete

• Tripoli

Cyprus

Alexandria •

AFRICA

EGYPT

Black Sea

Constantinople

BYZANTINE EMPIRE

SYRIA

• Damascus

• Jerusalem

Nile river

Red Sea

Caspian Sea

PERSIAN EMPIRE

Tigris river

Euphrates river

• Baghdad

Persian Gulf

Indus river

ARABIA

• Medina

• Mecca

Arabian Sea

Sahara Desert

500 km

500 miles

was elected as *khalifat rasul Allah* (Successor to God's Prophet) or 'caliph': the spiritual and political leader of the faithful. He died in 634, but before his death appointed a successor, another merchant and a member of the Quaraish, named Omar bin Khattab.

Under Caliph Omar's rule (634–44), Muslim Bedouin tribesmen won astonishing victories against the Byzantine and Persian empires, defeating the Byzantines in Syria and the Persians in Mesopotamia. They took Damascus in 635. In 637 they captured the Persian capital Ctesiphon. In 638 they took Jerusalem. In the 640s they established themselves in Egypt, capturing Alexandria in 646. By this time Omar was dead. Disputes over the succession gave rise to schism and centuries-long enmity between Sunni and Shi'ite Islam.

SUNNI AND SHI'ITE SPLIT
Omar was succeeded by Othman ibn Affan, another merchant and also one of Muhammad's original converts and once again a member of Quaraish tribe of Mecca. There was opposition to his appointment, gathered around the Prophet's cousin and son-in-law Ali, husband of Muhammad's daughter Fatima. When Othman was murdered in 656, two rival caliphs vied to replace him: on the

▼ *This image of a Moorish army is from a manuscript made for King Alfonso X of Castile and Leon (r.1252–84).*

one hand Ali, and on the other, Mu'awiyah, a member of Umayyad clan, who had earlier been appointed Governor of Syria by Othman. In 661 both Ali and Mu'awiyah were stabbed as they prayed in mosques in separate cities – Ali later died, but Mu'awiyah survived. Ali's supporters appointed his son Hassan caliph, but in a confrontation with Mu'awiyah he backed down; then when Mu'awiyah died in 680, Ali's second son Hussein claimed the caliphate. In an encounter with Mu'awiyah's son Yazid on 10 October 680, Hussein and all his followers were killed.

The split between Shi'ite and Sunni Muslims derived from this power struggle. Sunnis backed the descendants of Mu'awiyah – the Umayyad caliphs – as the rightful leaders of Islam, but Shi'ites declared them usurpers and argued that Ali had inherited the spirit of Muhammad and that leadership of Islam should be from his descendants. The Shi'ites' name came from that of the followers of Ali in the 7th century – the *shi'at Ali* (the party of Ali), whereas the Sunni were so called because they said they were following the *sunna* (example) of Muhammad.

AN ISLAMIC EMPIRE IN SPAIN
Muslim Arabs spread westwards from Egypt through northern Africa. Their advance was temporarily held up by the Berbers of the Atlas Mountains but after constructing the fortified city of Kairouan (in modern Tunisia) they subdued the Maghreb region of north and north-western Africa, then under the great Arab general Tariw ibn-Ziyad, crossed the Straits of Gibraltar and in just five years took virtually the whole Iberian Peninsula from its previous rulers, the Visigoths.

Arabs began to raid beyond the Pyrenees Mountains into southern and western France. In 732 at the Battle of Tours the marauding Arabs finally met their match in a redoubtable army commanded by Charles Martel ('the Hammer'), King of the Franks. Thereafter the Arabs withdrew into Spain and consolidated their possessions there.

▲ *St James makes a miraculous appearance in the legendary Battle of Clavijo in 844.*

UMAYYADS, ABBASIDS AND FATIMIDS
In the east the Umayyad descendants of Caliph Mu'awiyah ruled the Islamic empire from Damascus until they were ousted in 750 by their cousins and rivals the Abbasids, who established the capital of the empire at Baghdad in Iraq. The Abbasids came to power with Shi'ite support but ruled as Sunni Muslims. In 909 militant Shi'ite Muslims established a rival Fatimid dynasty (claiming direct descent from the Prophet's daughter Fatima) in Tunis and built their capital at Cairo.

By the second half of the 10th century the balance of power in the western Mediterranean was between a resurgent Byzantine empire, which had re-established itself in Syria; the increasingly weak Abbasid caliphate in Baghdad, which had nominal control over Iran, Iraq and the remainder of Syria; and the Fatimids of Cairo, who had extended their territory up through Palestine.

THE RISE OF THE SELJUKS
Then the Seljuk Turks erupted onto the scene. Originally from central Asia, these Turkmen tribes converted to Sunni Islam, conquered Afghanistan and eastern Iran, and in 1055 took control of Baghdad. In the 1070s the Seljuks delivered a crushing blow to the Byzantine army at the Battle of Manzikert, capturing Syria and most of Palestine from the Fatimids.

CHRISTIANS IN THE EAST
THE 'EMPIRE OF THE GREEKS'

The Latin Christians led by the pope in Rome, the faithful who were summoned by Urban II to the First Crusade, did not have a close or easy relationship with their counterparts in the Eastern Church and the Byzantine Empire.

CHRISTIAN ORIGINS IN THE EAST

Christian presence in the eastern Mediterranean dates back to the 1st century AD, when saints Peter, Paul and Barnabus established the first Christian community in Antioch – its members were the first people in history to be called 'Christians'. The origins of the Christian Byzantine Empire lie in the 4th century, when Constantine, the first Roman emperor to support Christianity, established the city of Constantinople as a new capital for the Roman Empire.

Constantine built the city as Nova Roma (New Rome) on the site of the trading city of Byzantium, according to legend created in 667BC by Greek colonists led by

▼ According to tradition, St Peter was the first Bishop of Antioch, then Bishop of Rome – and, as such, was the first pope.

▲ Constantine the Great (left) founded Constantinople, while his mother St Helena (right) played an important part in Jerusalem's rise as a centre of pilgrimage.

King Byzantas (or Byzas); New Rome was renamed Constantinople (the city of Constantine) after Constantine's death in AD337. In contrast to previous Roman emperors, who had persecuted Christians, Constantine announced that Christianity would be tolerated in the empire in 313 – traditionally he had won power after a vision had inspired him to fight under the sign of the Christian cross. He then laid the groundwork for the establishment of a Christian culture in the empire, although he was not himself baptized until shortly before his death. He called the Church's first ecumenical meeting, the Council of Nicaea, in 325. This council drew up the first statement of uniform Christian doctrine, the Nicene Creed.

Situated on the Bosphorus between the Black Sea and the Sea of Marmara, at the intersection of the mercantile routes of Asia and eastern Europe, Constantinople grew fabulously wealthy on the profits of trade. After the death of Emperor Theodosius I in 395, the Roman Empire was permanently split into eastern and western halves, ruled from Rome and Constantinople, respectively. Following the sacking of Rome by the Visigoths in 410 and the collapse of the eastern empire in Europe culminating in the deposition

of the last emperor in Rome, Romulus Augustus, in 476 by the Germanic king Odoacer, the city of Constantine was the capital of the Byzantine Empire.

EXPANSION AND DECLINE

In the 7th and 8th centuries the Byzantine Empire came under repeated attack by the swiftly expanding Muslim empire. Several times, from 674, the Arabs attempted to take Constantinople itself, but without success; they were finally driven back from the city when the siege of 717 was decisively defeated by the Byzantine emperor Leo III. In the period 863–1025 the Byzantine Empire expanded greatly and at one point in 976 the Arabs were driven back as far as the very gates of Jerusalem. But after the death of Emperor Basil II in 1025, the empire's fortunes declined once more, and in the mid-11th century the Seljuk Turks erupted into the region, culminating in the severe defeat of the Byzantine army by the Seljuks at Manzikert in Armenia in 1071. This defeat lost the empire all its lands in Anatolia.

▲ St Mark, author of the Gospel of Mark, is revered by Christians in north Africa, and was Bishop of Alexandria.

CONFLICT WITHIN

The name 'Byzantine Empire', it should be noted, dates from the 16th century, when it was first used by a German historian. The rulers and citizens of the empire called it 'Roman', whereas those in western Europe called it the 'Empire of the Greeks'. From the 9th century onwards the great powers of Europe were increasingly in competition with the Byzantine Empire to determine who was the successor of ancient Rome – as well as being in dispute over territories in Italy. In 800 Charlemagne was crowned *Imperator Augustus* (August Emperor) by Pope Leo III in Rome, in an attempt to revive the Roman Empire in the west; he also bore the title *Patricius Romanorum* (Protector of the Romans). In the 10th century Otto II of the Germans married a Byzantine princess – Theopanu, niece of the Byzantine emperor John I Tzimisces – but was in conflict with the eastern empire and declared himself 'Roman emperor'.

TENSION BETWEEN WESTERN AND EASTERN CHURCHES

There was also conflict between the Church hierarchies of west and east. In 1054, the leaders of the Churches – Pope Leo IX in Rome and Patriarch Michael Cerularius in Constantinople – excommunicated one another. The tension went right back to the 5th century, when, following the fall of Rome, the pope assumed the mantle of protector of Christians in the west. Rome was the burial place of the Apostle Peter and the popes claimed direct succession from him and ultimate authority over the entire Church; but the patriarchs of Constantinople claimed they were the highest authority, since Constantinople was the seat of the eastern Roman Empire.

Matters of doctrine also caused controversy: the Eastern Church allowed married priests but the Latin Church insisted officially on celibacy of the priesthood; the Latin Church allowed the use of unleavened bread in the Mass but the Eastern Church was against this. Another major disagreement arose over whether in the Christian Trinity of Father, Son and Holy Spirit, the Spirit derived from the Father or from both the Father and the Son. The Nicene Creed had declared 'I believe in the Holy Spirit, the Lord the giver of Life, who proceedeth from the Father', but western churches had added the words 'and the Son'. This *filioque* clause (so called from the Latin word meaning 'from the Son') had first been used in Spain in the 7th century, then had been backed by Charlemagne, and had finally been accepted by the papacy in 1014; but it was vehemently rejected by the Eastern Church as heresy. In 1089 Urban II sent an embassy to Constantinople asking for full relations to recommence between Western and Eastern Churches but the division – later known to historians as the 'Great Schism' – endured.

▼ The Byzantine Empire held territory in Italy. At Ravenna, the basilica of San Vitale contains this beautiful mosaic of Christ.

THE POWER OF THE PAPACY
POPES STRUGGLE FOR INDEPENDENCE

The second half of the 11th century saw concerted attempts by the papacy to establish the Church in a strong position independent of secular power. The idea of fighting as a form of Christian devotion was taken a stage further when popes presented struggles in support of the papacy as holy wars.

Pope Leo IX (ruled 1049–54) personally led troops to war against Norman adventurers in southern Italy in 1053. He set the precedent of promising his soldiers absolution of their sins and remission of penance as their reward. In this campaign the papal army was defeated at the Battle of Civitate by a Norman force led by Humphrey of Hauteville and containing Robert Guiscard. Ten years later the Normans were papal allies: after Pope Nicholas II (ruled 1059–61) invested

▼ *Pope Gregory VII grants absolution to German emperor Henry IV in 1077. This was an important but temporary victory for the papacy in the long struggle to establish its independence from secular rulers.*

▲ *Cluny Abbey in France was at the forefront of Church reform in the 10th to 12th centuries and its abbot was second in power only to the pope. Otho of Lagery, later known as Pope Urban II, was a prior there. As pope, he visited the abbey in 1095.*

Robert Guiscard as duke of Apulia, Calabria and Sicily, the Norman army fought under a papal banner in invading Muslim Sicily. Another branch of the Norman family also had a papal banner for William of Normandy's invasion of England in 1066.

GREGORY VII AND ST PETER'S SOLDIERS

Pope Gregory VII (ruled 1073–85) became embroiled in a long-running dispute with the German emperor Henry IV (reigned 1056–1105). The main issue of contention in what is known to historians as 'the Investiture Controversy' was whether Henry or Gregory should control

▶ *Pope Leo X and Patriarch Michael Cerularius of Constantinople excommunicated one another in 1054. The quarrel had begun centuries before in a dispute over which church had primacy.*

the church: it was focused on who should have control over bishops' investiture (appointment and presentation of symbols of office) in the German church; it followed a period in which the papacy had been very weak, and Henry IV's predecessor, Henry III, had appointed three German popes. Gregory set out to mobilize his own papal force, the *Militia Sancti*

Petri (the 'army of St Peter'). He told the knights in his service that they were 'vassals of Saint Peter' and as reward would receive Peter's blessing 'in this life and the life to come'.

Gregory and Henry IV clashed dramatically. In 1076 Gregory excommunicated Henry and declared him *anathema*, which meant he was excluded from the community of Christian believers and that none of his subjects had to keep oaths made to him. German nobles forced Henry to back down and in January 1077 he travelled to the pope's castle at Canossa in northern Italy, where Gregory made him wait outside, barefoot and clad in a hair shirt in the snow, before finally allowing him in to receive forgiveness. This decisively changed the balance of power between pope and emperor, but only in the short term: Henry and Gregory clashed again and Gregory excommunicated Henry again in 1080; Henry attacked Rome three times between 1081 and 1084 and on the third occasion Gregory had to be rescued from his castle of Castel Sant'Angelo in the city by his ally and vassal, the Norman adventurer Robert Guiscard.

REFORM AND PAPAL POWER

Gregory is remembered as a 'reforming pope', because he attacked such abuses in the church as simony (the sale of Church offices) and tried to impose celibacy on the priesthood. Both these campaigns were tied up with his efforts to establish the absolute supremacy of the papacy – simony was beneficial to secular leaders who used it to bring about the appointment of their own supporters in key positions, and he made use of the campaign for celibacy to counter the power of rebel bishops who allowed married priests. He was passionately committed to the spiritual renewal of the Church.

GREGORY VII'S 'CRUSADE'

Gregory is also notable for his attempt to launch a forerunner of the crusades – a military expedition to help Constantinople and the Christians in the East in 1074.

THE ISSUING OF INDULGENCES

Popes used the promise of forgiveness, the remission of penances and the granting of indulgences as a lure to mobilize armies in their support. The issuing of indulgences derived from the idea that a punishment remained due for a sinner even when he or she had won forgiveness for a sin through repentance and confession; a sinner might win God's eternal forgiveness through genuine repentance but still be liable for a temporal punishment.

In the early Christian Church 'canonical penances' were calculated to wipe a sinner's slate clean, to do away with the temporal punishment; then in the early medieval Church, parts of the canonical penance were commuted – a repentant sinner was told he or she would achieve the same benefit by donating a specified amount of money to the Church, by giving alms to the poor or by spending an allotted period of time in fasting or prayer. Indulgences were usually partial – they commuted part of the punishment. The first recorded instance of an absolute or plenary indulgence that promised the complete avoidance of temporal punishment was the speech by Urban II at Clermont in 1095, when he issued his call to arms in the First Crusade. He declared: 'Whoever, acting out of devotion and not for the sake of winning honour or riches, travels to Jerusalem to free the Church of God may substitute this sacred journey for all penance.'

▼ *Pope Urban II at Clermont, where he issued his call to take up arms.*

Gregory made the attempt in response to a call in 1073 from Byzantine emperor Michael VII for help against the Seljuk Turks. In a manner that would have many echoes in Urban II's declaration at Clermont in 1095, Gregory promoted the enterprise in 1074 as an act of charity on behalf of those he hoped to involve, and claimed that they would be following the example of Christ, acting under the mandate of God himself; he also offered the promise of 'eternal reward'. Gregory did manage to raise an army but the enterprise foundered and the expedition did not set out.

The First Crusade was a direct descendant of the holy wars that were fought in the name of the papacy, since it was launched by the pope and fought with the aim of establishing his supremacy over the Eastern Church and his rule over a united Christendom. From the outset it was conceived by those involved in it as an expression of papal power.

THE HOLY CITY OF JERUSALEM
PLACE OF CHRIST'S PASSION, SACRED TO THREE FAITHS

Several medieval maps survive to the present day in which Jerusalem is represented as the centre of the Earth, which was at that time believed to be flat. To Christians of this era, the city was the holiest spot in the world, the place where God, through his son Jesus Christ, had redeemed the fallen creation.

Jerusalem was and is sacred to Jews and Muslims, as well as to the followers of Christ. Jews revere Jerusalem as the city of David, founder of the united kingdom of Israel and Judah, and the place where his successor, Solomon, built a great temple. To Muslims Jerusalem is traditionally the third most sacred city in the world after Mecca, the Prophet's birthplace, and Yathrib, or Medina, the city in which he established the Islamic faith in AD620–30. Jerusalem is said to be the place from which the Prophet made an ascent into heaven – according to Muslim tradition,

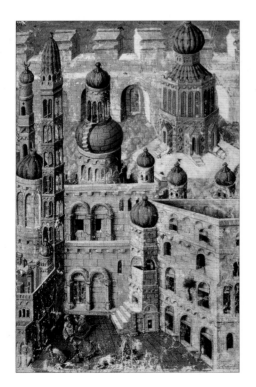

▼ *The Church of the Holy Sepulchre, believed to be built on the spot where Christ was crucified, was the crusaders' goal.*

Muhammad was taken up from Mecca by the Angel Gabriel one night in 620 and transported to Jerusalem, from where he ascended a golden ladder to heaven.

REPEATED VIOLENCE
By the time of the First Crusade in the 11th century, the city already had a long and bloody history. Following the era of David and Solomon the city was sacked by the Egyptian pharaoh Sheshonk I in 922BC, and then both city and Temple were destroyed by Nebuchadnezzar of Babylon in 587BC. This cataclysmic event, which resulted in the exile of the Jews in Babylon, was followed eventually by their return under Cyrus the Great of Persia and the building of a second Temple in 515BC.

Under the rule of the Seleucids (the rulers of a kingdom that grew out of the empire of Alexander the Great) in the 2nd century BC, Judas Maccabeus led his celebrated revolt to reclaim the city and cleanse the Temple. In the era of chivalry he became an unlikely role model for the crusader knights as a religious warrior.

ROMAN CITY
At the time of Christ, Jerusalem was part of the province of Judea in the Roman Empire. A Jewish revolt in AD66 resulted in a devastating attack led by the future emperor Titus, in which the city was almost completely destroyed and the Temple once again reduced to ruins. A new city named Aelia Capitolina was built by Emperor Hadrian, provoking another revolt in 132–35, put down again by Roman might; at this time Hadrian renamed the Roman province of Judea 'Syria Palaestina' after the Philistines named in the Bible. Jerusalem remained under Roman rule until the 7th century, although from the 4th century onwards this was under Christian emperors. The city became a well-established site of pilgrimage for Christians.

▲ *Jerusalem was depicted as being at the centre of the world in this map from an English psalter c.1262. Christ and two angels preside. The east is at the top, Europe and Africa at the bottom.*

CHURCH OF THE HOLY SEPULCHRE
Built by Emperor Constantine in c.325, the Church of the Holy Sepulchre was said to mark the site of Golgotha, or the Hill of Calvary, where Christ was crucified and then buried.

The church consisted of three parts: a basilica named the *Martyrium* built over the place of crucifixion, a colonnade called the *Triportico* built around the Hill of Calvary, and a rotunda called the *Anastasis* (Resurrection) containing the actual cave in which Christ was said to have been buried. The tomb itself was enclosed in a special structure beneath the rotunda called the 'edicule' (from Latin *aediculum*, meaning 'small structure'), and visiting the edicule understandably became a major focus for Christian pilgrims and subsequently crusaders.

AN ARAB CITY

Jerusalem was captured by Bedouin Arabs under Omar bin Khattab, the second caliph, or leader, of Islam, in 638. His successors, the Umayyad caliphs of Damascus and their successors, the Abbasid caliphs of Baghdad, ruled over Jerusalem for more than 600 years, until 969. These regimes were both supporters of mainstream Sunni Islam, but in 969 the rival Fatimid caliphs of Cairo in Egypt, who were Shi'ite Muslims, took control of the city.

THE DOME OF THE ROCK

The city's principal Muslim holy site, the Dome of the Rock, was constructed in 685–91 by the Umayyad caliph Abd al-Malik. It was a mosque built as a *masshad* (pilgrimage shrine) for Muslims, on the reputed site from which Muhammad ascended to heaven on his Night Journey. The site was also sacred on three counts for Jews: as the place where the patriarch

▼ *The army of Nebuchadnezzar, king of Babylon c.605–562BC, brings death and destruction to the city of Jerusalem. The illustration is from the* Commentary on the Apocalypse *(c.776) by Spanish monk Beatus of Liébana.*

Abraham had readied himself to sacrifice his son Isaac to please God; as the rock on which Jacob had dreamt of a ladder ascending to heaven; and as the site of King Solomon's Temple. The al-Aqsa Mosque was built nearby at around the same time. In the crusader era, contemporary reports suggest that many Christian pilgrims, ignorant of their history, believed the Dome of the Rock to be the biblical Temple of Solomon.

▲ *Christ's empty tomb is visible within the Church of the Holy Sepulchre in this 14th-century view of pilgrims visiting Jerusalem.*

The Umayyad, Abbasid and Fatimid caliphs were mostly liberal towards Christian pilgrims. There was a major outbreak of persecution in the early 11th century, when the Fatimid caliph al-Hakim ordered the destruction of Christian shrines, including the Church of the Holy Sepulchre in 1010. This aggression proved to be short-lived, however, and in the 1040s the church was reconstructed by Byzantine builders with the permission of Fatimid caliph Ma'ad al-Mustansir Billah.

In 1071, however, the Fatimids were ousted from Jerusalem by the Seljuk Turks, who were far less tolerant of Christianity, and were unwilling to allow pilgrims to come and go unmolested. The reported attacks by Seljuk Turks on Christian pilgrims to Jerusalem was one of the provocations and justifications of the First Crusade.

Immediately prior to the First Crusade, Jerusalem was in the hands of the Seljuk Turks, but during the crusade (in 1098) it was recaptured by the Fatimid Muslims, so it was from the Fatimids that the crusaders took it in July 1099.

THE PENITENTIAL JOURNEY
A LONG HISTORY OF PILGRIMAGE

The religious tradition of the pilgrimage, or penitential journey, has roots that travel down deep into history. Christians in the 10th and 11th centuries enthusiastically embraced the crusade as a form of pilgrimage, as a means of expiating their sins.

The tradition of making religious journeys to visit shrines dates back to at least the world of ancient Greece, when people would travel to visit the Temple of Diana at Ephesus in Asia Minor (now western Turkey) and other sacred sites. Christ's birthplace, Bethlehem, and the scene of his Passion, Jerusalem, were places of pilgrimage for Christians from as early as the 2nd century AD.

FIRST CHRISTIAN PILGRIMS TO JERUSALEM

Eusebius, an early 4th-century Bishop of Caesarea, made references in his *Historia Ecclesiastica* (History of the Christian Church) to travelling Christians making

▼ *Devout pilgrims patiently wait to receive a papal blessing before embarking on their voyage to the holy places in the East.*

religious visits to Jerusalem. In truth, there was little for Christians to see in the city before Constantine the Great began a programme of identifying sacred sites and building churches.

Before Constantine's time the Jerusalem of Christ's era was almost entirely covered with the new city of Aelia Capitolina built by Hadrian following the near-total destruction of the earlier city by the future emperor Titus in AD70. The only known site associated with Christ's Passion was the cenacle, or supper room, reputedly the place in which Christ shared his last earthly meal with his disciples and gave them the basis of the Christian Mass, or Communion service. The cenacle was in the house said to have belonged to Mary,

▲ *The 'True Cross' is identified when it miraculously heals a sick woman during St Helena's pilgrimage to Jerusalem.*

mother of Saint Mark, author of the biblical Gospel of Mark; she was a prominent early Christian and the house was a meeting place for the disciples and followers after Christ's resurrection.

Constantine identified the site of Christ's burial in an area that, according to Bishop Eusebius, had been built up with earth and used as the site for a temple of the Roman goddess Venus, probably during Hadrian's rebuilding of the city. Constantine excavated the mound and found a cave that was then identified as the place where Joseph of Arimathaea placed Christ's body after it was taken down from the cross. There, Constantine constructed the Church of the Holy Sepulchre in c.AD325.

THE 'TRUE CROSS'

According to a tradition first recorded by the late 4th-century Christian writer Socrates Scholasticus, Constantine's mother Helena – who also converted to Christianity – made a pilgrimage to Jerusalem in c.312–30 and, under the guidance of a local Jew, found Christ's cross together with those of the two robbers who were crucified alongside him. A miracle revealed which one of the three was the cross used to crucify Christ: each of the crosses was laid on a very sick woman and one of them, imbued with divine power because Christ's blood had been spilt on it, brought about a cure. Helena also supposedly found the inscription hung above Christ's head on the cross, which identified him as 'King of the Jews', and the nails used to fix Jesus to the cross: the relics were sent to Constantinople, where the nails were beaten to form the emperor's bridle and helmet.

According to some accounts Helena also took the cross itself back with her to Constantinople, but other versions indicate that parts of the cross were kept in the Church of the Holy Sepulchre: pilgrims were venerating relics of the cross there by about c.380. Shortly afterwards, accounts of pilgrimages indicate that religious travellers were also being told that they could see the Holy Lance that pierced Christ's side, the crown of thorns He wore and the pillar at which He was whipped.

A fragment of the cross was taken from Jerusalem by Persian Sassanid emperor Khosrau II when he took the city in 614, then recaptured by Byzantine emperor Heraclius when he defeated Khosrau in battle. After keeping the relic briefly in Constantinople, Heraclius returned it to Jerusalem, where it remained. It was hidden by Christians early in the 11th century, and reputedly found in August 1099 by Arnulf of Choques, the city's first Latin Patriarch. The fragment became the principal sacred relic of the Kingdom of Jerusalem, kept in the Church of the Holy Sepulchre, and carried into battle by the crusader armies. This was the relic whose loss to Saladin's army during the Battle of Hattin in 1187 caused such lasting concern and consternation.

PILGRIMAGE AS PENANCE

The pilgrimage was a form of penitential discipline. Making a pilgrimage was a form of penance, that is an act performed to win forgiveness of sins. A priest, or in more serious cases a bishop, would specify the particular pilgrimage that a penitent must undertake in order to earn forgiveness. While travelling, the pilgrim might be required to wear a heavy chain or a hair shirt to add to the penance.

THE POWER OF RELICS

The institution of the pilgrimage was supported by the belief – already powerful as we have seen by the 5th century, and strong right through the Middle Ages – in the spiritual force of physical relics of Christ and his saints. In addition to fragments of objects such as the Cross or the Crown of Thorns, pilgrims travelled to venerate miraculously preserved body parts of sacred figures, such as fingers or hair clippings. These relics were believed to be imbued with divine power and regularly, like Helena's piece of the cross, effected extraordinary cures. Pilgrimages did not have to be to Jerusalem or the Holy Land: penitents could make journeys to a wide range of sites closer to home that were associated with the lives of saints or sanctified by the possession of a holy relic.

THE GOLDEN LEGEND OF THE TRUE CROSS

The pilgrims who venerated pieces of the True Cross in various locations were eager to tell and hear stories of its origin. A story developed linking the wood from which the cross was made to the Tree of Life that grew in the Garden of Eden; the form in which this tale has survived is the *Golden Legend* written by Jacopo of Voragine, Bishop of Genoa, in 1260. According to this story, the cross was made of wood grown from a seed of the Tree of Life: as he lay dying, Adam persuaded his son Seth to get the seed from the archangel Michael; when he returned with it, Seth placed it in Adam's mouth. Adam was buried after he died and a great tree grew from the seed and lived for many hundreds of years. Finally it was cut down: the wood was used to build a bridge. It happened that the biblical Queen of Sheba crossed the bridge on her way to visit King Solomon: she saw the wood's true nature and worshipped it, then told Solomon that a piece of the wood would be instrumental in the establishment of a new covenant between God and the Jews. Solomon was afraid and had the wood buried, but 14 generations later it was unearthed and made into the Holy Cross on which Christ died.

◄ *The Queen of Sheba kisses the wood of the Cross in a fresco of the story by Piero della Francesca in the Church of San Francesco, Arezzo, Italy.*

CRUSADER PILGRIMS

A SACRED ENTERPRISE

Access to Jerusalem was the ultimate prize for the crusader armies, for their journey was a pilgrimage as well as a military campaign. Each crusader who took the cross vowed to enter the Church of the Holy Sepulchre and pray there.

PILGRIMS BEARING ARMS

At low points during the First Crusade, such as the long siege of Antioch and the delay following its capture, the rank and file of the army were inspired to endure by their desire to fulfil their pilgrimage vows. Following the taking of Jerusalem, and their visit to the Church of the Holy Sepulchre, many felt that their enterprise was complete and took off for home, despite the fact that the crusaders' hold on Jerusalem was tenuous and that a formi-

▼ *Amid brutal violence, the soldiers who recaptured Jerusalem at the climax of the First Crusade celebrated ecstatically. Their pilgrimage had reached its goal.*

dable Egyptian relief army under the command of Fatimid vizier al-Afdal Shahanshah was marching on the city.

Before the crusades, there was already, as we have seen, a well-established Christian tradition of the pilgrimage as a form of penitential discipline. There was also a precedent for armed pilgrimage: in 1064, 7,000 armed German pilgrims under the command of two archbishops and two bishops marched to Jerusalem – some apparently wearing crosses. In 1095 Pope Urban II conflated the idea of a holy war fought in the name of God and the papacy with the benefits of a penitential journey. Part of the explanation for the response to his call to take the cross and travel on armed expedition to Jerusalem was that it met a keenly felt need – it allowed people to make their piety public and to seek expiation for their sins.

For many, the highest expression of Christian faith in action remained the monastic or clerical life. For example,

▲ *Preaching the Second Crusade in 1146, Bernard of Clairvaux urges Christians to take up the cross of Christ, and demonstrate their willingness to share in His suffering.*

Aelfric Grammaticus (the Grammarian), 10th-century abbot of Eynsham in southern England, declared that monks were the proper soldiers of Christ, those who fought with the words of prayers rather than with the metal of swords. But not all

THE GERMAN PILGRIMAGE OF 1064–65

Various chronicle accounts survive of the German pilgrimage of 1064. It was led by Siegfried, Archbishop of Mainz, and William, Archbishop of Trier, supported by Otto, Bishop of Regensburg and Gunther, Bishop of Bamberg. According to one report, Bishop Gunther cut such a splendid figure on this voyage that when the pilgrims came to Constantinople the people suspected that he must be the Holy Roman Emperor himself, travelling in disguise.

As they moved on towards Jerusalem, the pilgrims met returning travellers who told horror stories about the treatment of Christians by Arabs. On Good Friday 1065 the German pilgrims themselves were attacked by Arab bandits and then besieged at an isolated farmhouse over the entire Easter weekend. But, inspired by their archbishops and bishops, the pilgrims trusted in God and in their weapons and drove back the besiegers on Easter Sunday, despite having gone three days without food or water. They captured some leading Arabs who had broken into the enclosure and used these men as hostages.

Another much-reported and horrific episode on the pilgrimage involved the rape of an abbess in full view of the travelling pilgrims by a gang of Arabs. The abbess was so badly injured that she died. One account of the pilgrimage, contained in the *Life of Bishop Altmann of Passau*, commented: 'Brought down by events like this and other humiliations in Christ's name, the travelling faithful won high praise in all quarters, from men and from angels above, because they elected to enter God's kingdom, suffering many tribulations.'

could follow this path. As Guibert, the Benedictine abbot of Nogent-sous-Coucy in France, wrote after praising the holy wars of the crusades as giving knights a chance to win their salvation: 'In this way they are not forced to give up secular affairs entirely by entering the monastic life of the clerical professions, as was once the normal practice, but can reach in some degree God's grace while following their own careers, with the freedom and in the dress to which they are used.'

THE CROSS OF SUFFERING

The men (and women) who took the cross did not call themselves crusaders. They were known by contemporaries as *cruces-ignati* – people marked with the cross. Nor did they call the enterprise a crusade. It was variously called a business, a journey or way and a pilgrimage. Urban principally promoted it as a military expedition.

When Bernard of Clairvaux came to preach the Second Crusade in 1146 – with such dramatic effectiveness that his sermons were viewed as a 'divine augury' and a 'miracle' – he emphasized the expedition to Jerusalem he was urging as an opportunity for Christians to win salvation and, on an individual level, to demonstrate their repentance. In his vision, the cross worn by the crusaders was a sign that they were willing to share in the suffering of Christ; what pain and difficulty they had to endure en route to victory would only improve the effectiveness of the enterprise in winning salvation for them.

In a sermonizing letter, which he despatched to the people of France and Bavaria in 1146, Bernard called the crusade 'Christ's business, in which is found our salvation' and called for urgency – 'now is the right time, now is the day of total salvation'. He summoned the vision of pagans defiling the Holy City, the place where so many Christian pilgrims had 'confessed their wrongdoings with tears and won forgiveness'; he said that the all-powerful God could of course cleanse the city with a battalion of angels, but that he preferred to test the mettle of his faithful Christian soldiers.

Bernard concluded with the following exhortation 'since your land is bursting with courageous men and is celebrated for the strength of its young warriors, gird yourselves like men and take up arms joyfully in the name of Christ.'

▼ *Bernard of Clairvaux and other crusade preachers painted a picture of terrible outrages perpetrated by Muslim 'Saracens' against the Christians in the East.*

A CALL TO ARMS

On 27 November 1095, in a stirring speech to a great crowd at Clermont in France, Pope Urban II set in motion preparations for the First Crusade, which was to prove the start of centuries of violence between European Christians and Eastern Muslims in the Holy Land. Of course, he did not know that his speech was the beginning of hundreds of years of religious conflict, and the pious knights and other European warriors who responded to his call to arms were not aware that they were embarking on the first of a series of wars of the cross – indeed, they were encouraged to believe that the war would be final, victory total and glorious. Urban made the claim that Christ offered the ultimate reward to the knights and infantrymen he was seeking to mobilize. According to the version of the speech recorded by eyewitness Fulcher of Chartres, Urban urged those who waged war to take their courage and martial vigour abroad and put it to good use in combating 'barbarians' and cleansing the Holy Land: 'Let those who have been used to fighting without justice in private wars against faithful men and women, now embark against the faithless infidel and bring to an end with a great victory this war which should have been launched long ago ... Let those who have been earning mercenary pay instead earn eternal reward.' This reward, promised by the pope on behalf of God, was the complete remission of sins, the glory of heaven.

▲ *The People's Crusade sets out for the Holy Land, led by Peter the Hermit.*

◄ *The wealthy and deeply devout Count Raymond IV of Toulouse was the first European nobleman to obey Christ's command – as relayed by Pope Urban – to take the cross. Many pilgrims travelled in his party.*

CONSTANTINOPLE UNDER THREAT

EMPEROR ALEXIUS'S CRY FOR HELP

In March 1095 Alexius I Comnenus, ruler of the Byzantine Empire, despatched envoys to the Council of Piacenza in Italy to ask Pope Urban II for help in fighting the Seljuk Turks. This appeal either convinced Urban to promote a holy war to come to the aid of Christians in the East and reclaim the Holy Land, or else gave him ammunition to justify a decision he had already made to ask the chivalry of Europe to fight for the cross in the East.

Alexius's appeal was one of a number he made in the 1090s. He wanted military help in launching a counter-attack against the formidable Seljuk Turks, who had defeated the Byzantine Empire at the Battle of Manzikert in 1071 and had established the Sultanate of Rum in central Anatolia in 1077. Since becoming Byzantine emperor in 1081, Alexius had succeeded

in halting the invasion of Byzantine lands in Greece by the southern Italian Norman lord Robert Guiscard in 1081–82, then in beating back the incursions of the Turkish Pecheneg nomads in the Balkans. He saw an opportunity in the death in 1092 of the Turkish sultan of Baghdad, Malik Shah, and the collapse of his empire in Iraq, Syria and Palestine. The time appeared to

▲ *Alexius made much of the barbarity of the Seljuk Turks. They were fierce warriors, but maintained a highly civilized court.*

be ripe to strike back against the Seljuks and to reassert Byzantine authority across many of its former lands.

To win the support of Western nobles, Alexius and his envoys emphasized the

▼ *Pilgrims arrive at Jaffa (top) and pay a toll before entering Tyre (bottom). Both cities attracted pilgrims because of their role in biblical and early Christian history, and became crusader strongholds.*

ALEXIUS I COMNENUS

Alexius I Comnenus, who ruled as Byzantine emperor from 1081 to 1118, proved himself one of the leading statesmen of his era. He came to power, by seizing the throne from Nicephorus III, just ten years after the empire's catastrophic defeat at the Battle of Manzikert by the Seljuk Turks, and ruled through the period of the First Crusade and the establishment of the crusader states of Jerusalem, Antioch, Edessa and Tripoli.

He made the crusader lords swear an oath to return to him the lands they gained on campaign and, although this was not honoured, by the crusaders' efforts he regained control of many cities including Nicaea, Sardis and Ephesus, as well as much of Anatolia. In his 37-year reign he restored the Byzantine Empire to a position of relative strength following its series of defeats at the hands of Normans and Turks. He founded the Comnenian dynasty of Byzantine emperors, who ruled until the late 12th century. In the words of an anonymous Greek biographer, he was a man 'great both in the power of his will and in deeds'.

◀ *The likeness of Alexius I Comnenus, Byzantine emperor between 1081 and 1118, adorns one side of this gold Byzantine soldo (penny coin).*

threat to Christians and their holy places posed by the pagan Turks. But he did not envisage a holy war – he wanted a mercenary army, whose soldiers he could control with financial incentives. He did not foresee the struggle for the Holy Land launched by the pope; fighting to recapture Jerusalem was never part of his plan – the city had, after all, been in Muslim hands since 638.

LETTER TO COUNT ROBERT OF FLANDERS

One of Alexius's appeals survives in the form of a letter dated 1093 written to Count Robert II of Flanders. Count Robert's father – Count Robert I of Flanders – had stayed with Alexius in Constantinople on his return from a pilgrimage and Alexius had reportedly been impressed by the strength of his escort. His letter tried to appeal on several different fronts, seeking to generate not only righteous anger but also a lust for riches.

The letter described how the Patzinaks (or Pechenegs) and Turks carried out forced circumcision of Christian babies and boys above the baptismal font, and forced them to urinate into its waters; it suggested that they not only abducted and raped Christian women (both virgins and

▲ *The crusaders were awestruck by the beauty and ancient treasures of the walled city of Constantinople. This map was made in c.1485 by the Italian cartographer Cristoforo Buondelmonti.*

venerable matrons), but also performed acts of sodomy on Byzantine men – including Christian clergy, monks and even bishops. He compared their acts to those of the 'impious Babylonians', who, according to biblical accounts, had mistreated the Jews in exile – suggesting

thereby that under the threat of the Turks, the Christian Byzantines were effectively in exile in their own lands.

Alexis lamented that the great expanses of the Byzantine Empire had been snatched away and suggested that the invaders were on the verge of capturing Constantinople itself, 'unless the help of God and faithful Latin Christians should come quickly to us'. He pointed out that the cities of the East – and notably Constantinople – were rich in holy relics and that God would punish any brave lord who refused to come to their protection; those who did come, he said, would win reward in heaven.

Later in the letter, however, Alexius also emphasized that these cities were additionally full of treasures and gold, and of beautiful women – 'Greek women possess a beauty beyond compare that would be a good enough reason to lure the brave armies of the Franks to Thrace'. The Latin Christian lords should not allow these beauties – neither treasures nor flesh and blood – to fall into pagan hands.

▼ *Byzantine forces besiege Messina in Sicily. In Italy, the Byzantines had for centuries been at odds with the Normans and other Europeans, whose help they now requested.*

RIGHTEOUS WARFARE
POPE URBAN II PREACHES THE FIRST CRUSADE

On Tuesday 27 November 1095 at the close of the Council of Clermont in central France, Pope Urban II issued a rousing call to arms, urging the Christian knights of Europe to travel to the aid of their brothers in the East and liberate the holy places of Jerusalem from unbelievers. The speech was the high point of a months-long tour of France promoting the crusade between August 1095 and September 1096.

The Council of Clermont, an assembly for church reform, had been running since 18 November and had been attended by around 300 prominent clerics. They had deliberated on clerical marriage, the elimination of simony (the practice of selling Church positions) and the excommunication of King Philip of France for committing adultery.

Word must have been circulated that the pope was planning to make a great announcement, for the crowd that gathered to hear him was too large to fit into the Cathedral at Clermont and the papal

▼ *Urban is escorted to Clermont, where he asked bishops and abbots to bring the leading lords in their areas to the council.*

▲ *In Fulcher of Chartres's account of the speech, Urban declared 'Let men who have grown used to waging private war against fellow Christians go now against the infidel and win a great victory in this war that should have been started long ago.'*

throne was therefore moved to a field just outside the city. There, Urban delivered the passionate address that launched the First Crusade.

URBAN'S SPEECH

We know that Urban was a highly intelligent man and a great orator and can tell from the response that the speech had an electrifying effect. But it is impossible to know for sure what he said. Five separate substantial accounts of Urban's speech survive, but all were written in the early 12th century in the light of later assumptions about the enterprise and after the First Crusade had ended in triumph at Jerusalem in 1099.

The earliest account was in the anonymous chronicle *Gesta Francorum* (Deeds of the Franks), probably written by a follower of Bohemond of Taranto in *c*.1100. This was used as a source by the other reports. Shortly afterwards, perhaps in 1101, Fulcher of Chartres, an ecclesiastic who travelled on crusade in the party of

Stephen of Blois and Robert of Normandy, wrote a history of the First Crusade that also included a major report of the speech; it is probable that Fulcher was actually present at the Council of Clermont. Another very important description of the speech was given by Robert the Monk, who reworked the *Gesta Francorum* in *c*.1106; he was almost certainly not present at Clermont.

A fourth account was written by the Benedictine historian Guibert, Abbot of Nogent-sous-Coucy, in his *Dei gesta per Francos* (Deeds of God carried out by the Franks) of *c*.1108. He used the *Gesta Francorum* as a principal source but also used material gleaned from discussions with crusaders he knew; he, too, was present at the Council of Clermont, so must have included his memories as an eyewitness in the report. A fifth version of Urban's speech was given by Balderic, Archbishop of Dol-en-Bretagne from 1107–30, who based his account – written 10–20 years after the speech – on the *Gesta Francorum*.

According to the account in the *Gesta Francorum*, Urban primarily focused on the instruction of Christ to his followers that they should take up the cross and follow him, and described how men should seek to save their soul and find reward in heaven by finding the way to the Holy Sepulchre in Jerusalem.

In Fulcher of Chartres's report, Urban presented the expedition as an opportunity for secular warriors to become soldiers in Christ's service. He condemned lawlessness and the actions of robbers and urged that the Truce of God, the general peace agreed on Church authority, should be honoured. Then he called on all present to hurry to the aid of Christians in the East against 'Turks and Arabs', and to 'drive that vile race from the territories of our friends'. He said: 'All who die on the journey, overland or across seas, or in fighting against pagans, shall be rewarded with immediate remission of sins.'

In Robert the Monk's account, meanwhile, Urban emphasized the need to fight for the conquest of the Holy Land more than hurry to the aid of the Christians in the East. He repeated many of the descriptions of pagan infamy listed in the supposed letter of Alexis I to Count Robert II of Flanders – such as forced circumcision of Christian boys, spilling of human blood in the font and brutal rape of Christian women.

▼ *According to Balderic, Urban called on knights to defend the Church of the Holy Sepulchre and other Eastern churches as they would defend their mother.*

▲ *Robert the Monk described Urban calling on Christians to go to the aid of their brethren because, in the words that became the battle cry of the crusaders, 'God wills it!'*

In Robert's account, the pope also emphasized the great history of the Franks and their pedigree as a fighting race – they were above all other nations in arms, and should be inspired by the deeds of their ancestors, great warriors such as Charlemagne: 'O bravest of soldiers, the sons of invincible forebears, do not forget the valour of your ancestors.' He added that France was crowded with men, nd that inevitable competition bred conflict, but that the Holy Land to which he called them was – as noted in the Bible – one that 'floweth with milk and honey'; it was 'a paradise of many delights' and, moreover, a place consecrated by the suffering of Christ. He personified the city of Jerusalem, which he said lay at the centre of the world: 'from you,' he said, 'she asks for help!' He added: 'Take on this journey for the remission of sins, in confidence of the undying glory of God's kingdom.'

Balderic of Dol's version emphasized particularly the desecration of holy places in Jerusalem by pagans and called powerfully on Christian knights to stop fighting one another and, instead, to combat Turks and others in the Holy Land. In this account, Urban declared 'may you find it is a beautiful thing to give your life for Christ in the city in which he gave his life for us all'; fighting Saracens, he said, was 'righteous warfare', and would deliver 'everlasting glory'. He also pointed out, however, that worldly wealth would be an auxiliary prize – for the enemy was in possession of great riches.

The account of Guibert of Nogent emphasized the notion, current in the 10th and 11th centuries, that the 'Last Days' were at hand prior to the Second Coming of Christ as described in the biblical Book of Revelation and suggested that Christian knights should go to Jerusalem to oppose pagans as part of this final conflict. In this version, Urban described the many sufferings of Christian pilgrims to the Holy Land at the hands of pagans. He promised that knights fighting in the holy war would have Christ as 'standard bearer and inseparable leader'.

GOD WILLS IT! GOD WILLS IT!

THE RUSH TO TAKE THE CROSS

At the end of Urban's speech, a great shout went up among those in the crowd: 'God wills it! God wills it! God wills it!' Adhemar, Bishop of Le Puy, stepped forward and fell to his knees before Urban, and asked to be allowed to take part in an expedition to the East. Urban appointed him to serve on the pope's behalf as leader of the crusade. Some men trembled and wept in the crowd, and others discussed Urban's words earnestly: almost at once, many came forward in imitation of Adhemar to pledge themselves to undertake the task to which Urban called them.

TAKING THE CROSS

According to some accounts volunteers at once began to mark themselves out by attaching a cross to their clothes, in homage to the cross of Christ; clerics and monks surrendered their cloaks to provide

▼ *A monk bestows the cross on a crusader. The symbol of Christ gave weight and meaning to each knight's journey eastwards.*

material from which people cut the crosses. Fulcher of Chartres reported that as soon as people took the oath to go on the expedition, they made 'shining crosses' from cloth of gold or silk and attached them to their shoulders.

It seems obvious from contemporary accounts that the events at Clermont were carefully stage-managed: doubtless Urban had instructed a cleric to set up the chant of 'God wills it! God wills it!' and arranged in advance that Adhemar would step forward and be the first to take a vow. According to Robert the Monk, Urban whipped up the crowd further by claiming that the fact that they all chanted the one phrase was evidence that God was at work among them, in line with Christ's promise that 'Where two or three are gathered together in my name there am I in the midst of them': though the words were issuing from many mouths, they had their origin in one place, in God. And he proceeded to specify that these words should become the battle cry of the crusading armies when they went to war in the East.

▲ *Crusader knights of the Minutolo family kneel in prayer, in a fresco from San Gennaro Cathedral, Naples. Over centuries families became associated with crusading as fathers and sons, uncles and nephews took the cross on different campaigns.*

The visual drama of 'taking the cross' by attaching it to clothing was also seemingly prearranged, with clerics briefed beforehand to provide the necessary material for the eager men in the crowd.

The taking of the cross was a symbolic visual act that gave added physical weight to the verbal vow taken by the participants. The *Gesta Francorum* reported that the Franks who undertook to make the expedition sewed the cross of Christ on their right shoulders. According to Robert the Monk, Urban instructed all those taking the vow to mark themselves with the sign of Christ's cross either on their forehead or on their chest, and said that when they had accomplished what he asked them to do, they should wear the cross on their back between their shoulders. Guibert of Nogent also reported that it was

Pope Urban's order that people sew the cross, made of any material, on their shirt, cloak or chain mail tunic. In this version, Urban added that any person who took the vow and then did not travel would be an outlaw for all time.

THE REMISSION OF SINS

Although the accounts of the speech at Clermont vary, we can be certain that Urban's appeal did promise the remission of sins for those who took part – the journey itself would bring the same benefits as a pilgrimage to Jerusalem.

The issues of sin and forgiveness were very important for people of all classes at this time, not least because it was commonly held that the expected Second Coming of Christ was imminent, and that the 'Last Days' of the world as described in the Bible were at hand. This meant that the feared Day of Judgement was also imminent, and that it was a matter of even greater than normal urgency to find officially sanctioned ways of seeking forgiveness for wrongdoing.

FIGHTING WITH GOD'S BLESSING

Urban II, who came from the minor nobility of the Champagne region of France, knew how to address the knightly class, and his appeal at Clermont and throughout the preaching tour of which it was a part struck a note that rang true with the warriors in his audience. The Church's initial response to the emergence of knights

▲ *Jerusalem, the Holy City, and navel of God's creation, was said to be calling out in her distress to the knights of Europe, begging to be freed.*

had been to try to stifle their enthusiasm for fighting – in the Peace of God and Truce of God movements, to limit knightly conflict to prescribed periods. But on the expedition Urban proposed should take place to the East, knights would be encouraged to fight, and would do so with the full blessing of the Church and of God. Moreover, in doing so they would gain spiritual blessings as well as impunity – as Christ's soldiers they would win forgiveness of their sins and ultimately their salvation after death.

THE QUEST FOR GLORY
MOTIVES OF THE KNIGHTS WHO UNDERTOOK THE FIRST CRUSADE

The primary motivation of the knights who departed on the First Crusade was religious. Taking the cross was an act of piety, a statement of faith.

Taking the cross as a knight was likened to becoming a monk, which in this period was put forward as the spiritual ideal for a Christian life. Those who took the cross were treated like the clergy, and acquired certain associated privileges – while on crusade they did not, for example, have to pay taxes or settle debts or carry out feudal military service. It was understandably a matter of concern for those considering going on crusade that they were leaving their family and property behind, but the Church promised protection on their behalf. In the account of Urban's speech at Clermont given by Guibert of Nogent, the pope announced that anyone who molested the property or family of a soldier of Christ while he was on pilgrimage to the Holy Land would be subject to 'a fearful anathema' – that is, excommunication.

▼ *Before embarking upon crusade a knight receives Holy Communion. Crusading was comparable to the quests in search of honour taken by knights in chivalric poems.*

GLAMOUR AND HONOUR

But there were also secular attractions for the crusaders in addition to these primary religious motives. The knights were seeking honour and glory as well. Glamour was attached to the crusade proposed by Urban: it was an adventure and, as we have seen, it allowed the knights of Europe to indulge their taste for conflict.

The code of chivalry, which in the late 11th century was in the early stages of its development, taught that knights must seek opportunities to practise their martial skills and to prove themselves worthy of the honour of being a knight. In Europe they could be frustrated in doing this by the Peace of God and by secular or ecclesiastical authority, but on crusade they were encouraged to do so. The knights were – and saw themselves as – an international elite: the landowners of northern France and of England and of southern Italy had more in common with each other than they had with their countrymen; the crusade gave them an enemy and a target, and the opportunity to ride out among their peers seeking glory.

THE LURE OF WEALTH?

For many decades historians argued that the crusaders also rode eastward in search of a fortune. The accounts we have of the appeal that was made to the knights of Europe certainly included the promise of wealth. Alexius Comnenus's letter to Count Robert II of Flanders pretended that in Constantinople there was more gold than anywhere else in the world – and that the city's churches were overflowing with silver and precious stones and fine silks as well as gold; moreover, he claimed that the riches of all the emperors of the ancient Roman Empire were hidden in the palaces of the city. In Balderic of Dol's account of Pope Urban's speech at Clermont, the pope promised the crusaders the spoils of the enemy: 'the

▲ *A knight offers his service to God. This celebrated crusading image is from the English Westminster Psalter of c.1250.*

possessions of the enemy will be yours, too,' he said, 'since you will make their treasures your spoils'.

The knights, of course, were happy to take what spoils of war came their way in line with conventional practice in the medieval period. But they did not set out principally to seek their fortune.

At one time, historians argued that crusade armies contained many younger sons, men who seized on Urban's call to reclaim the Holy Land as a chance to make a place for themselves in the world and win a fortune. This traditional account pointed out that within the feudal system in northern France and England, younger sons in noble families could not inherit their father's wealth and had limited opportunities for self-advancement. And even in southern Europe, where inheritances were shared out among all sons, many found their prospects were poor because the property was split so many times among

▲ *Committing to crusade required bravery, a willingness to risk all fighting far from home. Most knights were sustained by their faith that they were carrying out God's will.*

descendants that it became insignificant. However, modern historians dismiss this argument, pointing out the great expense of equipping oneself to go on crusade. To travel on crusade cost a knight many times his annual income.

From surviving charters and other documents we can see that the great majority of crusaders intended to return, if they did not die on the adventure overseas, and were not deliberately setting out to make a new life in a strange land. Moreover, it is simply not true that younger sons rather

▶ *Knights had to equip themselves at great expense with a horse, weapons and finery. Crusading was a chance to demonstrate social standing and chivalric qualities.*

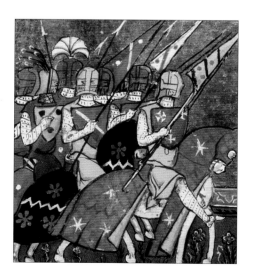

than their older siblings went on crusade – great lords and eldest sons travelled as well as their younger brothers. It is true that following the success of the First Crusade and the establishment of the crusader kingdoms of Jerusalem, Edessa, Antioch and Tripoli, a number of Europeans settled in the Middle East. But

historians now question whether these settlers were primarily crusaders, as was once assumed, or whether they were emigrants after the crusade taking advantage of the new opportunities.

There were certainly individual cases of young men who made their name and fortune on crusade, but they were not a general type among the crusaders. Many knights, in fact, made significant financial sacrifices to go on crusade – some had to mortgage their property to pay for the expedition – and pay high rates of interest on the loan; others sold their land – and often accepted a poor price because in France, for example, the 1090s were a time of agricultural depression. The fact that so many knights made substantial sacrifices to take the cross is testament to the power of Pope Urban's stirring appeal and runs quite counter to the proposal that knights travelled to the Holy Land out of financial self-interest.

WALKING TO THE HOLY LAND
THE PEOPLE'S CRUSADE

The sermon at Clermont may have been meticulously planned and the accompanying pageantry carefully staged, but the response to Urban's plea took him by surprise. In addition to a well-equipped military force of great princes, lords and knights of the kind Urban had hoped to mobilize, a vast army of peasants and poor townspeople also left their homes, determined to put their trust in God and make their way to the Holy Land.

PETER THE HERMIT
A monk and popular preacher from Amiens named Peter the Hermit toured northern France and Flanders on a donkey, calling for crusade volunteers. He was a small man, known as 'Little Peter' by his contemporaries, with a long thin face, like

▼ *Peter shows knights their duty. Byzantine princess Anna Comnena wrote that Peter had tried before to make a pilgrimage to Jerusalem, but had been tortured by Turks.*

that of his donkey, and eccentric habits – he dressed only in a cloak, was often unwashed and lived on nothing but wine and fish. Yet Peter had the orator's gift, the ability to transfix a large crowd; according to Guibert of Nogent, who met him, Peter's charisma was such that his acts and deeds seemed 'half divine'. Peter claimed that Christ himself had appointed him to preach the crusade – and even pretended that he had a letter from God to prove it. The crowds flocked after him.

This first wave of crusaders contained many hangers-on with little or no military equipment or experience of fighting, although the core of the group was adequately fitted out with horses and weapons. But remarkably there were only eight knights. The most notable of these was the experienced Walter of Sans Avoir in the Seine Valley. (He was not, as is commonly written, a penniless knight. This traditional reputation derives from a misunderstanding of his name – for

generations historians interpreted Walter Sans Avoir to mean he had nothing, that he was penniless; in fact, it refers to his feudal base, a place of that name in the Seine Valley.)

DEPARTURE FOR THE HOLY LAND
Pope Urban had declared the Feast of the Assumption of the Blessed Virgin Mary (15 August 1096) to be the starting point for the expedition, but the people who gathered to travel on what historians call the People's Crusade were impatient to depart. Peter the Hermit assembled his followers at Cologne, Germany on 12 April. His plan was to gather more followers by preaching among the Germans.

A French contingent of a few thousand under the leadership of Walter Sans Avoir could not brook even this minor delay and departed at once. They followed an overland route, and were in Hungary by 8 May. They then proceeded without incident as far as Belgrade, on the border of Byzantine lands. However, the governor of Belgrade refused them entry and the French crusaders looted the countryside – in the market town of Semlin, 16 of them were captured and stripped of their armour, which was hung from the walls of the castle there. Eventually the main group reached Nish (now in Serbia) and waited for a troop escort from the Byzantine emperor in Constantinople.

A second wave of around 20,000 left Cologne under Peter the Hermit's leadership on 20 April and followed the same route as the French pilgrims who had gone before. The first part of their journey was uneventful, but when they reached Semlin and saw the armour of the earlier crusaders hanging from the castle walls, they rioted and attacked the city, killing 4,000 locals. Afterwards, they crossed the River Save before attacking and looting Belgrade. At Nish, where they arrived on 3 July, the garrison commander was

▲ Faith drove them on. The unlikely looking forces of the People's Crusade march across Europe in an image from the 15th-century Les Passages faits Outremer.

initially peaceable and promised an escort to Constantinople if the crusaders would move quickly on, but then a skirmish broke out between locals and some German crusaders and the commander unleashed the full force of his garrison, routing the motley crusader force and killing about 5,000 crusaders. Peter the Hermit and the chastened survivors carried on, and on 12 July arrived at Sofia (now in Bulgaria), where they awaited a military escort from Constantinople.

CRUSADES AGAINST THE JEWS

Some sections of the great population mobilized for a crusade did not travel to the Holy Land, but carried out attacks against Jewish communities in France and Germany. The most serious slaughter was carried out by a 10,000-strong army commanded by Count Emicho of Leisingen, who claimed that Christ had appeared to him and promised to make him emperor if he would convert the Jews of Europe. The Church authorities largely tried to protect the Jews, but Jews were forcibly converted or killed in their thousands by the crusaders – especially in the Rhineland, where there were dreadful massacres in Worms, Mainz, Cologne and Trier. Count Emicho's troops massacred 800 Jews at Worms on 18 May and at least 1,100 at Mainz on 27 May.

Anti-Semitism had been current for centuries, but these were the first organized attacks against the Jews in European history. Some of the crusaders, including Count Emicho himself, felt that the Jews – culpable for the crucifixion of Christ – were just as much enemies of the cross as the Muslims, and believed that the crusading spirit could be given expression close to home. Feeling was also running high against the Jews among crusaders who had to borrow money to finance the crusade since, because money-lending was forbidden among Christians, they usually had entered into debts with Jewish lenders. Many of these crusaders now grew rich by stealing the Jews' money. Some historians refer to these attacks as the 'First Holocaust', linking them to the official attempt to exterminate the Jews by the Nazi government of Germany during the 1930s and World War II.

WHY DID SO MANY PEOPLE JOIN THE PEOPLE'S CRUSADE?

In the late 11th century there was a resurgence of belief that the Second Coming of Christ was imminent. This fired a popular desire to make a mass pilgrimage to Jerusalem and to return the Holy City to Christian control. At the same time, a series of celestial events – including a comet, a lunar eclipse and a meteor shower – seemed to reinforce the sense that the enterprise preached by Pope Urban and Peter the Hermit had God's blessing. In addition, there had been an outbreak of ergotism, or 'St Anthony's fire', food poisoning (caused by long-term consumption of cereals containing fungi). This poisoning results in convulsions and gangrene, and it was interpreted as evidence of God's displeasure and made people desire to expiate their sins by making a pilgrimage. Some historians argue that in the years prior to 1096, the peasants of northern Europe had been suffering very severely as a result of the plague, drought and famine and were seeking escape from these terrible conditions.

▶ For most people in Europe, life was harsh. Some may have seen the crusade as a chance for a new beginning.

JOURNEY TO PALESTINE

The vast contingent of pilgrims and soldiers led by the monk Peter the Hermit and the knight Walter of Sans Avoir was followed to Constantinople by no fewer than five armies commanded by minor royals and some of the leading noblemen of Europe – including Duke Robert of Normandy, eldest son of King William I of England, and Hugh of Vermandois, younger brother of King Philip I of France, as well as counts and noblemen such as Raymond of Toulouse, Godfrey of Bouillon and Bohemond of Taranto. The second wave of armies, some of whom travelled overland and some by sea, is known to historians as the Princes' Crusade to distinguish it from the earlier People's Crusade, which was so called because it contained many unarmed pilgrims and peasants. As had the People's Crusaders before them, the Princes' armies endured their share of mishaps and disasters before they ever arrived at the glittering capital of the Byzantine Empire; and, arriving there confident in the knowledge that they were riding to the help of beleaguered Christians, their leaders faced an uncertain welcome from an emperor suspicious of their motives, who in particular feared that they aimed to establish themselves as rulers in his territory. In the event, the two crusades merged – after a catastrophic defeat at the hands of the Seljuk Turks in Anatolia, the chastened remnant of the People's Crusade returned to Constantinople, joined up with the still fresh and confident armies of the Princes' Crusade and set off for Jerusalem.

▲ *A messenger is sent for help at the siege of Antioch.*

◄ *The main strength of a crusader army was in its mounted cavalry bearing lances, but the soldiers were also a very effective force when battle broke down into hand-to-hand combat.*

MORE THAN THE STARS OF HEAVEN
THE PEOPLE'S CRUSADE ARRIVES IN CONSTANTINOPLE

The two main branches of the People's Crusade, one under the leadership of impoverished knight Walter Sans Avoir and the other following charismatic monk Peter the Hermit, had both arrived at Constantinople by 1 August 1096.

Anna Comnena, daughter of the Byzantine emperor Alexius I, described how the armed contingent was accompanied by a vast crowd of crusader-pilgrims 'outnumbering the grains of sand on the sea shore or the stars sparkling in the sky, carrying palms and crosses on their shoulders'. This group included many women, children and old people. She wrote that 'to look upon them was like watching powerful rivers flooding from all sides to a confluence'.

▼ *Peter the Hermit's charismatic preaching convinced many to abandon home and loved ones to honour the cross. Arriving in the East, they began to realize the immense difficulty of the task they had taken on.*

ACROSS THE BOSPHORUS
Alexius had expected a disciplined and cohesive army to be sent from Europe; instead he was confronted with a motley band of largely ill-equipped travellers who expected to be fed and given assistance. He refused them entry into the city, and made them camp outside the city walls. Within five days he had ferried them all across the Bosphorus into Anatolia.

It may be that the emperor simply wanted to be rid of them, and sent them on without much help to face almost certain death; on the other hand, it is possible that the crusaders insisted on marching on towards Jerusalem despite his best efforts to dissuade them. Anna Comnena – whose account in the *Alexiad* (*c*.1148), a biography of her father, understandably cast Alexius in a sympathetic light – claimed that the emperor tried to persuade Peter to await the arrival of reinforcements before moving on, but that Peter insisted on crossing into Anatolia and pressing on

towards Jerusalem. Alexius also warned the hermit not to be drawn into battle, because he saw that the crusaders were evidently no match for the Turkish army.

The crusaders were joined by several contingents of Italians, newly arrived from home. The group marched on, pillaging the towns they came to until they reached Nicomedia (now Izmit in Turkey), where they quarrelled. The Italians and Germans, under the command of an Italian by the name of Rainald, separated themselves from the French under Geoffrey Burel. Peter the Hermit and Walter Sans Avoir were no longer in control of events.

RAIDS IN ANATOLIA
The crusaders established a camp at Civetot, on the Sea of Marmara (the inland body of water that connects the Black and Aegean seas). Groups set out from the main crusader camp, competing with one another in attempts to progress the crusade. A French contingent marched as far as Nicaea, wealthy capital of the Turkish sultanate of Rum, and looted the edge of the city – according to Anna Comnena's colourful version of events, they committed atrocities there, torturing venerable old men, killing children and even cooking babies over spits and eating them.

Meanwhile, a 6,000-strong German troupe took the city of Xerigordon. In response the Turks sent an army to lay seige to Xerigordon, which captured the only source of water, located outside the city walls. The Germans lasted eight days, and surrendered only after they were reduced to drinking their own urine and the blood of their donkeys to survive. In defeat, they were slaughtered, or forced to convert to Islam and sold into slavery.

CRUSADERS MASSACRED
The Turks then set a trap for the remainder of the crusaders. In the main camp at Civetot, Turkish spies spread a rumour

▲ *The dreams of glory summoned by Peter the Hermit fell apart in the unfamiliar territory of Anatolia, where the crusaders were ravaged by the Seljuk Turks.*

that the Germans had not only triumphed at Xerigordon, but had also taken Nicaea. The rumour spread like wildfire, and generated a clamour to travel swiftly on to Nicaea and share in the looting. Peter the Hermit was absent, having travelled back to Constantinople to negotiate for supplies; Geoffrey Burel convinced the entire remainder of the force, some 20,000 strong, that they should move out at once.

On 21 October at dawn they marched out of the camp towards Nicaea. Anna Comnena commented at this juncture that the 'Latins' (Italians and Europeans) were known for their love of money, and that when they went on a military campaign their lust for wealth grew even stronger, becoming so overpowering that it robbed them of their judgement and made them rush headlong, as here, into trouble. In her account, they simply ran out of the camp towards Nicaea, without arming themselves, clamouring for money, with no semblance of discipline: they were entirely unprepared for what followed.

The Turks had laid an ambush in a narrow valley just 3 miles (5km) from the crusader camp. There they set on the army led by Geoffrey Burel, provoking a wave of blind panic among them. The slaughter was most terrible. Anna Comnena reported that when after the battle men went to clear the battlefield they gathered together the corpses of the fallen crusaders and made not merely a mound or a hill but a grisly flyblown mountain. Only 3,000 crusaders survived, and they took refuge in an abandoned castle. The Turks pursued them there and laid siege, but in time a Byzantine force sailed across from Constantinople, chased the Turks off and freed the crusaders.

A RABBLE OR AN ARMY?

The conventional view of the People's Crusade has been that the people who made this long and fruitless pilgrimage were little more than a rabble roused by an unscrupulous charismatic preacher, and that their 'armies' contained no more than a handful of properly equipped and trained soldiers. However, it is worth considering that this first wave of crusaders maintained their discipline sufficiently to march all the way across Europe as far as

▲ *Peter distributes crosses to eager volunteers. He convinced many of his poorer followers that a host of angels would defend them if they came under attack.*

Constantinople and that in Anatolia they did win military victories before their ultimate defeat. Even granted this, however, the ill-conceived People's Crusade cannot ultimately be adjudged anything more than a disaster. Scores of thousands of people lost their lives – the 3,000 crusaders who survived defeat in Anatolia were the only survivors of the crusade.

After they were freed by the Byzantine relief force from the castle in which they had taken refuge, the survivors made their way slowly back to Constantinople, where they eventually joined up with the better equipped armies that had followed them from Europe.

▼ *The crusaders arrive in Constantinople. A significant proportion of the peasants on the People's Crusade died of starvation or were sold into slavery.*

PRINCES ON CRUSADE
THE LEADERS OF THE FIRST CRUSADE

The European princes and nobles who responded to Pope Urban's call to crusade travelled in five main armies to Constantinople by different routes. They began to leave in mid-summer 1096 and arrived at Constantinople at various times between November 1096 and May 1097.

The first army to arrive was that of Hugh of Vermandois, who as younger brother of King Philip I of France was a prince of a royal house and one of the highest-ranking of the crusaders. He was reputedly convinced to embark on the crusade by an eclipse of the moon in February 1096, which he interpreted as divine guidance. The chronicler William of Tyre called him 'Hugh Magnus' (Hugh the Great), but despite high birth Hugh did very little of note, being an ineffective soldier and leader. He certainly had a high opinion of himself, however: according to Anna Comnena, he sent a breathtakingly arrogant letter to Alexius, in which he declared: 'Be advised, O Emperor, that I am the King of kings, highest-ranking of

▲ Bohemond of Taranto's crusading feats won him the hand of Constance, daughter of King Philip I of France, in 1104.

▼ Godfrey of Bouillon. The crusade made him into a figure of legend, celebrated in literature as one of the 'Nine Worthies'.

all beneath the sky. My will is that you should attend me upon my arrival and give me the magnificent welcome that is fitting for a visitor of the noblest birth.'

Hugh's army travelled by way of Italy, where they were joined by a number of soldiers previously under the command of Count Emicho, leader of the German Crusade against the Jews – soldiers who had been dispersed by a Hungarian army. The army set sail from Bari across the Adriatic Sea, but were shipwrecked off the Byzantine port of Dyrrhachium (now Durres in Albania) and had to be rescued by the Byzantine governor of that locality before being escorted to Constantinople, arriving in November 1096.

GODFREY OF BOUILLON
The second army was from northern France and Belgium, led by Godfrey, Lord of Bouillon and duke of Lower Lorraine, with his younger brother Baldwin and his older brother Eustace III, Count of Boulogne. The army, perhaps 40,000 strong, set out from Lorraine in August

1096 bound for Constantinople: they followed largely the same route as the People's Crusade, through Hungary and the Balkans (part of the Byzantine Empire), where they crossed the River Danube at Belgrade and proceeded via Sofia and Adrianople (modern Edirne in Turkey) and arrived at the Sea of Marmara in mid-December. On 23 December they pitched their camp beneath the walls of Constantinople. In some accounts, this army was referred to as 'the Lorrainers'.

BOHEMOND OF TARANTO
The third army was made up of Normans from southern Italy and led by Bohemond of Taranto. Bohemond was the son of Norman adventurer Robert Guiscard and was an old enemy of Emperor Alexius, having fought against him during his father's failed invasion of the Byzantine Empire in the early 1080s. In his company

was his nephew Tancred, the son of Bohemond's sister, Emma of Apulia.

Bohemond did not hear Pope Urban's call to arms. He joined the crusade only in October 1097 after he encountered knights making their way towards the Holy Land by way of southern Italy, where he and his army – including Tancred – were besieging the town of Amalfi, which had rebelled against his authority. Among these knights was Tancred's brother William: learning of the purpose of their journey, the Normans under Bohemond elected to join the crusade. The army set sail in October 1096, crossing the Adriatic from Brindisi to Avlona (a seaport now in Albania) and marched overland to Constantinople, where it arrived on 9 April 1097.

RAYMOND OF TOULOUSE

The fourth army belonged to Raymond, Count of Toulouse, Duke of Narbonne and Margrave of Provence. He was the first noble knight to take the cross after Pope Urban's speech at Clermont, and was profoundly religious: according to one account in an Armenian chronicle, he had made a pilgrimage to Jerusalem before the First Crusade, and during the course of this journey lost an eye; he had also fought in Spain against Muslim armies. He was 55, the oldest and also the wealthiest of the crusading lords, and he might have expected to be named leader of the expedition, but Pope Urban gave no special position to any of the secular lords, vesting his authority in the papal legate Adhemar, Bishop of Le Puy, who travelled in Raymond's party.

Raymond, in the company of his third wife Elvira (the illegitimate daughter of King Alfonso VI of Castile) and Bishop Adhemar, departed from Toulouse with a large army and a significant contingent of unarmed pilgrims in October 1096. They took an overland route by way of Genoa and Venice and along the coast as far as Dyrrhachium, before heading inland. They arrived at the gates of Constantinople on 27 April 1097.

DUKE ROBERT OF NORMANDY

The fifth main army was jointly led by Duke Robert of Normandy, his brother-in-law Stephen, Count of Blois, and Count Robert II of Flanders.

Duke Robert of Normandy was the eldest son of King William I of England, who, on his deathbed, had bequeathed the duchy of Normandy to Robert and the English throne to his second son, William Rufus. The two brothers had been at war on and off since William Rufus had become King of England on the Conqueror's death in 1087: in September 1096, Robert pawned the duchy of Normandy to William Rufus in return for 10,000 silver marks, which he used to fund his part in the crusade.

Stephen, Count of Blois, was married to Robert's sister, the formidable Adela of Normandy, and according to contemporary accounts went on the crusade only because he was ordered to do so by his wife. (He was to be father of a king of England, for his son Stephen – born at

▲ Robert II, Count of Flanders, was one of the co-leaders of Robert of Normandy's section of the crusading army.

Blois in 1096 before the crusade – was King Stephen of England from 1135–54.) Count Robert of Flanders was an experienced campaigner and skilled knight, who had proved his worth by governing Flanders while his father had been away on a pilgrimage to Jerusalem from 1085–91. Also in this army was Bishop Odo of Bayeux.

This fifth army left northern France in October 1096, but was waylaid in southern Italy where Duke Robert and Count Stephen settled for the winter, enjoying the hospitality of local lords. But Count Robert of Flanders pressed on with his force, sailing from Brindisi and marching overland to Constantinople. The remainder of the army followed in the spring, leaving Brindisi in April and arriving in Constantinople in May 1097, just a month behind Raymond's army.

THE CRUSADERS IN CONSTANTINOPLE
NEGOTIATIONS WITH EMPEROR ALEXIUS

Alexius quite naturally viewed the princely crusaders with suspicion. The princes and lords had mobilized great armies and brought them on to imperial Byzantine territory officially to supply help to Christians in the East, but it was difficult to be sure of their true motives.

The emperor could not be certain that the Latin lords were not plotting to capture pieces of his empire for themselves. In any case, the crusaders were also talking of capturing Jerusalem, which Alexius still viewed as a possession of the Byzantine Empire, even if one that was temporarily in Muslim hands. Moreover, among the leaders was a major former adversary, Bohemond of Taranto.

Alexius determined to make each of the crusader lords swear an oath of allegiance to him, under which they would pledge to be his vassals and would promise to return any Byzantine lands that they won in the course of the crusade. In return, he would supply the crusade with provisions, money, horses, guides and a supporting

▲ *Constantinople had formidable defences. Its magnificent double walls, with 142 fortified towers and 11 gates, were built in 412–22 during the reign of Theodosius II.*

military force. In demanding personal oaths of loyalty, Alexius adopted the established practices of Europe: in his own domain he could expect the total obedience of his subjects, but in the feudal lands from which these lords had come, he knew, great men generally held they were bound only by oaths they swore in person to an emperor, a king or a suzerain (feudal superior).

HUGH OF VERMANDOIS

The first of the princely crusaders to arrive, Hugh of Vermandois, expected a grand welcome; Alexius was happy to provide gifts and to spout honeyed words, but he kept Hugh under close supervision – virtually as a prisoner – in a monastery. For all his self-aggrandizement, Hugh did not object when asked to swear an oath of loyalty as vassal to the emperor.

GODFREY OF BOUILLON

When the second main army arrived under Godfrey of Bouillon and his brothers, Alexius made them camp outside the

THE IMPACT OF CONSTANTINOPLE

The city of Constantinople amazed the crusaders. Emperor Alexius had decided to make the armies camp outside Constantinople's great city walls, but he allowed small groups of five or six at a time to enter the city in order to pray in the churches and see the sights. They were astonished by what they found – by the city's size and wealth, by its baths and sanitation and by the beauty of the churches and the rich collections of treasures and of sacred relics. Fulcher of Chartres wrote: 'Oh what a splendid and noble city! What fine monasteries, what elegant palaces we saw, what superb workmanship! How many superb works … It would take too long to describe the richness of all kinds of goods, of silver and gold, fine clothes and sacred relics.' The Frankish lords were also suspicious of, and perhaps a little intimidated by, the courtly ritual of the Byzantine Empire.

◄ *Constantinople retained its great beauty through centuries of conflict.*

▲ *Godfrey of Bouillon and his army praise God as they make the passage across the Bosphorus into Anatolia, moving closer to their ultimate destination, Jerusalem.*

city walls. Godfrey was unwilling to swear the proposed oath of loyalty, maintaining that he could not became a vassal of Alexius since his feudal lord was the German emperor Henry IV. He attempted to play for time, since he wanted to wait for the other European lords to arrive. Alexius, on the other hand, was concerned about what might happen if Godfrey, Bohemond of Taranto and other lords marshalled their armies at Constantinople at the same time: he was absolutely determined to move on Godfrey's troops before Bohemond arrived, but he could not do so until Godfrey agreed to swear the oath. Alexius cut off the food supplies to the crusader camp, but when this provoked an outburst of looting and then scavenging he began to provide food once more.

The waiting game continued until, growing desperate, Alexius cut off the food to the camp again. This time Godfrey and his army launched a military attack on Constantinople, which provoked panic among the citizens. Alexius decided to move the army on without requiring Godfrey to swear the oath but the men he sent with this message were attacked by the crusaders before they could deliver the information. Finally, Alexius lost his patience and unleashed the imperial military on the crusader camp. This was enough to bring Godfrey and his brothers to heel and on Easter Sunday, 5 April 1097 they swore the required oaths, recognizing Alexius as their overlord and promising to return to him any conquests they made in former Byzantine territories. The next day, Godfrey and his troops were transported across the Bosphorus.

THE NORMAN CONTINGENT

Three days later, on 9 April, Bohemond of Taranto arrived. According to contemporary sources, Bohemond declared 'I come by my own free will to be a friend to your Majesty'; Alexius housed him in magnificent quarters and gave him splendid gifts. Contemporary accounts report that Bohemond asked to be named as deputy or chief commander to Alexius in Asia, but Alexius was noncommittal. Bohemond was happy to swear the oath that Alexius suggested, although he set little store by it and had no intention of keeping it. They moved on: on 26 April the Norman army was transported across the Bosphorus and joined the troops of Godfrey of Bouillon in Anatolia. Bohemond's nephew Tancred, however, had refused to swear the oath and slipped out of Constantinople by night to escape having to do so.

RAYMOND OF TOULOUSE AND ROBERT OF NORMANDY

That very same day saw the arrival at Constantinople of the army of Raymond of Toulouse. It had not had an easy march, and had even come under attack from imperial forces. Raymond refused to swear an oath to Alexius as his overlord, but promised to return conquered lands.

The final groups of arrivals, Duke Robert of Normandy, his brother-in-law Stephen, Count of Blois, and Count Robert II of Flanders agreed to swear the oath. According to chronicler Fulcher of Chartres, who travelled in their company, swearing the oath was 'essential to make good our friendship with the emperor, for without his advice and help we would not be able to make the journey we planned'.

THE SIEGE OF NICAEA
THE CRUSADERS MAKE THEIR MARK

The princely and noble leaders of the First Crusade were now gathered in Anatolia at the head of an army of perhaps 60,000 men. They agreed that they should move first against Nicaea, the capital of the Turkish sultanate of Rum, for it was clear that the crusade could not safely advance beyond Nicaea towards Jerusalem if the city remained in Turkish hands.

The crusaders were not a united force, for there were many rivalries between lords, and regional, cultural and linguistic differences among the knights and

▼ *Under heavy attack by the forces of the Seljuk sultan, Kilij Arslan, the crusaders' rally was later attributed to heavenly aid.*

soldiers. In addition to the main army there were many non-combatants – women and children, some of them families of crusaders, as well as aged pilgrims and clergy – and the battered remnants of the People's Crusade. There was also a Byzantine force, around 2,000 strong, supplied by Alexius and under the command of an experienced general named Taticius; Alexius's order was that the crusaders would give the command of cities and territories they captured to Taticius.

CRUSADERS ENCAMP AT NICAEA

The crusader army arrived at Nicaea in instalments – the first groups, under Godfrey of Bouillon, Robert of Flanders,

▲ *During the siege of Nicaea, the crusaders lobbed the heads of corpses into the city.*

Tancred and Taticius arrived on 6 May and were reinforced a few days later by Bohemond of Taranto. On 14 May a large force under Raymond of Toulouse swelled their numbers, and the final contingent, under Robert of Normandy and Stephen of Blois, joined the camp on 3 June.

The city of Nicaea, on the eastern side of Lake Iznik, was an ancient Christian town, where, in AD325, the Church's first General Council had agreed the statement of Catholic Christian beliefs still known as the Nicene Creed. Situated just 50 miles (80km) from Constantinople, it was for centuries part of the Byzantine Empire, but had been captured by the Seljuk Turks in 1077. The crusaders surrounded it on three sides and settled in for a siege; they were unable, however, to blockade the lake approaches so the city could still bring in supplies. Emperor Alexius provided the crusader army with supplies and siege equipment.

ABSENT RULER RETURNS

Kilij Arslan, the Sultan of Rum, was not present to defend his capital. Not expecting any greater threat from the new wave of crusaders than he had experienced from the ineffective armies of the People's Crusade, he had departed to fight rival ruler Ghazi ibn Danishmend in Sivas (also known as Sebastea), several hundred miles away at the eastern edge of his territory. (The Danishmends were named after dynastic founder Ghazi ibn Danishmend; he had captured the Roman city of Sebastea and renamed it Sivas, making it his capital in *c.*1080.) When Kilij Arslan received messages to the effect that a large and apparently well-equipped army was besieging Nicaea, he made a hurried peace with Danishmend and rushed back.

By mid-May Kilij Arslan was in the vicinity of Nicaea, viewing the crusader forces with dismay. On 16 May he launched a surprise attack on the recently arrived army of Raymond of Toulouse, which was still setting up camp to the south of the town. It was a fierce clash, in which Raymond showed great skill to hold his force together until reinforcements sent by Godfrey of Bouillon arrived and decided the conflict in the crusaders' favour. A notable casualty, according to the account in a letter written by Stephen of Blois, was Baldwin, Count of Ghent. Kilij Arslan withdrew and gathered his forces in the hills to fight another day.

The siege of Nicaea lasted six weeks. The crusaders had only lightweight siege equipment and were unable to do significant damage to the town walls; they were

▼ *Nicaea's walls, about 32ft (10m) tall, ran for a total of 3 miles (5km). The west wall gave directly on to the lake.*

▲ *Nicaea was an important city for Christians, where a groundbreaking council had taken place in AD325 to formulate what became known as the Nicene Creed.*

limited to hurling small rocks, flaming missiles, beehives, the heads of corpses and other foul objects at the defenders. They could not smash their way into the town and since the town garrison could bring in supplies across the water of the lake, there was no hope of starving them out. There seemed to be no end in sight.

OUTMANOEUVRED BY ALEXIUS

Emperor Alexius was keeping a close watch on events from a camp at Pelecanum nearby. He wanted to regain control of Nicaea in good condition for the Byzantine Empire, and so wanted to prevent the crusaders destroying its defences, overrunning the city and looting its wealth. With typical cunning, he went behind the backs of the crusaders, opening secret negotiations with the Turks in Nicaea. He promised them good treatment if they would surrender to him; if they did, he would protect them with his own troops against the crusaders.

On the morning of 19 June the crusaders prepared to launch a major attack on the town and saw to their initial puzzlement and then dismay that the Byzantine standard was flying above the walls. The Byzantine troops were in control of the city. They acted as guards, only

allowing the crusaders inside the walls in small groups. Alexius laid on food and wine for the crusading army and made gifts of jewels and gold to the leaders, but the crusaders remained deeply unhappy at having been outmanoeuvred and denied the riches they had expected to gain from looting.

In the aftermath, Alexius had a stand-off with Tancred: he refused to give Tancred his share of the gold unless the prince swore an oath of fealty. Tancred insisted that his loyalty was to Bohemond, not to Alexius; and he demanded as much gold as all the other lords put together, plus the amount it would take to fill Alexius's campaign tent. The tense situation was only resolved when Bohemond persuaded Tancred to give way.

Despite the crusaders' disappointment at the outcome in Nicaea, the future looked bright. Stephen of Blois wrote to his wife Countess Adela declaring they would be in Jerusalem in just five weeks. In fact, the crusaders' journey to the Holy City was to take more than two years.

MEN OF IRON
THE BATTLE OF DORYLAEUM

Near Dorylaeum (modern Eskiehir) on the Anatolian plateau, the crusaders were attacked by a Seljuk Turkish army led by Kilij Arslan, Sultan of Rum. The battle, on 1 July 1097, was fierce and long – from the third hour to the ninth, according to the Frankish chronicle the *Gesta Francorum*. After weathering a Turkish assault, the crusaders were reinforced when the rear of their army caught up and turned the tables to win a great victory.

BUILD-UP TO THE BATTLE

Following the capture of Nicaea, the crusaders set out eastwards across the Anatolian plateau towards their ultimate goal, Jerusalem. In the vanguard of the army were around 20,000 Normans under Bohemond of Taranto, his nephew Tancred and other noblemen; in the rear, around a day behind, were some 30,000 Franks led by Raymond of Toulouse, Godfrey of Bouillon and other lords. Kilij Arslan, who was smarting at the loss of his capital city Nicaea, had retreated to the mountains and, in alliance with Ghazi ibn Danishmend, prepared an ambush for the Christian invaders. The Turkish army was probably about 20,000–30,000 strong – although the contemporary crusader accounts claim it was much bigger, with Raymond of Aguilers suggesting 150,000 and Fulcher of Chartres reporting 360,000 men under Kilij Arslan's command.

Bohemond noticed that Turkish scouts were watching the crusaders' vanguard, and on the evening of 30 June, three days' march out of Nicaea, set up a defensive camp near the town of Dorylaeum. At once, he sent a messenger riding at breakneck speed back to the army's rearguard, with an urgent summons for the Franks to come to the rescue of their comrades.

DAWN ONSLAUGHT

The Turks attacked at dawn the next day, 1 July. Bohemond ordered his knights to form a defensive line, while the foot soldiers and women took refuge in the camp. He ordered that no one was to try to charge the attackers – they were to put all their efforts into holding them at bay. The plan was to defend the camp until the rest of the army caught up.

Rather than engaging the crusaders in a pitched battle of foot soldiers and cavalry of the kind fought in Europe, the Turks surrounded the camp and attacked from all sides. The Turkish army was all cavalry: its horsemen swept in from every direction, then swerved away at the last moment, sending a storm of spears and arrows into the camp. The attack was strange and terrifying for the crusaders – as Fulcher of Chartres wrote, 'this form of warfare was not known to us'. The *Gesta*

▼ *Heavily armoured crusaders clash head on with the Turks. At Dorylaeum the Franks were amazed at the size of the Turkish army, while the Turks marvelled at the ferocity of the crusaders' charge.*

▲ *When properly deployed, a fully armoured cavalry backed up by foot soldiers and archers was a formidable force.*

Francorum reported, 'the Turks were attacking us from all sides … we were not able to resist or weather the force of so many'. The defence was brave, but seemed ultimately hopeless.

Many of the pilgrims who accompanied the soldiers were killed, and those huddled in the camp feared that they would be slain. According to contemporary accounts, while some women ran tirelessly back and forward bringing water to the cavalry, others seem to have been quickly convinced that defeat was inevitable and set about making themselves as attractive as possible as a way of averting death by winning admirers among the Turks.

REINFORCEMENTS TO THE RESCUE

For six hours the army of Kilij Arslan and his allies kept up the assault. They were breaking through the crusaders' defences and an end to the battle was in sight. But at this moment, the rear of the crusaders' army rode in to the rescue.

On their arrival, a group of knights under Raymond of Toulouse attacked the Turks from the flank. Then the crusader cavalry drew up swiftly in battle formation, with Godfrey of Bouillon and Hugh of Vermandois aligning themselves to the right of Bohemond, and Stephen of Blois and Robert of Normandy to the left. They attacked, a great wall of cavalry, bristling with lances, thundering across the field.

THE LURE OF RICHES

The battle continued. The crusaders were no longer in desperate straits, but they were unable to drive the Turks off. According to the *Gesta Francorum*, the crusaders marvelled at the size of the Turkish army and knowing that these essentially nomadic men carried their riches with them, they looked forward to seizing some of the wealth they had missed out on when they had been denied the chance to sack Nicaea. They declared: 'Let us all be one in faith in Christ and in the victory of the Holy Cross because this day, God willing it, we shall become rich!'

Then knights under the papal legate Bishop Adhemar of Le Puy launched a surprise attack on the Turks from the rear, having ridden round under cover of some low hills. The army of Kilij Arslan, now tiring, and fearing being surrounded, broke and fled. The crusaders rode in triumph through the enemy camp, setting it afire and looting the riches in its tents.

VICTORY FOR THE 'MEN OF IRON'

The Turks' casualties were very heavy. Probably around 4,000 crusaders died; among them was Tancred's brother, William. Disaster had been very close at Dorylaeum: defeat would have brought the crusade to a premature end, but victory reinforced the crusaders' belief in their holy mission.

▼ *The Turks were astonished by the determination of the Norman and Frankish knights. Impressed by the chain mail armour that allowed the knight to withstand the blows of swords and points of arrows, and their indomitable strength under attack, they dubbed the crusaders the 'men of iron'.*

DEFENDER OF JERUSALEM
GODFREY OF BOUILLON

French knight Godfrey of Bouillon did not play a leading role in the First Crusade until its final stages, when he was one of the first Christians into Jerusalem on 15 July 1099 and after its capture became the first ruler of the Latin Kingdom of Jerusalem. He died only a year later, but he succeeded in consolidating the kingdom, and within a century of his death had become a hero of medieval legend, celebrated in chansons about the crusade that were told by *trouvères* (troubadours) at the noble courts of Europe as early as the 12th century.

Born in 1060 in northern France or Belgium, perhaps in Boulogne-sur-Mer, Godfrey was lord of Bouillon, a castle and village in the Ardennes forest of France, and from 1087 duke of Lower Lorraine. Most of Godfrey's life before he left in his

▼ *At Jerusalem Godfrey and the crusaders emulate the example of Joshua and the Israelites at Jericho in marching around the city prior to launching their attack.*

mid-30s on crusade was spent asserting his right to the lordship of Lower Lorraine against attempts by Henry IV, King of Germany and ultimately Holy Roman Emperor, to take these territories away.

FINANCING THE CRUSADE
In 1095, inspired by Pope Urban's call to crusade, Godfrey either sold or agreed loans against his substantial landholdings and thereby raised a large force of knights. He also accepted money from Jewish communities in the Rhineland who were desperately attempting to buy safety in the face of repeated atrocities by crusaders. With his brothers Baldwin and Eustace, Godfrey embarked with an army of perhaps 40,000 from Lorraine in August 1096. They reached Constantinople in November, the second of the princely armies to arrive, following that of Hugh of Vermandois, brother of Philip I of France.

When the following year the crusaders set out for Jerusalem, Godfrey and his knights played only a supporting role in the conflicts en route, such as the capture of Nicaea and Antioch, while in between those two events, he and his contingent were part of the force that rode to the rescue of the beleaguered vanguard of the crusader army at the Battle of Dorylaeum. After Antioch, he took part in the march on Jerusalem and the siege of the city and was one of the first knights to climb the walls when it was taken on 15 July 1099.

DEFENDER OF THE HOLY SEPULCHRE
A week later, in a meeting of the crusade leaders in the Church of the Holy Sepulchre in Jerusalem on 22 July, Godfrey was elected ruler of the newly established Latin Kingdom of Jerusalem. He did not accept the title of king in a city where the crusaders believed that Christ himself was the only true ruler, and was known either as *Princeps* (Prince) or as *Advocatus Sancti Sepulchri* (Defender of the Holy Sepulchre).

According to the *Gesta Francorum*, Godfrey's task as ruler was to 'subdue the pagans and defend the Christians'. He set about ensuring the survival of the new kingdom, which was by no means certain, for the great majority of the crusaders departed, leaving him with a force of only 300 knights and 2,000 infantry and without a fleet with which to mount naval blockades of Muslim cities along the coast. He agreed truces with the cities of Acre, Ascalon and Caesarea and, most important of all in the short term, succeeded in defeating the Egyptian army in the Battle of Ascalon.

DEATH AND LEGACY
On 18 July, less than a year after his election, Godfrey died in Jerusalem. He was around 40 years old. Accounts of how he died differ: the Muslim chronicler Ibn al-Qalansi reported that Godfrey was shot by an arrow while besieging Acre, but

Christian chroniclers wrote that he fell ill in Caesarea in June and succumbed to the illness on 18 July in Jerusalem – some versions allege he was poisoned by the emir of Caesarea.

Godfrey was succeeded by his younger brother Baldwin – according to the chronicler Radulph of Caen, before he died he called the Patriarch of Jerusalem and leading secular lords and warned them, saying they needed to consider formally who should succeed him, but they asked him to nominate his successor and when he named Baldwin they were pleased and pledged to be loyal subjects to him.

THE LEGEND OF GODFREY OF BOUILLON

It was Godfrey's position as the first ruler of Jerusalem and his achievement in securing the future of the Latin kingdom there that established his towering reputation in medieval legend. In the stories that

▼ The enduring fame and memory of Godfrey of Bouillon is honoured by a fine equestrian statue in Place Royale, Brussels.

▲ The clergy, knights and citizens of the young Kingdom of Jerusalem mourn Godfrey at his funeral on 23 July 1100.

quickly began to circulate, he was presented as an exemplar of fearless chivalry and a man of immense strength – in one story he wrestled a bear into submission, in another he beheaded a camel with one skilful stroke of his sword. William of Tyre, whose chronicle of the Kingdom of Jerusalem was written in the late 12th century when the myth of Godfrey was already established, described him as taller than average, with solid limbs, a brawny chest and 'strong beyond any comparison'; William reported that the hero was good-looking, with blond hair and beard. Godfrey was certainly an intelligent man and a forceful character, but there is little evidence that he was truly devout, and he was certainly not the paragon of Christian virtue that he became in his legend.

THE MARCH ACROSS ANATOLIA
AND THE ESTABLISHMENT OF THE COUNTY OF EDESSA

Following their victory in the Battle of Dorylaeum, the crusaders rested for two days and then marched onwards to the south. They headed across the Anatolian plateau bound for Antioch in Pisidia and thence on to Iconium.

A HELLISH SUMMER
It was summer and the gruelling heat took a heavy toll on the army. According to chronicler Albert of Aix, the suffering was terrible: children, women, animals and soldiers died at the roadside from thirst and heat exhaustion; some women gave birth in the dust and were too weak to do anything but stagger on, abandoning their babies in the roadway; when a river was reached, many more people and their ani-

mals died from drinking too much. Albert claims that 500 people died in a single day from the effects of the heat. It seemed to the crusaders that far from arriving in the paradise of a land flowing in milk and honey, as promised by Urban II, they had arrived in hell.

Near Heraclea, the crusaders had to muster the strength to fight a Turkish army under two emirs from Cappadocia; the battle was soon over, for the Turkish army – perhaps made nervous by reports of the crusaders' exploits at Dorylaeum – dispersed and fled when Bohemond gathered his finest knights and charged at speed with couched lance.

In September the crusaders arrived at the Cilician Gates, the daunting pass

▲ *The people of Edessa pay homage to Baldwin I, King of Jerusalem.*

through the snow-covered Taurus Mountains that lay between the Anatolian plateau and the Mediterranean coast. By this stage almost all the travellers' pack animals had died and many knights were without horses, having to ride on oxen and force dogs to pull carts.

The weather was still hot and dry and the crusaders decided that if they took the pass, they would be vulnerable to guerrilla attacks from the Turks. The main body of the army now marched north-east, away from the Cilician Gates, into easier wooded country towards Armenian lands. In these territories, the crusaders could expect a welcome: the Armenians were Christians who had been evicted from their lands in the southern Caucasus by Byzantine forces and so had little affection for the emperor of Constantinople. They were also enemies of the Turks.

FIGHTING OVER TARSUS
A smaller force of around 100 knights and 200 foot soldiers under Tancred elected to split off from the main army, risk the passage through the Cilician Gates and attempt an assault on the Turkish-garrisoned town of Tarsus on the plain beyond. At Tarsus, Tancred succeeded in driving out the Turks and raising his own banner, with the help of reinforcements of 500 knights and 2,000 foot soldiers led by

---

FIRST-HAND ACCOUNTS OF THE FIRST CRUSADE

Such was the impact made by the crusaders' success in liberating Jerusalem that several histories were written soon afterwards. *Gesta Francorum* (Deeds of the Franks) was written almost immediately after the capture of Jerusalem in *c.*1100 by an anonymous follower of Bohemond of Taranto. Fulcher of Chartres, a churchman who travelled in the party of Stephen of Blois, also wrote a history of the crusade perhaps as early as 1101–06. The history of Raymond of Aguilers, chaplain to Raymond, Count of Toulouse, is rich in accounts of visions and miracles – including the discovery of the Holy Lance at Antioch. Radulph of Caen was chaplain to Bohemond of Taranto and he wrote a biography of Bohemond's nephew, Tancred, in *c.*1112. Albert of Aix (also known as Albert of Aachen) wrote a 12-volume history of the First Crusade and the early history of the Latin Kingdom of Jerusalem in *c.*1125–50; Albert's is the most detailed chronicle of the First

Crusade. Among other first-hand accounts of events of the time are Anna Comnena's biography of her father, Emperor Alexius, and the writings of Armenian Christian Matthew of Edessa. There are also later accounts of events of the First Crusade written by Muslim chroniclers, including Ibn al-Athir and Sibt Ibn al-Jawsi.

▼ *In the aftermath of the crusade, churchmen recorded God's triumphs.*

Baldwin of Boulogne, brother of Godfrey of Bouillon. The two knights then disputed the spoils: Baldwin had led his men through the Cilician Gates not to help Tancred but in order to prevent him (and thereby his uncle Bohemond) from taking control of the coast.

Rival lords were coming into open and bitter conflict as they disputed control of captured territories. In this instance, Baldwin had many more knights and soldiers than Tancred, so Tancred gave way. When more of Bohemond's knights arrived at Tarsus, Baldwin refused to open the city gates and they were put to the sword in an attack by Turkish troops. Tancred moved on and took control first of Adana and then of Mamistra. Baldwin followed. The two armies fought, but finally agreed to withdraw from the coast.

ON TO ANTIOCH

The main army had a terrible time crossing the Anti-Taurus Mountains that stood inland, behind the Taurus range. By this time it was October and heavy rains had begun – in wet conditions, the steep tracks were almost impassable. The army limped across the mountains and moved on

▼ *During the lengthy siege of Antioch, various plots to take the city by stealth were attempted, and rumours of secret truces and intercepted messengers were rife.*

▲ *Baldwin of Boulogne, seen here in a particularly viciously-fought battle against the Seljuk Turks, became the King of Jerusalem in 1100.*

towards the city of Antioch. Tancred, meanwhile, had captured Alexandretta, crossed into Syria and was reunited with the main army as they prepared to besiege Antioch in October 1097.

BALDWIN ESTABLISHES THE COUNTY OF EDESSA

For his part, Baldwin headed north-east to the town of Edessa, an important and wealthy Armenian town to the east of the River Euphrates, while the main army settled in for the siege of Antioch. Edessa was governed by an Armenian Christian

named Thoros, who had only two years earlier captured it from the Turks. Thoros's position was far from secure: he was surrounded on all sides by Seljuk emirs who were all too keen to depose him. He was happy to welcome a fellow Christian in Baldwin, and to accept the support of his fighting men. Baldwin, clearly sensing possibility, demanded that Thoros adopt him as his son and heir, which he did in a public ceremony.

Shortly afterwards, Thoros was killed during a revolt by the townspeople, who were said to hate him because he was a Greek Orthodox rather than an Armenian Orthodox Christian. Baldwin became ruler, calling himself Count of Edessa. Thoros's death was highly convenient for Baldwin, but we do not know for sure that he masterminded it – indeed, his contemporary supporters vehemently denied that he had any involvement.

Baldwin thereby established the County of Edessa, the first of the crusader territories that would be created in the course of the First Crusade.

BOUND FOR JERUSALEM

The extraordinary events of June 1098 at Antioch were the turning point of the First Crusade. In that month the crusaders twice went from despair to wild elation. At the start of June they were bogged down in a siege of the city that they had been enforcing since October 1097 with little progress, and were expecting the arrival within days of a vast Seljuk Turkish army led by Sultan Kerbogha of Mosul, who had every intention of lifting the siege.

One of their leaders, Stephen of Blois, abandoned the enterprise and departed for home. They were starving, and frightened, and desperate. Then they took the city through cunning and subterfuge on the night of 2 June, and rejoiced wildly and raucously. But within three days they were plunged into despair again, when Kerbogha arrived and besieged them. Within the city they wondered if the entire crusade would come to nothing, but after visions of St Andrew and the discovery of what was purportedly the Holy Lance – the spear with which Christ's side was pierced on the cross – morale soared. On 28 June the crusaders threw open the gates of Antioch and rode out behind Bishop Adhemar bearing the Holy Lance to take on the huge army of Sultan Kerbogha. Despite being vastly outnumbered, they won, and claimed it as a miracle. Antioch was safe, and as soldiers of Christ riding in a divinely ordained mission to liberate Jerusalem; the crusaders must triumph.

▲ *The town of Latakia was one of the key ports in Syria. The crusader armies were dependent on it for the delivery of supplies.*

◄ *The crusaders at last reach Jerusalem, and give thanks and praise to God for a hard-won achievement that has taken so much longer than expected.*

THE SIEGE OF ANTIOCH

A LONG STRUGGLE TO WEAR DOWN THE CITY'S DEFENCES

The crusader army drew up before Antioch in October 1097. The city lay in a vital position on the route from Anatolia into Syria, and the crusader lords knew that they had to capture it before moving southwards through Syria and on down the Mediterranean coast towards the city of Jerusalem.

FORBIDDING DEFENCES

At once the crusader lords saw that capturing Antioch was a daunting task, for it had 400 towers set in 25 miles (40km) of defensive walls running across very hostile terrain. A siege would be difficult – the city stood on the bank of the River Orontes, so was very well supplied with water, and there were even areas of pasture set safely within the forbidding walls. Military attack was impossible from the north, because of the river, and from the south because of the forbidding bulk of Mount Silphius, site of Antioch's citadel. Writing home, Stephen of Blois called the city 'unassailable' and by general consensus the city was deemed to be impossible to take by force: the Arabs had captured it in AD637, and since that time it had only been taken twice – by the Byzantine Empire from Arabs in 969 and by Seljuk Turks from the Byzantines in the 1080s – both times by treachery.

In October 1097 when the crusaders set up camp before the city, Antioch was in the hands of a Turkish governor, Yaghi-Siyan, ruling on behalf of the Seljuk sultan in Baghdad, Barkiyaroq. The citizens were mostly Christians, a combination of Orthodox Greeks, Armenians and Syrians, most of whom disliked their governor heartily. Taking a precaution against possible treachery, Yaghi-Siyan made himself more unpopular by expelling the leading Christian citizens and jailing the Patriarch of Antioch, a very senior ecclesiastic on a par with the patriarchs of Constantinople and of Jerusalem.

TO ATTACK OR TO BESIEGE?

The crusader lords discussed how to proceed: Raymond of Toulouse argued for a military assault, but Bohemond urged a siege and an attempt to foster treachery within the city. Caution prevailed, and the army settled in for a siege. As autumn passed into winter, they had to deal with dwindling food supplies, regular sallies by the garrison and the taunting behaviour of Yaghi-Siyan, who put the Patriarch of Antioch in a cage, and hung it from the walls to enrage the Christians without. Stephen of Blois wrote to his wife, reporting that: 'We have lived through great

▲ *Like the cities of Nicaea and Jerusalem, Antioch was surrounded by massive walls that demanded the construction of siege towers for any attack to be successful.*

suffering and evils beyond counting. Many people have exhausted their finances, and others were saved from starvation only by the kindness of God. The cold is excessive and there are terrible deluges of rain.' In these months, having come so far, thousands of the poorer crusaders died of starvation; some people ate their horses, while there were even reports of cannibalism among the most desperate.

TWO RELIEF ARMIES ROUTED

The need for food grew so severe that in late December Bohemond and Robert of Flanders risked riding out on a foraging expedition up the fertile valley of the River Orontes. There they encountered a large Turkish army under Sultan Duqaq that was marching from Damascus to raise the siege of Antioch. In a tense battle, the crusaders recovered from a disastrous start, in which Robert of Flanders and his men were almost defeated, to launch a powerful counter-attack that drove the Turks off. Bohemond and Robert returned safely to Antioch, but without the supplies they had been seeking.

The New Year brought little comfort. Godfrey of Bouillon and Raymond of Toulouse fell ill. Robert of Normandy left the siege, withdrawing to Laodicea in Anatolia (near modern Eskihisar in Turkey). In February the Byzantine general Taticius took his troops north, either in search of supplies or else because he judged it more important to consolidate Byzantine gains in Anatolia than continue

▲ *Wearing his mitre in battle, papal legate Adhemar of Le Puy takes the battle to the Seljuks at Antioch. He carries the Holy Lance discovered within the city.*

▼ *During the long months of the siege at Antioch, the crusaders spent a great deal of time building siege equipment to drive home their assault, but they made little progress.*

a hopeless siege. Many began to despair, losing their faith in what they were doing; some deserted, including Peter the Hermit who was caught and forcibly brought back to Antioch by Tancred.

Then a fresh threat emerged: news arrived that a large relief army under Radwan, Seljuk ruler of Aleppo, had approached and had set up camp at Harenc, only 25 miles (40km) from Antioch, in preparation for launching an attack on the besieging army. The crusaders struck first: Bohemond led a company of knights out by night and surprised Radwan's army, winning a stunning victory despite being vastly outnumbered.

SIEGE EQUIPMENT

In March an English fleet under Edgar the Atheling, a claimant to the throne of England, arrived at St Symeon, the port of Antioch, with supplies, siege equipment and building materials. The crusaders tightened their grip on the city by building tall siege towers and a fort called the 'Castle of Raymond' opposite the city's Bridge Gate; Tancred established a position in a monastery opposite St George's Gate. Spring turned to summer and although the city was almost entirely encircled, the crusaders were no closer to taking it by force. It was clear that they would need to find someone in the city who was willing to betray his masters.

THE FALL OF ANTIOCH
THE CRUSADERS CAPTURE THE CITY

In May 1098 the crusading army encamped around Antioch received news that a mighty relief army was approaching under the command of the powerful Sultan Kerbogha of Mosul. It was clear that they needed to take the city before Kerbogha arrived, otherwise his force would either destroy the crusader army or drive it away – and all their efforts and suffering during the eight-month siege would have been wasted.

THE CRUSADERS ABANDONED
At this crucial moment Stephen of Blois, who had been elected commander-in-chief of the besieging army, abandoned the crusade. Deciding that the enterprise was doomed to failure and taking a sizeable contingent of French soldiers with him, he marched back towards Constantinople to take a ship for Europe.

▲ *Betrayed to its besiegers, Antioch is overrun. The city has a European look in this 15th-century French illustration.*

His timing could not have been worse, for Bohemond had found the ally he had been seeking within Antioch. This man was an Armenian, a Christian convert to Islam named Firuz, who commanded key defence towers overlooking the Gate of St George. Firuz had been fined for hoarding foods and according to some versions had discovered that his wife had been seduced by his superior officer. He was happy to have his revenge and profit by it.

BOHEMOND TAKES THE CITY
On the night of 2 June 1098 the crusading army feigned a retreat from the city walls. To Antioch's Turkish governor, Yaghi-Siyan, it looked as if the news of

Sultan Kerbogha's imminent arrival had forced the invading Christians to take fright and abandon the enterprise, or else to lift the siege in order to fight Kerbogha's army in open countryside.

But in the middle of the night, the treacherous watchman Firuz let down a rope beside the Gate of St George and allowed Bohemond to climb into the city. At the top, in the darkness, Bohemond felt his hand seized by another and heard a voice whisper: 'Long life to this hand.' He was followed in by a group of 60 knights. They succeeded in surprising the watchmen and guards and at dawn opened the Gates of St George and of the Bridge.

LOOTING AND DESTRUCTION
Meanwhile the main army had returned under cover of darkness and now they swept into the city. Terrible scenes followed, as the starving crusaders gave vent to their fear and greed, raping and killing, looting and burning. Many of the Christian citizens burst out from their houses into the streets to seek revenge against the Turkish overlords, but were killed in the confusion and lawlessness by the blood-crazed crusaders.

A few Turks survived by taking refuge in the citadel under the command of a son of Yaghi-Siyan. As for Yaghi-Siyan himself, he escaped on horseback, but fell and was knocked unconscious during his flight to the mountains; his companions left him for dead, but some Armenians found him and, recognizing his face, cut off his head. They brought the corpse and its head to Bohemond in Antioch and were given a substantial reward.

The crusaders, when their heads cleared, praised God. Another victory had been achieved that had seemed impossible. They had taken the impregnable city of Antioch. It was beginning to seem as if their success in the crusade truly was to be guaranteed by God.

THE TAFURS

The most intense members of the crusader army were the Tafurs, poor soldiers originally part of the People's Crusade who were fired with wild religious fanaticism. According to Guibert of Nogent they marched barefoot and without weapons, living on the roots of plants, as a kind of holy army, and led by their own king of the Tafurs. They were notorious among the enemy – their name comes from the Arabic *tafuria*, meaning 'poverty-stricken'. They were always associated with the most extreme behaviour of the army, for instance performing acts of cannibalism during the siege of Antioch or later at Maarrat an-Numan, and were said to have urged on soldiers to acts of cruelty against the enemy at Antioch and in Jerusalem. The Tafurs were later celebrated as the deserving poor in the crusade chanson, the *Chanson d'Antioch*, which suggested that God had led the crusaders to victory because of the Tafurs' religious devotion.

► *The 'king' of the Tafurs was reputedly a wealthy Norman knight, who took pity on their plight and gave up his position and comforts to become their leader.*

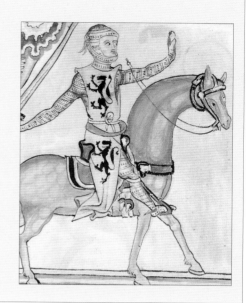

TRAPPED INSIDE THE CITY

But in the days following their victory, the Christians' delight turned to fear once more. Sultan Kerbogha arrived on 6 June and set his army before the city. The besiegers became the besieged.

There was little food within Antioch. Kerbogha's troops took possession of the citadel and the crusaders had to fight determinedly to prevent them flooding over its walls into the city.

The crusaders pinned their hopes increasingly desperately on relief from Emperor Alexius, who had set out with an army from Constantinople in the spring. But these hopes were empty: Alexius had met the fleeing Stephen of Blois, who had described the critical situation at Antioch. Alexius, convinced that the crusaders' cause was lost, had turned back.

The crusaders' numbers were cut further by desertions – those who fled were derided as 'rope-danglers', presumably because they used ropes to climb from the city walls. By this stage, the Christian army probably numbered no more than 30,000. The crusaders' position was desperate.

► *Flooding into the city after months of frustration, the crusaders ran amok. Terrified citizens jumped to their deaths to avoid being torn limb from limb.*

MIRACLES AT ANTIOCH

FIRED WITH BELIEF, THE CRUSADERS DEFEAT SULTAN KERBOGHA

In early June, as we have seen, the crusaders were at the lowest of ebbs. Once the euphoria of breaking into Antioch had died down, they found themselves besieged and starving in the city.

Then, on 11 June, a priest named Stephen of Valence reported to the papal legate Bishop Adhemar that he had had a vision of the Blessed Virgin Mary and of Christ himself and that Christ had promised to come to the army's aid. Around the same time, a Provençal peasant named Peter Bartholomew reported that he had had a whole series of visions of St Andrew, who had revealed that the Holy Lance – the spear with which Christ's side was pierced on the cross – was within Antioch, buried beneath the Church of St Peter. There were other portents, including a meteor that seemed to fall directly on to Sultan Kerbogha's besieging army.

▼ *Soldiers fall to their knees in awe as Peter Bartholomew presents the Holy Lance (the spear that pierced Christ's side on the cross). The illustration is from an edition of William of Tyre's crusade history made for King Edward IV of England.*

THE DISCOVERY OF THE HOLY LANCE

On 14 June an excavation was carried out in the Church of St Peter: at first the digging soldiers found nothing, but then Peter leapt into the hole, dressed only in a shirt, and triumphantly brandished a length of metal that he declared to be the lance. A few sceptics doubted, but most were swept up in a wave of delirious rejoicing. Here was proof that God was on their side. They need fear no more.

THE DEFEAT OF KERBOGHA

The leaders prepared for battle and on 20 June elected Bohemond commander-in-chief. Bishop Adhemar ordered a three-day fast (not much of a challenge, since most were already without food) in repentance of their sins and preparation for battle. At first light on 28 June the soldiers attended Mass then flung open the city gates and marched out to take on the army of Sultan Kerbogha.

They marched behind Bishop Adhemar holding the Holy Lance and priests dressed in white and carrying crosses

▲ *Reported visions of the Blessed Virgin Mary and of Christ himself in Antioch, together with the discovery of the Holy Lance, raised feelings among the crusaders to such a fever pitch that they came to believe themselves invincible.*

while they prayed aloud. Their chances of success seemed to be nil. The encircling army was vast. The crusaders were weak from hunger. In previous encounters on crusade, their strength had been the mounted charge of knights with couched lances, but now they had only around 200 horses left alive. Many of the knights had to fight on foot.

According to the *Gesta Francorum,* as the crusaders emerged from the city they saw a great host on white horses and bearing pure white banners charging to their aid. This was – they afterwards reported in awe – nothing less than a heavenly army commanded by saints George, Demetrius and Mercury riding in to ensure that God's will was done. This was in line with the prophecies of the Last Days in the biblical Book of Revelation,

▶ *At Antioch the crusaders built this façade in front of a cave believed to have been used as the very first Christian place of worship by St Peter and followers in c.AD40–50.*

which declared that the heavenly armies following the Word of God 'were upon white horses, clothed in fine linen, white and clean'.

The crusaders, calling on God's name, charged the Turkish army. Amazingly, the Turks broke up and fled. A letter written by the leaders of the crusade to Pope Urban II, describing the victory, declared 'from the very first clash on the battlefield we drove the enemy back'.

Kerbogha had split his force between an advance group near Antioch's Bridge Gate and a main camp no less than 3 miles (5km) away. Charged by the crusaders, the advance group fled just as Kerbogha arrived with the main army from the camp. The main force then also abandoned the battle – perhaps partly because they were surprised by the discipline and ferocity of the crusaders' assault but principally, according to Islamic sources, because the sultan's rivals in the army wanted to prevent Kerbogha capturing Antioch and so called off their men at the very last moment.

Finally Kerbogha set fire to the sun-dried battlefield in a last desperate attempt to change the course of the conflict, but to no avail. The crusaders were afire with belief, and fought like men possessed; they had no desire to flee since behind them was only the empty city where they had been starving to death. In the citadel above the city, the Turkish garrison watched Sultan Kerbogha's army flee and knew that their chance had gone. They sent a message of surrender to Raymond of Toulouse. The crusaders had complete control of the city. The letter to Pope Urban II continued: 'the right hand of God fought on our side … our Lord Jesus Christ brought the entire city of Antioch to the Roman religion and faith.'

THE HOLY LANCE AND ITS EFFECT ON THE CRUSADERS

In the medieval era Christians had a deep and powerful belief in the miraculous powers of relics of the life of Christ and other biblical figures. The astonishing effect of the Holy Lance on the crusaders can partly be explained as an effect of this belief. In addition, the majority of the crusaders were under extreme mental and physical stress – starving and desperate for hope – which would increase the likelihood of mass hysteria. The relic supposedly discovered by Peter Bartholomew was presented as the lance used by a Roman soldier to pierce the side of Christ while he was hanging on the cross, an event described only in the Gospel of St John and said to be the fulfilment of a prophecy in the Book of Psalms concerning the Messiah. Many crusaders in Antioch must have known and chosen to forget that a spear said to be the Holy Lance had been found in Jerusalem, where it was seen by many Christian pilgrims in and around the 5th–6th centuries AD; by the time of the First Crusade, this other spear was being kept in Constantinople.

▶ *In John's Gospel, the soldier was said to have pierced Christ's side with the lance rather than break his legs, which was normal practice with the crucified.*

THE PRINCE OF ANTIOCH
BOHEMOND OF TARANTO

Bohemond of Taranto, the Calabrian-born Norman knight who established himself as Prince of Antioch, was an inspirational leader of men and by far the most effective general among the knights of the First Crusade. He was also powerfully ambitious and primarily self-interested; the realization of his dream of establishing a personal principality meant far more to him than the official aims of the First Crusade. He did not even take part in the triumphant conclusion of the crusade, the capture of Jerusalem, having remained in Antioch to consolidate his position there.

BOHEMOND'S APPEARANCE AND CHARACTER

Anna Comnena, daughter of the Emperor Alexius, met Bohemond in Constantinople at the start of the First Crusade and left a vivid portrait of the man. She reported that Bohemond was astonishingly tall – she claimed he was 18 inches (45cm) taller than the tallest men; he had a narrow waist but broad chest and shoulders and very strong arms; he had a sturdy frame, she said, but a slightly stooping stance. His skin, she reported, was noticeably white, but his cheeks were red; his hair was light brown and worn shorter than was normal among the crusaders, cut just above the ears. He had grey eyes, which suggested (according to Anna) that he was a man of indomitable courage and great dignity. People were astonished at the sight of him.

Anna noted that Bohemond's size and strength made him frightening – even his laugh, she remembered, caused people to be nervous; in fact the mere mention of his name made people jittery. But he certainly also had charm. It was clear that courage and love ran deep in him, and he found expression for both these qualities in warfare. His intelligence was sharp – he always made ambiguous, non-committal replies to questions, and his mind 'ran

▲ *Bohemond climbs into Antioch on the night of 2 June 1098 after the watchman let down a rope ladder. He then threw the gates open to admit his fellow crusaders.*

over all possible outcomes' and 'dared all things'; his actions were often unpredictable, for he rushed into undertakings. Overall, he was 'like no other man ever found in the Byzantine Empire, whether a foreigner or a Greek'. It is a measure of the impression that Bohemond made that Anna's account, with its vivid details, was written around 40 years after she met him and that he was the only one of the crusader lords she described so closely.

THE YOUTHFUL GENERAL

Bohemond's father was the powerful Norman adventurer Robert Guiscard. As a baby, the future prince of Antioch was christened 'Mark' but as he grew was given the name 'Bohemond' by Guiscard in tribute to a legendary giant of that name. In 1080–85, in his early 20s, Bohemond proved himself a great general during Guiscard's daring invasion of the Byzantine Empire, and in 1082–84 while commanding the Norman army when

Guiscard was recalled to Italy, he won two major victories over Emperor Alexius. Bohemond was forced to abandon the campaign in 1084 through illness, and returned to Italy. Guiscard's death in 1085 was followed by a succession conflict in which Bohemond fought his half-brother Roger; this was ended by a settlement, favourable to Bohemond, imposed by Pope Urban II.

In 1096 Bohemond joined the First Crusade: in some accounts, he was besieging the rebel town of Amalfi (near Naples) when he encountered knights riding to the crusade and, impressed by their zeal, opted to join them. In other versions, such as that of the 11th-century Benedictine chronicler Geoffrey Malaterra, Bohemond saw the crusade from the start as a chance to continue his father's attack upon the Byzantine Empire and to carve out a principality there for himself.

A LEADER OF MEN

Throughout the early part of the First Crusade, Bohemond was the effective commander of the enterprise, an inspirational general and leader for the crusaders. At Dorylaeum through his quick thinking and tactical nous he averted disaster and held off the Turkish attacks until the main force of the crusader army could arrive. During the difficult months of the siege of Antioch Bohemond again proved his excellence as a general – not only defeating a large force under Sultan Duqaq that he encountered during a foraging mission, but also routing and driving back a substantial relief army under Radwan, Seljuk ruler of Aleppo.

Bohemond then almost single-handedly brought about the capture of Antioch through clandestine negotiations with the rebel Firuz within the city and a daring night-time raid. Afterwards, when the crusaders were besieged within the city by Sultan Kerbogha, when despair was

▲ The crusader army had feigned a retreat but turned around and flooded into Antioch after Bohemond had opened the gates.

mounting and desertions were commonplace, he remained inspirationally upbeat, touring the defensive positions, making sure that they were manned and lifting the spirits of the defenders with the example of his courage and self-belief.

After the discovery of the Holy Lance, Bohemond was privately sceptical that a miracle had occurred, but he knew well enough how to marshal the outpouring of emotion among the rank and file: he was elected commander-in-chief of the army by the lords, and in this capacity planned the army's tactics and oversaw the astonishing victory over the besiegers on 28 June 1098.

SEEKING CONTROL IN ANTIOCH

Throughout this period, however, Bohemond was also plotting to outmanoeuvre the other crusader lords and establish a private holding in his name at Antioch. He was even apparently willing to put this objective above the success of the crusade itself: during the siege his men spread discontent within the crusader camp, suggesting that a military assault would never succeed and that their cause was hopeless, so that when he established contact with an ally within the city and with the news that Sultan Kerbogha was approaching fast, he could negotiate hard, knowing that he held all the cards. From the other leaders he wrung the concession that he could keep Antioch if they won it. He proceeded with the capture of the city only when he knew that it would be his.

Bohemond remained in Antioch when the main crusading force marched on towards Jerusalem in January 1099. He watched the conquest from afar, and then visited Jerusalem at Christmas 1099 to fulfil his vows. On this occasion, wily as ever, he engineered the election of Dagobert of Pisa as Patriarch of Jerusalem to counteract the strength of the Lorrainer faction under Godfrey of Bouillon, who was by that time the effective king of Jerusalem.

AFTER THE CRUSADE

In 1100 Bohemond launched an attack on Danishmend, the warlike emir of Sivas (Sebastea), but was captured and thrown in jail. He stayed there for three whole years until being ransomed in 1103 by Baldwin of Le Bourg, at that time Count of Edessa and later King Baldwin II of Jerusalem. In the following year, Bohemond was heavily defeated by a Seljuk army after he attacked and besieged the city of Harran. After this setback Bohemond returned to Europe, where in 1105–06 he was hailed as a conquering hero for his part in the crusade.

Now Bohemond felt that he was poised for enduring greatness and after raising a large army he launched an attack on the Byzantine Empire. The enterprise failed, and Bohemond was forced to accept a peace treaty in 1108 by which he became the emperor's vassal. He died, humiliated and with his dream of creating a powerful independent principality broken.

However, he was able to pass Antioch on to his heirs, and was assured of everlasting fame for his reputation as a charismatic diplomat and general. Without his leadership, the crusade would have foundered at Dorylaeum or Antioch before it ever reached Jerusalem.

▼ On his death in 1111, Bohemond was buried in this mausoleum at the Cathedral of San Sabino in Canosa di Puglia, Italy.

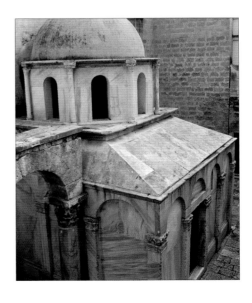

THE WAY TO THE HOLY CITY
DELAY IN ANTIOCH PRECEDES THE MARCH SOUTH

The capture of Antioch appeared to open the way to Jerusalem. The army's morale was sky high, bolstered by the conviction that with the Holy Lance in their possession they were invincible because they fought with God's blessing. But this impetus and energy was wasted, allowed to drain away, while the princely and noble leaders of the crusade were locked in dispute over what should be done with Antioch.

Raymond of Toulouse insisted that Antioch be returned to Alexius in order to honour the vow that he and other lords, including Bohemond, had made while in Constantinople, to return captured lands to the Byzantine Empire. Bohemond claimed the city for himself and, as we have seen, before beginning the assault he had negotiated an agreement with the other lords that he should keep it; he argued that because Alexius had not come to the crusaders' aid when they were besieged in Antioch, and left them to God's mercy, that the vow no longer held. Nevertheless, Raymond sent a message to Alexius with Hugh of Vermandois to the effect that they would return Antioch to the empire if the emperor now agreed to bring an army to help them in the conquest of Jerusalem.

THE UNTIMELY DEATH OF BISHOP ADHEMAR

Just over a month after the capture of Antioch, the crusaders lost their spiritual leader when Bishop Adhemar, the papal legate, died of a plague that swept through the city. Adhemar's death was a great setback, for he had been a guiding presence, presiding over councils of leading lords, reminding all involved of the original purpose of the undertaking and attempting to restrain the leading lords from personal conflicts that might derail the crusade.

He had also been a visible leader of the army and played a major part in determining battle tactics. For example, prior to the siege of Antioch a crusader force under Robert of Normandy captured the Iron Bridge across the River Orontes 15 miles (24km) from Antioch, defeating a garrison sent from the city to do so; in this battle, on Bishop Adhemar's advice, they used a tortoise formation – the crusaders held their shields above their heads to form a protective barrier to hold off arrows fired by the defenders, and were able to advance largely unscathed and overpower the garrison. The formation was inspired by the *testudo* formation of the ancient Roman army, which the bishop probably read about in a Roman military treatise.

▲ *The crusader army finally began its march southwards from Antioch towards Jerusalem. Rank and file soldiers were convinced Heaven was lighting their way.*

THE ATTACK ON MAARRAT AN-NUMAN

The months dragged on, with little happening. Groups of crusaders raided the countryside around Antioch; some went north to join Count Baldwin in Edessa. In December an expedition was mounted to take the strategically significant town of Maarrat an-Numan to the south of Antioch. The army captured the town and slaughtered its 20,000 population and then, finding little or no food, they were allegedly reduced to cooking and eating some of the freshly slain inhabitants.

JERUSALEM BECKONS

The Holy City to which the crusaders were ultimately headed was no longer in the hands of the Seljuks. In 1098, while the crusaders were occupied at Antioch, an army of the Fatimid Vizier of Egypt, Al-Afdal Shahanshah, had retaken Jerusalem and Palestine as far north as Beirut – lands which they had only lost to the Seljuks in the early 1070s. The Fatimids had

---

CANNIBALISM AMONG THE CRUSADERS

According to accounts by Tancred's biographer Radulph of Caen, and in a letter to Pope Urban II, the troops at Maarrat an-Numan were driven by desperation and maddening hunger to commit acts of cannibalism. Guibert of Nogent, who discussed incidents of cannibalism in his *Historia Hierosolymitana*, reported that perhaps because of incidents such as this or perhaps because of wild rumour and speculation, the Turks and other 'Saracens' became convinced that it was common practice among the crusaders, whom they regarded as savages, to eat the flesh of their dead enemies. He then described an act of provocation by the Tafurs, who openly spit-roasted a slain Turkish prisoner in view of the Turks in order to madden and anger them – they had no intention of eating the man's flesh. It is probable that accounts of crusaders eating flesh were propaganda on behalf of Christian writers seeking to make the crusaders seem fierce.

---

declared that the city was open to Christian pilgrims, who could come and go safely – the city's holy places did not need rescuing.

Although the crusaders did not know this, the Byzantine emperor Alexius had effectively disowned them, declaring to the Vizier that he could not control and did not support them, and renewing an alliance with Fatimid Egypt. Yet the bulk of the crusaders were desperate to march on Jerusalem, determined to fulfil their vows to reach the city and worship in the Church of the Holy Sepulchre, and driven by the conviction that they were engaged in a divinely inspired war fighting for Christ and his saints.

While the leading crusaders continued to hesitate, the lesser lords and knights – together with members of the army's rank and file – urged the continuation of the crusade. They offered to recognize Raymond of Toulouse as leader of the crusade if he would command them on the way to Jerusalem. Raymond accepted, giving way in the stand-off and allowing Bohemond to keep Antioch.

Finally, in mid-January 1099, walking barefoot as a pilgrim, Raymond finally left Antioch and began the journey southwards towards Jerusalem, leading a force of 5,000 crusaders. Tancred and Robert of Normandy followed with their troops almost immediately, while Robert of Normandy and Godfrey of Bouillon caught up around a month later.

PROGRESS SOUTHWARDS

The crusaders encountered little opposition as they marched south, partly because local lords – following the defeat of Kerbogha and the advance of the Fatimids – thought that dealing with the Christians was a way of exploiting the changing balance of power to their own advantage, and partly because the rulers simply wanted

▼ As the crusader army advanced through the Holy Land, its reputation for ferocity and acts of barbarity preceded it.

▲ Local lords were willing to make deals with the crusaders so they would pass by and become someone else's problem.

to keep the crusaders moving on, avoiding the devastation that would follow from conflict, and making the bedraggled army another ruler's problem.

The crusaders captured the port of Tortosa, strategically important for maintaining their supply line, and then passed Tripoli on the coast of Lebanon on 16 May without attacking, after its emir agreed to pay them protection money and supplied them with horses and provisions. They proceeded down the coast past Beirut and into Fatimid-held territory, past Acre and Caesarea to Arsuf, about 50 miles (80km) north-west of Jerusalem, from where they headed inland towards the Holy City.

They stopped for four days at the town of Ramla, which they found deserted of its Muslim garrison but well supplied with food. Here, according to Fulcher of Chartres, they installed a bishop in the Church of St George and left a Christian garrison holding the fortress before setting out once more for Jerusalem on 6 June.

ROBERT OF JERUSALEM
CRUSADER KNIGHT COUNT ROBERT II OF FLANDERS

French knight Robert of Flanders fought bravely in the major sieges and battles of the First Crusade, including the capture of Jerusalem in 1099, and when he returned to Europe after fulfilling his vows he won acclaim and adulation for his part in events that were quickly becoming the stuff of legend. Hailed as Robertus Hierosolimitanus (Robert of Jerusalem) and as 'Robert the Crusader', in the ensuing decades his fame was almost equal to that of Godfrey of Bouillon.

THE 'ARDENT WARRIOR'

The eldest son of Robert I, Count of Flanders (the nobleman known also as Robert the Frisian), Robert the younger had ruled the county as regent while his father had undertaken a pilgrimage to Jerusalem in 1085–91. After his father's death in 1093 he took power as Count Robert II, but within two years had committed to the First Crusade. He was already an experienced knight, and on the crusade he proved himself a great general and soldier, often in close association with Bohemond of Taranto. *Gesta Francorum* described Robert as an 'ardent warrior'.

EXPLOITS ON CRUSADE

Robert travelled on crusade in the company of Godfrey of Bouillon, leaving northern France in October 1096. In Constantinople he was easily persuaded to swear the oath of loyalty to Emperor Alexius in the company of Bohemond and Godfrey. After taking part in the siege of Nicaea, Robert marched on in the vanguard of the crusader army with Bohemond of Taranto – the part of the

THE CULT OF ST GEORGE

Robert played a significant part in the establishment of the cult of St George in Europe, for on his return he brought with him a precious relic, supposedly the arm of St George, which had been given to him as a gift by Emperor Alexius. Robert gave the relic to the Church of Anchin in Flanders, which established the church as a pilgrimage centre. He also founded the Monastery of St Andrew at Betferkerke near Bruges.

▼ *An artist's impression of Count Robert and Godfrey of Bouillon depositing trophies, supposedly won in the Battle of Ascalon, in the city of Jerusalem.*

army that came under attack in the Battle of Dorylaeum. He and his men fought bravely to keep the Seljuk Turks under Kilij Arslan at bay until the arrival of the main part of the crusader force, then fought on in the centre section of the crusader army alongside Raymond of Toulouse, when it launched the counter-attack that managed to decisively break the Turkish advance.

In the long siege of Antioch, Robert took part in key manoeuvres at the side of Bohemond of Taranto. In December they rode out to forage for food in the fertile valley of the River Orontes and, on 30 December, they together encountered and defeated a relief army sent by Duqaq, the Seljuk ruler of Damascus. As at Dorylaeum earlier, the charge of the Frankish and Norman knights riding with lances couched was too much for the Turkish horsemen to endure. When Antioch was subsequently taken, Robert was among the first of the crusaders to enter the city with Bohemond.

Then on 28 June 1098, when the Christian army broke out of the city to attack Sultan Kerbogha's besieging force – behind the Holy Lance, to the sound of prayers chanted by priests and in the face of a blinding vision of heavenly warriors under St George riding to their rescue – Robert together with Hugh of Vermandois commanded the first regiment to emerge, which deployed along the riverbank in a line. Contemporary accounts of the battle suggest that leadership was exemplary, for the crusader deployment and tactics were highly disciplined. After this battle, Robert took part with Bohemond in the capture of the citadel of Antioch, which had held out against the crusaders when the rest of the city had fallen.

LOYAL TO BOHEMOND OF TARANTO

Subsequently, Robert backed Bohemond in the dispute with Raymond of Toulouse over whether the crusaders could keep the city or must return it to Alexius. In December that year he rode out with

Raymond of Toulouse to attack the strategically important town of Maarrat an-Numan to the south of Antioch: Robert took part in the siege and capture of the town and presumably also in the massacre of its 20,000 inhabitants. He probably did not become involved in the alleged instances of cannibalism in which, according to Radulph of Caen, the starving crusaders cooked and ate the freshly slaughtered locals, both adults and children – this was most likely limited to the rank and file, while the nobles and commanders would have had the resources to buy scarce and overpriced food.

The crusaders recommenced their movement towards Jerusalem in January 1099, led by Raymond of Toulouse. Robert of Normandy and Tancred swore oaths to become Raymond's vassals and marched in his army, but Robert of Flanders and Godfrey of Bouillon refused to swear and initially remained in Antioch with Bohemond, subsequently joining the army at the siege of Arqa in March.

Robert largely remained with the army all the way down the coast to Jerusalem, except that at one point he and Tancred made a diversion into Samaria to find wood for building siege engines to use in the expected siege of Jerusalem. Robert then took part in the siege and capture of Jerusalem and in the subsequent Battle

▲ *The ancient port of Latakia in Syria, taken by Count Robert and Raymond of Toulouse in 1099, became an important holding of the Principality of Antioch.*

of Ascalon, in which the crusaders drove off a Fatimid army commanded by al-Afdal Shahanshah, Vizier of Egypt. Having been warned of the approach of the Fatimid army, the crusaders rode out to meet them and caught them by surprise in their camp near Ascalon. In this battle, he fought in the centre of the crusader force with Tancred, Robert of Normandy, Eustace of Boulogne and Gaston of Bearn, while Godfrey of Bouillon commanded the left wing and Raymond of Toulouse led the right flank. The crusaders triumphed despite being outnumbered by as many as five to one.

HOMEWARD BOUND

Robert of Flanders left Jerusalem in the company of Robert of Normandy and Raymond of Toulouse at the close of August 1099. On route to Constantinople, they conquered the Syrian port of Latakia, which became part of the crusader Principality of Antioch. In Constantinople, both Roberts declined an offer from Emperor Alexius to remain there in his service and took ship for Europe and a wildly enthusiastic homecoming.

JERUSALEM! JERUSALEM!
ARRIVAL AT AND BESIEGING OF THE HOLY CITY

As spring turned to summer in 1099 the crusaders neared their goal day by day. They were encountering little opposition, and even receiving a welcome of sorts, but they got an inkling of the locals' true attitude when a carrier pigeon was killed by a hawk above their camp and was found to have been carrying a message from the governor of Acre calling on faithful Muslims to take up arms and repel the Christian invasion.

A WELCOME IN BETHLEHEM

Christian inhabitants of Bethlehem sent out envoys begging the crusaders to liberate them from Egyptian occupation. Tancred and Baldwin of Le Bourg accepted the call and were welcomed as a liberating army by citizens and priests. The sight of their banner flying above Christ's birthplace was an enormous boost to the crusaders. They were further cheered by an eclipse of the Moon that occurred at that very time – they interpreted it as portending the imminent eclipse of the crescent, the symbol of Islam.

'MOUNT JOY'

On 7 June 1099, the very day after the taking of Bethlehem, the crusader force crossed the hill known as Mountjoie ('Mount Joy') to generations of pilgrims and saw the walls of Jerusalem before them. 'Jerusalem!' went up the cry, and echoed down the lines. According to William of Tyre, the crusader-pilgrims fell to their knees and sobbed tears of joy, offering prayers of gratitude that God had led them to their destination; they cast off their shoes and bowed low to the ground in order to kiss the earth of the Holy Land. It had taken them three years to get there,

▲ At last the crusaders see the cherished city of Jerusalem. They offer prayers to God for having delivered them to their goal.

a long period of suffering and desperate exertions in which the pull of the Holy City and of their pilgrims' vows had inspired them to carry on. Now Jerusalem's walls were spread out before them. But their task remained a daunting one, for this city was one of the world's most strongly fortified, in a commanding position with deep valleys on two sides, to the east and west.

Assault was really only feasible from the north, for in the south on Mount Zion conditions could not support anything other than a small encampment. Expecting a siege, its governor, Iftikhar al-Daula, had prepared well, bringing in provisions and poisoning wells around the city, and sending urgent communication to Cairo calling for a Muslim relief army. He also expelled the city's Christian inhabitants to prevent any of them betraying Jerusalem to the crusaders.

AN ATTACK IN FAITH

The crusader army was not large enough to surround the city fully. On the northern wall, Godfrey of Bouillon arrayed his troops, alongside those of Robert of Flanders and Robert of Normandy, while to the south was the army of Raymond of Toulouse. In the gruelling heat of the summer and with very little water available, the crusaders decided to act quickly. They launched an attack on 13 June, although they had insufficient siege equipment. They had been spurred on by a hermit who reported that he had been told in a vision that if they proved their faith by attacking at once even without the necessary equipment God would grant them instant success. The attack failed, and brought home to the besiegers their urgent need for wood and other equipment with which to build proper siege towers.

Then, as if in answer to their prayers, Tancred found a hidden collection of

▲ *Exaltation strengthened the crusaders' resolve to take the city into Christian hands.*

timber in a cave, and six English and Genoese ships put in at Jaffa bearing wood, nails, bolts, ropes and other supplies. Hidden from sight of the Jerusalem garrison, the crusaders set to work building two siege towers. They even took apart two ships to get more wood.

THE EXAMPLE OF JOSHUA

As at Antioch, they were working against time, for they received a warning that Governor Iftikhar al-Daula's cry for help had been answered, and a large relief army was on its way from Egypt. But they found time to mount a penitential procession around the city. A crusader priest named Peter Desiderius had been visited by the late Bishop Adhemar in a vision, and been instructed that if the army marched barefoot around the city walls Jerusalem would fall within nine days. This was inspired by the example of Joshua, Israelite leader in *c*.1200BC, who, according to biblical accounts, led his army seven times around the city of Jericho – and, as promised by God, the walls of the city fell down and the Israelites captured it. The entire crusader army held a three-day fast and on the second day, Friday 8 July, marched barefoot around the city, singing hymns. Members of the garrison gathered on the walls to jeer at the soldiers, who proceeded to the Mount of Olives to hear sermons by Peter the Hermit and others.

Five days later, the siege towers were ready. The plan was to mount the main assault on the north wall, using the two towers, one commanded by Godfrey of Bouillon and the other by Robert of Normandy, while a second assault was led by Raymond's force from the south side.

▼ *Godfrey rallies foot soldiers and knights at Jerusalem. Victory now seemed as certain as that of Joshua at Jericho.*

THE HOLY CITY CAPTURED

THE CRUSADERS' TRIUMPH – AND SHAME

After dark on the night of 13 July, the crusaders began to move their siege towers up to the walls of Jerusalem. They worked beneath a murderous storm of arrows, missiles, pitch and Greek fire. All night and all the next day, while behind them the mangonel hurled great rocks at the walls of Jerusalem, sweating and toiling beneath a searingly hot sun and through great clouds of dust, they laboured at hauling the machines forward.

At last, on the morning of 15 July, Godfrey of Bouillon's tower was close enough to the wall to make a bridge across on to the city ramparts near Herod's Gate. Godfrey and his brother Baldwin fought bravely on the tower. At around noon, despite the defenders' desperate attempts to repel them using fire and boiling water, the first crusaders made it on to the ramparts from Godfrey's tower. Among the first across were two brothers from Flanders, Lethold and Gilbert of Tournai. Just afterwards, the second tower under Robert of Normandy established a bridgehead to the wall.

THE CITY TAKEN

The defenders on the north wall retreated in order to take refuge in the al Aqsa mosque. Crusaders clambered over the walls and opened gates from within, and their comrades flooded into Jerusalem, unleashing a frenzy of bloodletting.

During the long struggle to get the towers up to the walls, according to the author of the *Gesta Francorum*, the crusaders had been surprised by how difficult it was, 'numbed with astonishment and extremely frightened'. Now, in the moment of triumph they had dreamt of for years, they unleashed their pent-up emotions in a bloodbath. According to the same author, 'the defenders of the city fled … and our men, following Lethold, ran after them, slaughtering them and dismembering them all the way to the Temple of Solomon. And in that place there was so much killing that the blood

▼ *The besiegers endured a heavy assault from the battlements as they moved their siege towers, little by little, up to the walls.*

came up to our ankles.' According to the Provençal chronicler Raymond of Aguilers, 'in the streets and squares of the city, piles of heads, hands and feet could be seen. People were making their way over the corpses of men and horses. But this is only to describe the minor horrors …'

The defenders of the north wall were pursued by Tancred and his men, and surrendered to him, promising to pay a large ransom. They took refuge in the al Aqsa mosque praying for their lives. Tancred claimed the Temple quarter in his name, and set his banner flying above the building. The Jews of the city also fled for their lives, taking refuge in their main synagogue, by the Western Wall.

The *Gesta Francorum* account goes on to describe how the pilgrims followed the soldiers into the city and also slew 'Saracens' indiscriminately to left and right. At the Temple of Solomon, it reports, attackers and defenders 'fought a furious battle all day so that their blood flooded all over the Temple. At last the pagans were defeated and our men took a good number of men and women prisoner in the Temple. They killed whichever prisoners they wished and chose to allow others to live.'

THE HONOUR OF RAYMOND OF TOULOUSE

On the south wall, meanwhile, the defenders kept Raymond of Toulouse's attack at bay until they saw that behind them the city had been lost. Then they made a swift retreat to the citadel, the Tower of David, and finally surrendered there to Raymond. He gave his word that they would have safe passage out of the city – and, remarkably, amid such chaos was able to honour it, escorting them from Jerusalem as far as the Muslim garrison in the port of Ascalon. This honourable enactment of the safe escort was a brief interlude of restraint.

THE CITY IS STRIPPED

The account given by Fulcher of Chartres describes how crusaders ran into deserted houses and seized whatever they found. Whoever was first into a building was able to claim it – 'in this way, many poor folk became rich'. For it was a frenzy of greed, as well as of bloodletting. According to the *Gesta Francorum*, 'the crusaders seized silver and gold, mules and horses, and buildings full of all manner of riches'.

A VIOLENT CLEANSING

It was normal practice in 11th-century warfare for an army to loot a city it had conquered after a long siege. The attack on the inhabitants of Jerusalem had an extra intensity, fuelled as it was by papal and priestly rhetoric about the need to sweep the city clean of 'Saracens'. After the killing, the soldiers and pilgrims piously gave thanks to God in the Church of the Holy Sepulchre. Fulcher of Chartres presented this dreadful slaughter as a purgative cleansing: 'O day so fiercely longed for! ... O deed above all other deeds! ... [the crusaders] desired that this place, for so long made unclean by the pagan practices of its inhabitants, should be cleaned of its filth.' Raymond of Aguilers declared that: 'after the city had

▼ *In the 15th century, when this illustration was drawn, the battle for Jerusalem was reimagined as a civilized encounter.*

been taken, it was a rich reward to see the devotion of the pilgrims at the Holy Sepulchre; the manner in which they clapped in their exulting, singing a new song to the Lord.'

The slaughter continued for almost two days. Tancred was not able to protect the Muslims in the al Aqsa mosque. On 16 July the crusaders forced their way into the building and killed every man, woman and child. The synagogue, filled with refugees, was burned to the ground. A letter from the crusade leaders to the pope declared proudly that in the portico of Solomon and in his Temple, 'our men rode in the blood of the Saracens even up to the knees of their horses'. A reference, perhaps, to the Book of Revelation, whose apocalyptic accounts of the Last Judgement were familiar to the crusaders: 'And the winepress was trodden without the city, and blood came out of the winepress, even unto the horses' bridles.'

▲ *The crusaders dedicated their attack to Christ and proclaimed a desire to win Jerusalem for God.*

▼ *In the heat of the moment, bloodlust took over from pious righteousness, and one act of barbarity was followed by another.*

AFTER THE VICTORY
THE CITY SECURED WITH TRIUMPH AT ASCALON

In the immediate aftermath of the slaughter of 15–16 July, the crusaders had had to deal with cleaning the city, since the piles of corpses made such a terrible stench. The *Gesta Francorum* reports that the bodies of the Saracens were dragged out of the city and burned in huge pyramids. The smoke hung over the city in a dreadful pall.

DEFENDER OF THE HOLY SEPULCHRE

On 22 July, the eighth day after the taking of Jerusalem, the crusaders elected Godfrey of Bouillon to rule the city as Defender of the Holy Sepulchre. The first choice had been Count Raymond of Toulouse as king, but he declined the offer saying no mortal man should wear a crown in the city that belonged to Christ. Godfrey agreed with this statement, but came up with a compromise title that allowed him to take power.

▼ *With the city of Jerusalem secured, normal rules of pillage did not apply, and the victors became rich overnight.*

In many ways, Godfrey was an understandable choice. He had proved himself pious, steadfast and brave. Among the other lords, Bohemond had established himself in Antioch and Baldwin in Edessa, while Robert of Normandy had truly joined the crusade in order to liberate Jerusalem and was now set on returning to France. Raymond's refusal of power in Jerusalem is less easy to understand, given that he had shown himself elsewhere to be ambitious and not averse to putting political ambition above Christian piety. It is possible that his refusal was a ploy to prevent any of the lords claiming the kingship or that he considered Jerusalem too difficult a prize to defend and was planning to establish a principality in Tripoli.

JERUSALEM'S FIRST LATIN PATRIARCH

Then on 1 August Arnulf of Choques, the chaplain in Robert of Normandy's army, was elected Patriarch of Jerusalem. Arnulf had been one of the most prominent sceptics voicing doubts about the validity of Peter Bartholomew's claims that he had

▲ *When the Church of the Holy Sepulchre gave up a piece of the True Cross it was seen as a further validation of the attack.*

discovered a piece of the Holy Lance in Antioch, and his opposition had played a major part in forcing Peter to undergo a trial by fire in April during the march south, after which the visionary had died. During the siege of Jerusalem, Arnulf had made a statue of Christ to stand on one of the siege engines. Then, on 5 August, he announced that he had discovered a piece of the True Cross (the cross on which Christ had been crucified) in the Church of the Holy Sepulchre. This became one of the most treasured possessions of the Kingdom of Jerusalem.

Arnulf's election was supported by Godfrey, and in return Arnulf backed Godfrey's decision to make the Kingdom of Jerusalem a secular state rather than one under Church — and ultimately papal — rule. He imposed the Latin form of Christianity, barring the priests of other denominations, such as the Orthodox Greeks and the Coptic, Armenian or Georgian Christians, from the Church of the Holy Sepulchre. He also reportedly authorized the torture of other Christians to force them to reveal where they had hidden other parts of the True Cross. The events of these first weeks of the Kingdom of Jerusalem created a fierce hatred in the Eastern churches for the Latin Christians that would endure for centuries.

BATTLE OF ASCALON

Godfrey's first job as ruler was to repel the Fatimid relief army summoned from Egypt by Jerusalem's governor, Iftikhar al-Daula, before the fall of the city. The Fatimids had raised a force of perhaps 50,000 men under the command of Vizier al-Afdal Shahanshah, who intended to mount a siege of Jerusalem. On 10 August, Godfrey received reports from scouts that the Muslim army was massing in the vicinity of Ascalon, a port about 35 miles (55km) east of Jerusalem. Godfrey led his army out of Jerusalem to confront the Fatimid force, with Robert of Flanders and Arnulf; they were followed the next day by Raymond of Toulouse and Robert of Normandy. On the way, at Ramla, they met up with Tancred and Eustace of Boulogne, Godfey's brother.

In total, the crusader force numbers totalled around 10,000, with probably as few as 1,200 knights and the rest infantry. They were severely outnumbered by the Fatimids, although not as badly as is suggested in the *Gesta Francorum*, which claims the Egyptian army was 200,000-strong. The crusaders had their relics to comfort them: they marched behind Arnulf carrying the piece of the True Cross he had found and Raymond of Aguilers carrying the relic of the Holy Lance.

On 11 August the crusaders discovered a large number of goats, cattle, sheep and even camels grazing near Ascalon: they presumed the creatures were intended as a source for food for the large Fatimid army, although a few captives taken in a small encounter by Tancred indicated that the animals were intended as a decoy in the hope that the crusader army would lose its discipline and begin pillaging.

When the crusader scouts discovered the precise location of the Fatimid force, the Christian army marched on with the animals in tow, making their army seem larger than it otherwise would have done.

The two forces met in open conflict outside Ascalon. Most contemporary accounts suggest that the crusaders caught the Fatimids unprepared and that the battle was quickly over. It began with an exchange of arrows, and then the two main contingents fought at close quarters with lances, the kind of battle in which the crusaders were at their best. The Fatimids broke and fled, some into the city, some into the sea. They abandoned their camp, and all its treasures, which were claimed by Tancred and Robert of Normandy.

QUARREL OVER ASCALON

The crusaders rejoiced, but prepared for a second battle. However, after spending the night in the abandoned Fatimid camp, they discovered the next day that the Fatimid survivors had begun a retreat to Egypt. The city lay at their mercy, but its garrison declared that it would only surrender to Raymond of Toulouse – doubtless because he had behaved honourably in providing safe escort for Iftikhar al-Daula and his troops during

▲ *The crusaders rejoice as the symbol of Christ's Passion is raised at the end of their long and desperate campaign.*

the capture of Jerusalem. Raymond and Godfrey quarrelled over the spoils: Godfrey refused to accept the surrender on these terms, declaring that the city should come to him as ruler of Jerusalem, Raymond, furious at being thwarted again by Godfrey; marched back to Jerusalem, with Robert of Normandy. Godfrey alone was not strong enough to capture Ascalon, and so it remained in Muslim hands. Allowing this to happen was a grave mistake, for taking Ascalon would have been an important step towards consolidating the fledgling Kingdom of Jerusalem.

CRUSADE COMPLETED

For the great majority of the crusaders, the enterprise was now at an end and most went home. At the end of 1099 Godfrey remained in Jerusalem with only around 2,000 foot soldiers plus perhaps just 300 knights – in the estimation of William of Tyre. Robert of Normandy and Robert of Flanders were among those who departed for Europe and with them Godfrey sent word that the Kingdom of Jerusalem needed reinforcements.

THE
SECOND CRUSADE

Christians in the Holy Land and in Europe rejoiced at the outcome of the First Crusade. They believed that God's will had been done, that in 'liberating' Jerusalem from its Fatimid rulers they had overcome bleak odds with divine help and through their resolute faith: at Antioch in June 1098, in the course of the long journey towards Jerusalem, the crusaders reported being led into battle against an army commanded by Sultan Kerbogha of Mosul by heavenly warriors and the saints George, Demetrius and Maurice. Therefore it came as a terrible shock when Muslim powers in the Middle East, having regrouped, fought back. In 1119 the Artuqid Turkish general Ilghazi, ruler of lands in northern Iraq, northern Syria and eastern Anatolia, won a devastating victory over a Christian army in an encounter near Aleppo called 'the Battle of the Field of Blood' by Christian commentators. When on Christmas Eve 1144 Imad ed-Zengi, the ruler of Aleppo and Mosul, retook the city of Edessa from the crusaders after undermining the walls, he shook the whole of Christendom. Pope Eugenius III called a second crusade and the superb oratory of French Abbot Bernard of Clairvaux inspired Louis VII of France, Conrad III of Germany and Frederick, Duke of Swabia to commit themselves to the enterprise.

▲ *Tancred, hero of the First Crusade and Prince of Galilee was a staunch defender of the Kingdom of Outremer and won a foothold in the County of Tripoli when he gained posession of the powerful Crusader fortress of Krak des Chevaliers. Here he is pictured during his wedding to the daughter of the King of France in 1107, just two years before he died.*

▶ *A parliament was convoked at Vezelay in Burgundy in 1146, and Bernard of Clairvaux preached before the assembly on March 31. Louis VII of France, his wife, Eleanor of Aquitaine, and the princes and lords present all prostrated themselves at the feet of Bernard to receive the pilgrims' cross.*

THE LAND OVERSEAS

The many settlers who stayed after the First Crusade in 1099 created an outpost of Latin Christendom in the East. The land in which they made their homes became known as *Outremer* – from the French word meaning 'overseas'. Outremer encompassed the four crusader states established during or as a result of the First Crusade: the County of Edessa; the Principality of Antioch; the Kingdom of Jerusalem; and the County of Tripoli.

The settlers organized life along familiar lines, introducing the feudal system and imposing the rites of the Latin Church on other Christians. But in many respects, also, they went native. Fulcher of Chartres, who became chaplain to King Baldwin I of Jerusalem, wrote: 'We were once Westerners, but now we are men of the East. You may once have identified yourself as a Roman or a Frenchman, but here, in the present, you are a man of Galilee or of Palestine.... For we do not remember the lands of our birth; to the majority of us they are unfamiliar, foreign lands.' He went on to describe how the lords of the new estates came to appreciate local customs and food and married local women, whether Armenians, Syrians or even 'Saracens' – of course, he added, 'only to those who have been baptized'. It is clear that for the settlers life in Outremer represented the start of something permanent. When the soldiers of the Second Crusade arrived in 1148, they were shocked to find that the leading men of Outremer in their eyes were more like 'Saracens' than Christian princes.

▲ *The coastal crusader citadel of Sidon, in Lebanon.*

◀ *The impressive remains of Krak des Chevaliers at Qal'at al-Hisn in Syria are an enduring symbol of the might of the military orders and the kingdoms of Outremer.*

THE FOUNDATION OF OUTREMER
EDESSA, ANTIOCH, JERUSALEM AND TRIPOLI

The first crusader states had been established in 1098 en route to Jerusalem, when Baldwin of Boulogne created the County of Edessa based on the ancient city of that name (now Urfa, Turkey), and Bohemond of Taranto established the Principality of Antioch in Syria.

THE KINGDOM OF JERUSALEM
The third state, the Kingdom of Jerusalem, did not technically come into existence until 17 months after the Christian conquest of Jerusalem on 15 July 1099. As we have seen, Godfrey of Bouillon, refused to be called king in the city where Christ wore a crown of thorns and took the title 'Defender of the Holy Sepulchre'. But following Godfrey's death in July 1100 his brother Baldwin, no longer 'of Boulogne' but 'of Edessa', had no such qualms, and was crowned king on 25 December 1100 by Daimbert, Patriarch of Jerusalem.

Daimbert had arrived in Jerusalem from Rome in 1099. The Archbishop of Pisa, he had been sent from Italy as the new papal legate, the replacement for Bishop

▲ *The crusaders called this fortress on Mount Hermon 'L'Asibebe'. In English it is called Nimrod Fortress after the biblical hunter – and 'Citadel of the Mosquitoes'.*

▼ *Baldwin of Boulogne became Baldwin of Edessa and then, on the death of his brother Godfrey, King Baldwin I of Jerusalem.*

Adhemar of Le Puy, who had died of the plague in Antioch. Daimbert engineered the removal from office of the recently elected Patriarch of Jerusalem, Arnulf of Choques, on the grounds that Arnulf's election had been illegal, and took his place. He allowed Arnulf to occupy the lesser position of Archdeacon.

Then Daimbert set to work to bring about the creation of the papal state in the Holy Land that had been Pope Urban II's dream. He recognized the rule of Bohemond as Prince of Antioch and Tancred as Prince of Galilee, thus guaranteeing their independence from Jerusalem. From Godfrey he won the assurance that on his death the church would inherit control of Jerusalem – according to William of Tyre, Godfrey's plan was to cede rule to the Church in the Kingdom of Jerusalem and to carry on crusader conquest as far as Egypt, where he would establish his own secular kingdom.

But when Godfrey died unexpectedly, fate and conspiracy among the secular lords combined to prevent Daimbert achieving his and the papacy's wish of establishing a theocracy (a state ruled by God through churchmen). At the time of Godfrey's death, Daimbert was away on a campaign with Tancred against Haifa, and Baldwin was secretly summoned to come to Jerusalem and take power. When

Daimbert heard that Godfrey had died and that Baldwin was marching on Jerusalem, he wrote to Bohemond offering him rule of Palestine under Daimbert's authority – and asking him to prevent Baldwin reaching Jerusalem. The letter was intercepted, however, and Bohemond was captured while attempting an attack on Danishmend, emir of Sivas (Sebastea).

Baldwin marched into Jerusalem and secured his power base. Daimbert was forced to crown him king. Baldwin gave his previous holding, the County of Edessa, to his cousin Baldwin of Le Bourg. Early in 1101 Tancred abandoned his rule as Prince of Galilee, moving to take up power in Antioch – he reigned as regent for Bohemond, who was in Danishmend's jail (where he remained until 1103).

THE FOURTH CRUSADER STATE
The crusader state of the County of Tripoli was created in the course of the war waged by Raymond of Toulouse, from 1102 onwards, against Fakhr al-Mulk, emir of the coastal city of Tripoli (now in Lebanon), in power there as a vassal of the Fatimid caliphs in Cairo. Raymond died

in 1105, before the city fell, naming his cousin William-Jordan as regent and his infant son Alfonso-Jordan as heir; but subsequently, one of his illegitimate sons, Bertrand, who had been serving as regent of Toulouse in his father's absence, arrived in the Holy Land. Bertrand and William-Jordan agreed, as a result of King Baldwin I's intervention, that they would each keep the conquests they individually made. Bertrand was the main beneficiary, for he captured Tripoli and became sole ruler when William-Jordan died a little while afterwards; Alfonso-Jordan meanwhile returned to France with his mother.

Bertrand ruled the County of Tripoli as a vassal of the king of Jerusalem. Within his realm, the castle of Krak des Chevaliers was given to the military order of the Knights Hospitaller in 1142.

THE GEOGRAPHY OF OUTREMER

The County of Edessa was the farthest north of the crusader states and set in a remote, landlocked position, with half of its territory lying far away from the Mediterranean, on the east bank of the River Euphrates; the other three states were all coastal domains. The Edessa territory west of the Euphrates was governed from the castle of Turbessel, strongly fortified against attacks from the Seljuk Turks of the Sultanate of Rum, which lay to the north. To the west lay Armenian Cilicia, parts of the Byzantine Empire where the crusaders had made conquests, including the city of Tarsus.

▲ The majority of Outremer territories were coastal, and the Christian lords grew rich on trade passing through their ports.

▼ Krak des Chevaliers, the 'Castle of the Knights', in the County of Tripoli, was the foremost crusader fortress of Outremer.

The Principality of Antioch bordered the County of Edessa to the south-west, and ran down to the Mediterranean coast. When Tancred was regent in 1100–03 he expanded the Principality north-west to take the cities of Tarsus and Latakia from the Byzantines. To the south was the County of Tripoli, leading south again to the Kingdom of Jerusalem. By the mid-1100s, when the Kingdom was at its largest, it extended north to south from Beirut (now capital of Lebanon) to Rafia (modern Rafah in the Gaza Strip). In the north it was separated by the district of Lebanon from the Emirate of Damascus; in the south-east it ran all the way to the Arabian desert and even encompassed the Red Sea port of Aïla (modern Elat). After the First Crusade, some parts of Cilicia remained in European hands, but they never formed into a state or principality.

GOVERNMENT OF THE CRUSADER STATES
THE FEUDAL HIERARCHY IS EXPORTED TO OUTREMER

The crusader states were governed on the lines of the feudal system. The crusaders imported this social system from Europe because in their eyes it had God's blessing as the perfect way to create stability within a hierarchy of duties and responsibilities. Each man had his place, by divine plan, beneath the king. Detailed accounts of the government of the Kingdom of Jerusalem survive, and we know that the other crusader states had a parallel system.

THE KING OF JERUSALEM
Within the Kingdom of Jerusalem, the king was paramount. Great lords held land as his tenants in chief – men such as Tancred, Prince of Galilee, or Eustace Grenier, Lord of Caesarea. These lords in turn packaged land out to their tenants or rear-vassals. Only Catholic Christians were permitted to hold fiefs – Jews, Muslims and all other Christians were excluded from the system.

As in Europe, the lords and their vassals were required to provide military service – for example, Caesarea was required to provide 100 knights, as was Galilee; even the inhospitable lordship of

▼ *The port of Caesarea, a major crusader possession on the Mediterranean coast, dates back to around the time of Christ. It was built by Herod the Great in c.25BC.*

Oultrejourdain (the land east of the Jordan river containing the Negev Desert) had to raise 60 knights.

In 1166 the second tier of tenants, the rear vassals, took vows of liege homage to the king – at that time, Amalric. The chief city of Jerusalem was naturally reserved for the king himself, part of a royal domain that he governed directly.

THE KING'S POWER STRUCTURE
The king's most senior officers were: a seneschal, with control of royal castles and the treasury; a butler, in control of the royal household; and a constable, in charge of the military establishment. The collection of revenue from the countryside largely used pre-crusade methods, and then the moneys were passed via scribes and bailiffs, through local treasuries to the Grant Secrete, or principal treasury.

The king's power was limited by the great lords as tenants-in-chief and the rear-vassals, in their capacity as members of the High Court. The king took an oath in its presence, and was forbidden to seize any lord's fief-holding unless the decision was approved by the Court. The High Court, and not the king, made the kingdom's laws or assizes – the Assizes of Jerusalem. (These are sometimes wrongly said to have been drawn up by Godfrey of Bouillon.) Under these assizes, if the king broke his oaths, his feudal dependants had the legal

right to resist. In addition, if two members of the royal family came into dispute over succession to the throne, the Court had the power to determine the new king. However, the Court met only when summoned by the king so, if necessary, he was able to sideline its powers.

The High Court also functioned as the kingdom's highest legal tribunal, and there was no appeal against its judgements. Beneath it was a network of burgess courts to judge cases involving Western settlers; these courts had the power to impose the death penalty or to send offenders into exile. In addition, within the larger fiefs there were courts of knights and burgesses. These courts were limited to Latin Christians. Other Christians used a separate group of port and market courts. For Muslims and Jews, cases were divided into spiritual or secular: spiritual cases were judged by the existing religious authorities of qadis or rabbis, while secular ones went to newly established native courts called the Courts of the Syrians.

Assemblies of leading citizens – including senior churchmen, top members of the military orders and prominent townsmen as well as the king and nobles – were occasionally held to debate matters of consequence such as the necessity of levying taxes to pay for wars or policy problems such as where help could most profitably be requested among western lords. These meetings were called *parlements*.

THE INDEPENDENCE OF MAJOR LANDOWNERS
As in feudal Europe, the king often struggled to impose his will on the most powerful lords, who possessed strongly fortified castles and their own military forces – for example, Reynald of Châtillon, lord of the important fief of Montreal from 1174, was largely a law unto himself and waged a private war against Muslims, ignoring the royal policy of his king,

THE MILITARY ORDERS

One of the principal difficulties for the crusader authorities was the low number of settlers. They made repeated attempts to attract immigration from Europe, but they remained vastly outnumbered – a ruling minority with a very large subject population of Syrians, Greeks and Muslim Arabs who could not be relied on if the kingdom came under attack. By the 1180s, only an estimated 35 per cent of the population was European in origin.

The establishment of the military orders such as the Knights Hospitaller, the Knights Templar and the Teutonic Knights helped to boost the Kingdom's strength. The increasingly wealthy orders, funded by lavish donations in Europe, were able to buy castles and land from impoverished noblemen among the settlers and were an important means of maintaining order.

However, the ultimate loyalty of the military orders was to the papacy; they were not bound by feudal ties to the king, and technically did not owe military service in the defence of the kingdom, although in practice they fought in all the major campaigns. They also had the right to negotiate directly with Muslims.

Baldwin VI. The lordship of Montreal was a wealthy one, for its main castle, Al-Shaubak (also known as Montreal) controlled lucrative caravan routes from Damascus to the Red Sea and Egypt.

THE RICHES OF THE KING

This difficulty was balanced by the fact that the king's domain made him richer than any of his lords: it contained the ports of Tyre and Acre as well as the city of Jerusalem. The king imposed customs duties at ports along the Mediterranean coast, and taxed overland trade caravans; he also had a monopoly on some local industries and was the only lord permitted to coin money in the realm; he had the right to claim shipwrecks; he could also, with the approval of his *parlement* or the High Court, levy one-off taxes – as when, in 1182, Baldwin IV imposed a tax of 2 per cent on all incomes, including those of the Latin Church, in order to raise money to fight Saladin. These large and varied incomes made the kingship of Jerusalem very profitable indeed: the king of this small eastern kingdom was probably richer than most European princes in the 12th century. And he was able to use his wealth to hire mercenaries.

THE POWER OF THE CHURCH

After the king, the Patriarch of Jerusalem was the most important person in the kingdom. The Latin Church in Palestine quickly became powerful, establishing a number of monasteries on land donated by wealthy crusaders and ruthlessly

▲ *The prosperity of Outremer depended on trade. The king of Jerusalem amassed great wealth from taxes on desert caravans.*

sidelining other Christians, such as the Coptic, Syrian, Greek Orthodox and others. The Patriarch was elected by the clergy, then acclaimed by the people: his position was subject to the approval of the pope, who would confirm the Patriarch's powers after the election.

▼ *The city of Tyre, an important port on the Mediterranean coast, had a Christian community from the 2nd century onwards. Its Muslim rulers surrendered in 1124.*

LIFE IN THE CRUSADER STATES

THE RICH ENJOY LOCAL LUXURIES

▲ *In this image of Bertrand of Saint-Gilles receiving submission from Seljuk qadi Fakhr al-Mulk it can be seen how the Westerners adapted their lifestyle to the climate and landscape of Outremer.*

In Jerusalem and other cities of the crusader states, the great lords and many of their retainers lived in fine style. They had their pick of the cargoes of Chinese silk, rare stones and spices that were brought to the Mediterranean coast overland from central Asia by camel caravan; in addition, they chose from the finest locally produced cotton and glassware.

In their city dwellings and their castles, they surrounded themselves with the finest luxuries, including silk wall hangings, woven carpets and beautifully carved Arabian furniture; the richest even used gold and silver plates. They adapted to the local diet, learning to enjoy dates, olives, watermelons, lemons, oranges and sugar cane, and to spice up their foods with pepper, ginger and cinnamon; they dressed in flowing robes, and began to wear open-toed sandals; some even adopted the turban. They married beauties among the local womenfolk – often in addition to European wives. Many lords kept elaborate Arabian-style gardens as havens from the dust and heat.

LIFE IN THE COUNTRYSIDE

The majority of the Europeans lived in the cities and castles but there was some settlement in the countryside. Some occupied existing villages and towns. In the Mediterranean port of Caesarea, for example, the crusaders who captured the town in 1101 simply drove out the Muslim population and made their homes in the existing city. Initially they just adapted mosques to use them as churches. In the longer term, they dismantled the Great Mosque and built in its place the Catholic Cathedral of St Peter.

There were also new settlements, in which land was given to European peasants in return for a 10 per cent tithe paid to the local secular or religious landowner. For example, the village of Magna Mahumeria (modern day al-Bira) north of

Jerusalem was established on these lines in 1120 by canons of the Church of the Holy Sepulchre on land bequeathed to them by Godfrey of Bouillon.

For poor Eastern Christians and Jews in the parched countryside, however, life probably seemed to have changed very little as a result of the crusade: their Muslim landlords had been replaced by Christian lords, but little else was different. The Muslims, of course, had to come to terms with being cast among the poor.

One way in which the feudal system in the East was different to that in Europe was that the Christian lords were largely absentees, for they chose to live in Jerusalem or other cities rather than on their estates. Although technically they were the property of the Latin Christian master who owned their land, the Muslims, Jews and Eastern Christians had a significant amount of freedom. There was freedom of religion in that in the countryside, Jews, Muslims and Eastern

THE KING'S ARMY

The king's feudal subjects were required to perform military service, but unlike in Europe there was no time limit set on this; as a result, knights and soldiers were rewarded with pay. But the feudal army, given the small Western population of the kingdom, was always likely to be too small to mount an effective defence of Jerusalem and its environs. In addition to perhaps a few hundred knights, the king of Jerusalem used his immense wealth to hire a large force of mercenaries, including Seljuk or Greek mounted archers called *Turkopoles* (from the Greek for 'offspring of Turks'), Lebanese archers and Armenian and Syrian infantry. This force numbered around 20,000.

▲ *The crusaders drove the local inhabitants out of Caesarea in 1101 and simply took what they found for their own use.*

Christians could follow their own faith and in religious matters at least were subject to their own authorities.

The farmers grew cereals and summer crops such as maize and millet. They kept vineyards, orchards and olive groves, and a few grew sugar and cotton. They paid a tax of up to one-third of their arable crops and one-half of the produce from olive groves and vineyards.

RELIGIOUS FREEDOM

In the cities, Muslims, Jews and Eastern Christians had their freedom – except that Jews and Muslims were allowed only to visit Jerusalem and were officially not permitted to live there. The Armenians, Jacobites and Maronite Christians were allowed to worship according to their own rites, but as we have seen were excluded from the Church of the Holy Sepulchre.

The degree of tolerance that developed between the Catholic Christians and other groups was a matter of necessity. For example, trade connections had to be made with Muslims and Jews. The Catholics' treatment of Jews was considerably better in the crusader states than in 11th–12th-century Europe, and there were no pogroms against the Jews in the crusader states.

MERCHANT ENCLAVES

Within the cities – particularly the coastal ports, such as Tyre and Acre – were colonies of merchants from the cities of Genoa, Venice, Pisa, Marseille, Narbonne and so on, who lived in independent, self-contained districts under the control of their own consul; they were not subject to the feudal system and did not have to perform military service. These merchant colonies had landholdings on the edges of cities, where they grew sugar cane and cotton. They were allowed a monopoly on trade between the Kingdom and Europe and sent home ships heavily laden with highly profitable cargoes. Ships from European ports brought goods necessary to the settlers' way of life, although most adapted quickly to local conditions.

The ports grew very rich. Traders from the Byzantine Empire, Syria, Iraq and north Africa worked alongside those from the European mercantile cities of Europe. Taxes imposed by the authorities could be as high as 25 per cent. The most valuable trade of all was in spices leaving the Mediterranean ports bound first for Constantinople and then on to the towns and cities of western Europe. Among the richest and most profitable of the ports was Acre. The Muslim geographer Ibn Jubayr, born in Valencia, described Acre in 1185 as 'a trading stop for all ships. It is a major attraction for vessels and caravans, the meeting place for Christian and Muslim traders from all around the area. Its streets are hard to walk, so crowded are they by men from all countries.'

▼ *Acre was a key crusader city, which was taken, lost and recaptured many times.*

PRINCE OF GALILEE
TANCRED OF HAUTEVILLE

A Norman lord from southern Italy, Tancred of Hauteville rode on the First Crusade with his uncle Bohemond of Taranto and afterwards established himself first as Prince of Galilee and then as regent of the Principality of Antioch and the County of Edessa. Through his feats of bravery leading up to, during and after the capture of Jerusalem in 1099, and his staunch defence of the independence of the crusader state of Antioch against the Byzantine Empire, Tancred won enduring fame as a knight that made his name resonate down the centuries.

Grandson of the great Norman–Italian adventurer Robert Guiscard, Tancred shared his name with the founding father of the Hauteville clan, the relatively minor 11th-century nobleman from near Coutances in Normandy, whose sons – including William Iron-Arm, Guiscard himself and Roger, Count of Sicily – travelled south to achieve greatness. Tancred

▼ *Tancred (right) meets King Philip I of France prior to marrying the king's daughter, Cecile.*

the Crusader certainly lived up to the expectations that such ancestry aroused. His life was recorded in the *Gesta Tancredi in Expeditione Hierosolymitana* (The Deeds of Tancred on Crusade to Jerusalem), written in Latin by Norman churchman Radulph of Caen in the years after 1112, based on eyewitness accounts.

IN CONSTANTINOPLE AND CILICIA

Tancred took part in the early episodes of the crusade. Notably in Constantinople, when other crusader princes swore oaths to Alexius in which they promised to return any conquered lands to the Byzantine Empire, doubtless with the full intention of breaking them, Tancred avoided taking the oath at all by slipping out of the city at night.

He took part in the siege of Nicaea and the Battle of Dorylaeum, but Tancred first made his name on the crusade when taking Tarsus during an excursion in Cilicia in 1097; in this part of the crusade he came into open conflict with Baldwin of Boulogne (later King Baldwin I of

Jerusalem). Tancred went on to capture Adana, Mamistra and Alexandretta, before taking part in the siege of Antioch.

In the course of the siege at Antioch, when spirits in the camp were very low and members of the crusader armies were sorely tempted to abandon the adventure, Tancred encountered no less a figure than Peter the Hermit attempting to flee and make his way back to Constantinople. Peter was the itinerant French monk who had preached the crusade so enthusiastically in Europe and become one of the leaders of the 'People's Crusade'. Tancred forced him to return to the crusaders' camp before Antioch.

A BROKEN PROMISE TO PROTECT MUSLIM PRISONERS

During the capture of Jerusalem in 1099 Tancred took hundreds of Muslim prisoners and famously pledged to protect them from the rampaging soldiers who had taken over the city, in return for the offer of a large ransom. He flew his banner over the al Aqsa mosque where the prisoners were gathered, but on the second day of looting he allowed the Muslims to be slain – man, woman and child.

AFTER THE FIRST CRUSADE

In the aftermath of victory, Godfrey of Bouillon, newly elected as Defender of the Holy Sepulchre, gave Tancred the title Prince of Galilee. Then, in the following year, when his uncle Bohemond was taken prisoner during an ill-fated military expedition against Danishmend, the emir of Sivas (Sebastea) in eastern Anatolia, Tancred became regent of the Principality of Antioch. He extended its territories by seizing land from the Byzantine Empire, and resisted attempts by Emperor Alexius to bring him to heel.

In 1104 Tancred also became regent of the County of Edessa, when its ruler Baldwin of Le Bourg was taken prisoner

▲ *Tancred raises his banner above Bethlehem. He and Baldwin of Le Bourg established a crusader presence in Christ's birthplace before the attack on Jerusalem.*

by the Seljuk Turks at the Battle of Harran. In 1105–06 when Bohemond, having been released, returned to Europe to raise reinforcements, Tancred remained as regent in Antioch. He attempted to hold on to the regency of Edessa when Baldwin was released in 1107, but later agreed to relinquish his claim.

HUSBAND OF A PRINCESS

Around this time, Tancred married Cecile, daughter of King Philip I of France; she had travelled to the Holy Land to become the wife of Bohemond of Taranto, but that marriage had not taken place. He remained very powerful in Antioch and staunchly defended the Principality's independence from the Byzantine Empire – despite the fact that Bohemond, having been defeated in battle by Emperor Alexius, had signed the humiliating Treaty of Devol in 1108, in which he agreed that Antioch should be a vassal state of the empire. In 1100, moreover, Tancred gained a foothold in the crusader state of Tripoli when he gained possession of the powerful castle of Krak des Chevaliers.

DEATH AND REPUTATION

Just two years later, however, Tancred died of typhoid while still in power in Antioch. He had no children, but his memory was kept alive in Radulph of Caen's *Gesta Tancredi*. In addition to his status as a warrior in the key engagements of the crusade, Tancred demonstrated considerable strength of purpose and political nous, as he carved out a position for himself as the pre-eminent Catholic Christian magnate in northern Syria.

AFTERLIFE OF A CRUSADER

In the 16th century, Tancred was a hero of the epic poem *La Gerusalemme Liberata* (Jerusalem Delivered) by Italian poet Torquato Tasso. The poem used historical events from the First Crusade as a frame on which to hang a chivalric romance, and borrowed many narrative elements from the *Orlando Furioso* of Tasso's fellow-Italian, Ludovico Ariosto. In Tasso's work, the character of Tancredi falls in love with a Muslim warrior maiden, Clorinda, a character based on Bradamante in the Orlando; Tancredi himself is loved by Princess Erminia of Antioch, who betrays her city to the crusaders because of her love for him.

Italian composer Claudio Monteverdi used parts of Tasso's poem in his operatic dialogue *Il Combattimento die Tancredi e Clorinda* (The Fight Between Tancred and Clorinda), composed in 1624. In 1759 French writer Voltaire wrote a tragedy about the hero called simply *Tancrède*, and this, together with Tasso's poem, formed the basis of the opera *Tancredi in Siracusa* by Gioacchino Rossini in 1813.

▼ *In* La Gerusalemme Liberata *the distraught Erminia finds Tancredi heartbroken by the death of Clorinda.*

KRAK DES CHEVALIERS
AND OTHER GREAT CRUSADER CASTLES

The crusaders built a string of formidable castles in Outremer. Like castles in Europe, these functioned both as garrison points from which to dominate the surrounding countryside and as strongholds to which troops could retreat when under attack; they were either maintained as lordly residences or were garrisoned by the military brotherhoods. The foremost of all the crusader castles was Krak des Chevaliers (Castle of the Knights), built at Qal'at al-Hisn in Syria, and today celebrated as one of the finest surviving medieval castles in the world.

The first fortress on the site, which occupied a commanding position 2,300ft (700m) above sea level and dominating the valley between Tripoli and Homs, was built in 1031 for the Muslim emir of Aleppo. It had a Kurdish garrison and in Muslim chronicles was known as the 'Castle of the Kurds'. During the First Crusade, Raymond of Toulouse captured it in 1099 then abandoned it when he headed southwards with the rest of the

▼ *The inner enclosure at Krak des Chevaliers, enlarged by the Knights Hospitaller, incorporated some of the stonework of the original structure.*

crusader force to Jerusalem; Tancred, Prince of Galilee, then took the fortress in 1110 when he was regent of Antioch. Raymond II, Count of Tripoli, gave the castle to the Knights Hospitaller in 1144.

It was during its time under the care of the Hospitallers, who held it until it was taken by the Mamluk Sultan Baibars in 1271, that Krak was developed into the largest crusader castle in Outremer. The Hospitallers built an outer wall with a thickness of 10ft (3m) and with seven guard towers to make the fortress a con-

▲ *According to legend the crusaders found the Holy Grail at Caesarea. They built a castle there, but in 1265 the Mamluks razed it after taking the city.*

centric castle. (A concentric castle has two sets of defensive fortifications, a lower outer wall enclosing an outer bailey overlooked by a higher inner wall protecting the inner bailey. Its garrison would initially man the outer walls, but under heavy attack could retreat to the inner bailey and then any attacking force would have to

WELSH CRUSADER CASTLES
The future King Edward I of England visited Krak des Chevaliers when he travelled on crusade in 1271–72. He was impressed with its formidable concentric defences and, with the help of architect Master James of St Georges, reproduced them where possible in the castles he raised in Wales. Master James was so called after the castle of St Georges d'Espéranches that he built, but his masterpiece is considered to be Beaumaris, the concentric castle on the isle of Anglesey.

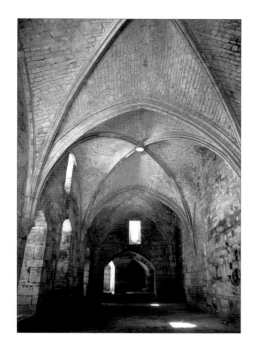

▲ *At Krak des Chevaliers the Knights Hospitaller built a vast central keep with a superb vaulted stone roof. The castle is one of the best-preserved crusader fortresses.*

cross the outer walls and outer bailey under heavy attack from the garrison before even beginning their assault on the formidable walls of the inner bailey.)

The Hospitallers refashioned the buildings of the inner ward in the Gothic style. They included a storage chamber almost 400ft (120m) in length and stables with the capacity to hold 1,000 horses, in addition to a well, bakery and a sizeable meeting hall and chapel.

Historians have estimated that there was room in the fortress for a garrison of up to 60 Hospitaller knights and around 2,000 infantrymen and that the storage chamber, supplemented by further storerooms that had been excavated in the cliff beneath the fortress, could hold enough supplies to enable the garrison to survive a siege of five years.

After Krak was rebuilt by the Hospitallers it never fell to military assault: the one time it was captured was through trickery, when Sultan Baibars forged a letter purporting to be from the garrison's commander in Tripoli, which commanded the defending knights to resign.

OTHER CRUSADER CASTLES

Belvoir, another concentric Hospitaller stronghold, was situated around 12 miles (20km) south of the Sea of Galilee and controlling the Jordan Valley. Following the Battle of the Horns of Hattin in July 1187, Belvoir withstood a siege by Saladin's forces for 18 months, before finally surrendering on 5 January 1189.

Margat, on the route between Tripoli and the port of Latakia and overlooking the Mediterranean, was the Hospitallers' headquarters in Syria. Originally an Arab fortress, it was captured by the Byzantines in 1104, then taken by Tancred and made part of the Principality of Antioch before being passed to the Hospitallers in 1186.

Montreal in the Transjordan (on the eastern side of the River Jordan) was built by King Baldwin I of Jerusalem on a hill dominating the plain of Edom and overlooking Muslim pilgrimage and caravan routes from Syria to Arabia. Reynald of Châtillon gained possession of the castle on his marriage to Stephanie, daughter of Philip of Milly, in 1183. From this stronghold Reynald emerged to raid Muslim caravans, and even planned an attack over

▼ *The 90ft (27m)-deep ditch at Saone Castle near Latakia in Syria is a powerful deterrent to attackers. But Saladin succeeded in taking the fortress in 1188, and it is also called 'the Castle of Saladin'.*

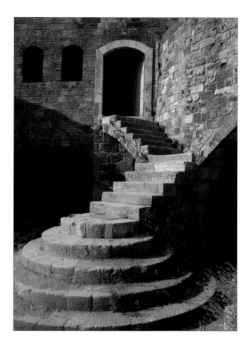

▲ *Steps lead to an inner retreat at the Castle of Saint-Gilles in Tripoli, named in honour of crusader lord Raymond of St Gilles, Count of Toulouse and of Tripoli.*

the Red Sea on Mecca; his repeated provocations reputedly enraged Saladin. After defeating the crusaders at the Horns of Hattin, Saladin personally executed Reynald; then, after taking Jerusalem in October 1187, he made it his business to capture Montreal. It took him almost two years, but the castle fell at last in May 1189 – after a devastating siege in which the defenders reputedly went blind from a severe lack of salt in their diet, and also were said to have sold their children and their wives to obtain food.

Saone, around 15 miles (24km) northeast and inland of Latakia in north Syria, was one of the biggest of the crusader fortresses, covering 12 acres (5ha) in a triangular fortification atop a rocky outcrop surrounded by precipices. On the eastern side, the crusaders dug an extraordinary defensive ditch 90ft (27m) deep, 60ft (18m) wide and 450ft (140m) long. In its construction, they shifted an estimated 2.4 million cubic feet (70,000 cubic metres) of rock, which they used in raising the castle's great towers and walls. Saone was besieged and captured by Saladin.

BY SEA FROM ITALY
CRUSADING PILGRIMAGES OF THE EARLY 12TH CENTURY

Several expeditions were mounted from Europe to Jerusalem in the aftermath of the First Crusade. Some were armed pilgrimages, others were called by the pope and preached as military crusades.

THE CRUSADE OF 1101

The first of these, generally known as 'the Crusade of 1101', set out almost immediately after the end of the First Crusade in response to calls for reinforcements from the original crusader lords. After the capture of Jerusalem and the defeat of the Egyptian army at Ascalon in 1099, the crusaders sent word back to Europe that they needed strengthening if they were to hold on to what they had won.

According to Genoese soldier and historian Caffaro di Caschifellone, two Genoese traders named William and Primus Embriaco had in the summer of 1099 sailed to Jaffa with two galleys, which were broken up to provide wood for making the siege machines used to take Jerusalem. Afterwards, they acquired vast riches at the Battle of Ascalon from the abandoned camp of al-Afdal Shahanshah, vizier of Cairo, and with this treasure and messages calling for reinforcements had sailed for Europe, arriving in Genoa on Christmas Day 1099.

▼ *The exploits of the crusaders were depicted proudly all over Europe, but the disastrous failure of the Crusade of 1101 in Anatolia brought a change in attitude.*

As a result of the call for help, a new crusade was called by Pope Paschal II, the successor to Pope Urban II. In particular, he urged the crusade on those who had taken part in the First Crusade but turned back, and those who had taken the vow in 1096, but not departed. The crusade had three main parts, all of which were crushed by Turkish armies in Anatolia.

The first phase began when an army consisting largely of Lombard peasants under Archbishop Anselm IV of Milan departed Milan in September 1100. On arriving in the East, the army pillaged Byzantine territory and even parts of Constantinople itself, so Emperor Alexius swiftly moved them on across the Bosphorus, where they waited for reinforcements. In May 1101 this first army was joined by a French–Burgundian–German force under Stephen of Blois (the same count who had travelled on the First Crusade) and a Byzantine army under Raymond of Toulouse, who was now in the service of Emperor Alexius. The combined crusader force suffered a devastating defeat at the hands of a Seljuk army at the Battle of Mersivan in June 1101; Raymond and Stephen of Blois both escaped and fled back to Constantinople.

▲ *The establishment of the Kingdom of Jerusalem, and in particular its capture of Mediterranean ports, opened a sea route from Europe to the Holy Land. It was taken by pilgrims and later crusaders.*

Meanwhile, a second crusader army from Nevers in France had arrived, but failed to meet up with the first; the second army was trounced by Seljuk leader Kilij Arslan at Heraclea Cybistra. A third army under Hugh of Vermandois and William IX of Aquitaine then arrived: around half of the force was again slaughtered by the Seljuks, although the other half travelled by ship directly to Palestine; Hugh of Vermandois was mortally injured in the battle with the Seljuks and died at Tarsus in October 1101.

Survivors of all three waves united and pressed on, but the expedition was by this stage more pilgrimage than crusade. They arrived in Jerusalem at Easter 1102. Many then went home, but some remained to fight with King Baldwin I of Jerusalem against an Egyptian army at Ramla, a battle in which Stephen of Blois was killed.

The First Crusade had given the crusader armies an aura of invincibility, but the Seljuk Turks' devastating victories in

1101 proved to the Muslim world that the armies of Europe were in fact far from unbeatable. The major consequence of the defeats was that the land route to Jerusalem from Constantinople could no longer be made safe, and so passage to the crusader states had to be by sea. With Jerusalem under Christian rule, ever larger numbers of Europeans wanted to make a pilgrimage there, and merchants from the Italian cities such as Venice and Genoa grew rich transporting them there.

THE EXPLOITS OF 'SIGURD THE CRUSADER'

In 1107–11 King Sigurd I Magnusson of Norway led an armed expedition to support the Kingdom of Jerusalem. Sailing with 60 ships, en route to the Holy Land he visited Lisbon and fought Moorish pirates off the Balearic islands; after arriving in Jerusalem, he fought alongside Baldwin I in 1110, helping the crusaders capture the coastal city of Sidon (modern Sayda, Lebanon). He returned home the following year, taking as a gift from Baldwin a piece of the True Cross that he housed in a castle at Konghelle (modern Kungälv, Sweden). Sigurd's adventure

▼ *Sidon, an ancient city on the coast of Lebanon, became a major lordship within the Kingdom of Jerusalem following its capture by crusaders including King Sigurd I Magnusson of Norway in 1110.*

earned him the title of Sigurd Jerusalemfarer (the Crusader), although his expedition was really more pilgrimage than crusade.

BOHEMOND'S 'CRUSADE' OF 1107–08

Around the same time, Bohemond of Taranto led a military expedition from Europe that is sometimes identified as a crusade. Bohemond was one of the leaders of the First Crusade who had established himself as Prince of Antioch, but after defeats at the hands of Muslim powers he had returned to Europe to raise an army in 1105–06. He led a military expedition to the East in 1107–08, but rather than using it to consolidate the position of Antioch he launched an attack on Emperor Alexius and was again defeated. The episode was ended in 1108 by the Treaty of Devol, in which Bohemond became a vassal of Alexius and agreed to allow a Greek Orthodox Patriarch to have authority in Antioch.

Two further crusades took place in the 1120s. The first was proclaimed by Pope Calixtus II in 1122 and is also known as the 'Venetian Crusade' because the main response came from the city of Venice. The city sent a large fleet, which was waylaid at Corfu before finally reaching the Holy Land, where it took part in the siege of Tyre. Tyre was captured in 1124 and became one of the key trading posts for

▲ *In a highly-charged atmosphere, Doge Dandolo of Venice forced the crusade leaders to swear an oath to support an attack on Zara. From this point, Venice rose to wealth and prominence on through trade with the Byzantine Empire.*

the Kingdom of Jerusalem. Calixtus also offered Christian soldiers fighting Muslims in Spain 'the same remission of sins we have offered to the defenders of the Church in the East' and the crusade he called had also found expression in campaigns against Spanish Islam waged by Alfonso I of Aragon in 1125.

Another crusade was launched in 1128, partly recruited by Hugues of Payens, the French knight who was a co-founder of the Knights Templar. This expedition attacked Damascus in November 1129 but failed to take the city.

CONTROL OF THE COAST

Partly with the help of these expeditions and partly by their own strength, the armies of the crusader states won control of the key ports along the Mediterranean coast of what are now Syria, Lebanon, Israel and Palestine in the quarter century after 1099. In 1101 they took Arsuf and Caesarea, Haifa and Acre in 1104, Beiry and Sidon in 1110 and Tyre in 1124. The only significant port left was Ascalon.

MUSLIM RESURGENCE

The Europeans who fought in the First Crusade and subsequently established the crusader states of Jerusalem, Antioch, Edessa and Tripoli benefited from division among their opponents. Fierce rivalries between Muslim lords meant that in many cases, they preferred to ally themselves with the crusaders than with their countrymen. But in the 12th century great Muslim generals such as Ilghazi, Zengi, Nur ed-Din and Saladin began to develop unity and inflict great defeats on the Christians. These men mobilized their armies and people with the call to jihad, or holy war. The capture of Edessa at Christmas 1144 provoked European Christians to mount the Second Crusade of 1147–49; the abject failure of that enterprise only boosted Muslim morale and inspired Nur ed-Din to further great exploits of jihad. Then, in 1187, Saladin annihilated the strength of the crusader states at the Battle of the Horns of Hattin, and later that year recaptured Jerusalem. According to his biographer Imad ed-din al-Isfahani, Saladin envisaged an even more sweeping holy war. After Hattin he declared: 'When Allah grants me possession of the rest of Palestine I shall divide my lands, make a will laying down my wishes, and then embark by sea to the Franks' faraway lands, and pursue them there, so as to clean the earth of all those who do not believe in Allah.'

▲ *Qalaat ar-Rahba in Syria was built by the great Muslim general Shirkuh.*

◄ *The culmination of the Islamic fight back in the Holy Land was the recapture of Jerusalem by Saladin's army on 2 October 1187, seen here through the eyes of a 19th-century artist.*

THE FIELD OF BLOOD

A GREAT TURKISH VICTORY NEAR ALEPPO

The first major victory in the Muslims' fightback against the crusaders came in 1119, when a vast Turkish army assembled by the emir of Damascus and the Artuqid Turkish ruler and general Ilghazi entirely devastated a Christian army commanded by Roger of Antioch. The defeat was so heavy that it became known to Western chroniclers as *Ager Sanguinis* (Field of Blood).

BACKGROUND TO THE CONFLICT

Things looked very grim for the Muslims of northern Syria at the close of the 12th century's first decade. In 1109 the crusaders captured and sacked Tripoli after a siege of five years. In May 1110 they took Beirut. On 4 December Sidon also fell and was sacked. In Baghdad the Seljuk Turkish sultan, Muhammad, faced calls to mount a jihad, or holy war, against the invaders.

Muhammad sent his general Mawdud, who was also governor of Mosul, to attack the crusader state of Edessa. The attack failed but there were many Christian

▼ *Imposing city walls embody the power of the Artuqid dynasty at Diyarbakir, Turkey.*

casualties. In 1113 Mawdud raised another army to mount a new wave of jihad, but the enterprise came to a premature end when he was murdered in Damascus by a militant Shi'ite assassin. Fulcher of Chartres recorded Christian relief – 'the Lord had allowed this man to be a scourge unto us for some time, but afterwards His will was that the general should die a lowly death by the actions of an unimportant man.'

Mawdud's place as leader of jihad was taken by Ilghazi, a highly gifted general who had fought in Mawdud's army. The Artuqid dynasty to which Ilghazi belonged had been established in the late 11th century by Artuq ibn Ekseb. Starting out in the service of the Seljuk Turkish sultanate, Artuq's descendants built an independent powerbase in the province of Diyarbakir (now south-eastern Turkey).

Ilghazi took power at Mardin in that province in 1108. In 1118 the citizens of Aleppo asked Ilghazi to become ruler of their city, which was in turmoil: Aleppo's ruler Alp Arslan had been assassinated by his eunuch, who had seized power and then been killed himself.

THE BUILD-UP TO THE BATTLE

The following year Ilghazi marched on Antioch. The Principality of Antioch was in the hands of Roger of Salerno, nephew of Tancred; Roger had succeeded his uncle as regent when Tancred died in 1112.

Roger brought trouble upon himself: when Ilghazi marched into the Principality, Roger and his army were safely ensconced in the fortress of Artah, near to the city of Antioch, and he overconfidently ventured forth to meet Ilghazi, ignoring orders from King Baldwin II to wait for reinforcements from Jerusalem, and advice from the Latin Patriarch of Antioch, Bernard of Valence, that they should remain in Artah. As a result, the Christian army was vastly outnumbered by the Turks. Roger established himself in the mountain pass of Sarmada, while Ilghazi was engaged in besieging the fortress of al-Artharib. Roger sent a contingent under Robert of Vieux Pont to try to lift the siege but they were outmanoeuvred when Ilghazi feigned a retreat and were easily defeated.

On the morning of Saturday 28 June 1119 Roger's army awoke in their camp at the Pass of Sarmada to find themselves

Western historians suggest the more sober figure of around 3,700, but accept that only a handful of Christians survived.

THE AFTERMATH OF AGER SANGUINIS

Although the city of Antioch had been left wide open to attack, Ilghazi failed to press home his advantage by advancing, and instead, he returned to Aleppo to celebrate his victory. Yet the total victory at the Field of Blood was of major significance: it delivered a great shock to the crusaders, and it proved to the Muslim world that their armies did not have to rely on the might of the Seljuk forces to defeat the European soldiers.

entirely surrounded by Ilgahzi's men. They may have suspected that this day might be their last and went to their deaths after the archbishop of Apamea had heard the confessions of the whole army.

▲ *The power of mounted soldiers – especially the devastatingly effective Turcopole archers – was decisive at the Battle of the Field of Blood.*

▼ *Armies on the march in crusader-era Syria relied on roads and bridges built by the Romans. This bridge, across the River Afrin in northern Syria, dates to c.3AD.*

THE BATTLE

Descriptions of the battle survive from both sides. The Christian perspective was given in an account by Walter the Chancellor, the Norman crusader who served as chancellor of the Principality of Antioch, in his *Bella Antiochena* (Antioch Wars); the Muslim view was recorded by Kamal ad-Din, a Muslim historian of Aleppo. When battle was joined, the crusaders began well but then fell into disarray when their Turcopole mounted archers were driven back into the main line under Roger's command. Roger, who was fighting under a great jewelled cross as his standard, was slain, slashed in the face with a sword and his head sliced open down to the nose. His army fled – according to ad-Din 'the arrows flew thick as a locust swarm, falling on cavalry and infantry alike' and forced the Christians into disorganized retreat. They were pursued without mercy, and cut down in the hillside vineyards nearby.

Ad-Din claims that Roger's army numbered 15,000 and that all but 20 were killed in the battle and the ensuing chase.

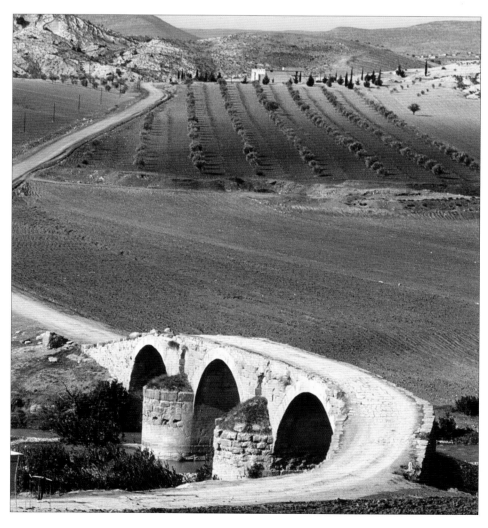

THE CAPTURE OF EDESSA
THE RISE OF IMAD ED-DIN ZENGI

Turkish general Imad ed-Din Zengi stunned the Christian world on Christmas Eve 1144 when he succeeded in capturing the capital of the crusader state of Edessa. In the 25 years since the defeat of Roger of Antioch by Ilghazi at the devastating *Ager Sanguinis*, there had been defeats for the crusader lords, notably at the hands of Ilghazi's fearless nephew Balak, but always the status quo was more or less maintained in the crusader states. Now Zengi's triumph at Edessa cast doubt on the very survival of Outremer, the Christian kingdom overseas. Among Muslims, Zengi was hailed as *al-Malik al-Mansur*, the 'victorious king'.

BALAK
Ilghazi did not long survive his triumph at the Ager Sanguinis – he died three years later, in 1122, having never risen to those heights of military success again – but his nephew Balak took up the torch and swiftly became a scourge of the crusader kingdoms. In 1122 he captured Joscelin of Courtenay, Count of Edessa, and the following year took captive no less a person than Baldwin II, King of Jerusalem.

In 1124 Balak became ruler of Aleppo and began to retake territory from the crusaders in northern Syria. But he died the same year, having been shot in the chest with an arrow while besieging the castle of Manbij. In a few years he had made a great impression on the crusaders – after recording the news of his death, Fulcher of Chartres wrote in his chronicle: 'Then we all gave thanks to God because Balak, the furious dragon who had stamped on Christianity, was brought low at last.'

THE ORIGINS AND EMERGENCE OF ZENGI
In Balak's wake, Imad ed-Din Zengi leapt to prominence. Zengi was the son of a governor of Aleppo who, after his father's execution for treason against the Seljuk sultan Malik Shah in the late 11th century, had been raised in Mosul. According to legend, Zengi was the son of Ida of Austria, mother of Leopold III, who had travelled with the Crusade of 1101 and disappeared, presumed dead, during the crusaders' defeat at Heraclea Cybistra by Kilij Arslan. The legend recounted that rather than being killed she was carried

▲ *The formidable citadel of Aleppo. The city was Imad ed-Din Zengi's base when he established his power after 1128.*

off to life in a harem, where she later gave birth to Zengi. However, this tall story is impossible on grounds of chronology, and cannot be true.

Zengi established himself as ruler in Mosul in 1127, then in Aleppo the following year. Over the next 15 years or so he worked tirelessly to extend his power in the region, fighting whoever came his way – his Turkish rivals, the Byzantine emperor or the crusader lords. Zengi repeatedly attempted to gain control in Damascus and in 1137, when the Damascenes allied with the crusaders, he ambushed the army of King Fulk of Jerusalem and then besieged them in the fortress of Barin, north-east of Tripoli, before allowing Fulk to buy his freedom and return home to Jerusalem.

ATTACK ON EDESSA
King Fulk's death in 1143 led to a joint succession by his wife Melisende (daughter of King Baldwin II) and his son

Baldwin III, but Melisende effectively ruled alone, with the help of the Constable of Jerusalem, Manasses of Hierges, and initially largely excluded Baldwin III from power. Zengi sought to take advantage of this situation and in 1144 turned against the County of Edessa.

Joscelin II, Count of Edessa, had made an alliance with Kara Aslan, the Artuqid Turkish ruler of Diyarbakir and had marched the bulk of his army out of Edessa to support Kara Aslan in a campaign against Aleppo. Zengi moved swiftly, mounting a siege of the city of Edessa in November 1144. Within its walls Hugh II, the Catholic archbishop, and Basil, the Armenian bishop, combined to lead the defence; Count Joscelin II, hearing of the developments, went to the town of Turbessel, (now Tilbesar in Turkey) and sent out a plea for help from the other crusader states. Queen Melisende sent an army led by Manasses, but Raymond of Antioch was unable to help.

At Edessa, Zengi built siege engines and set to work undermining the walls of the city. The defences were poor, for the population of the city, according to chronicler William of Tyre, were traders who 'knew

▼ *Fulk of Anjou became King of Jerusalem when he married Melisende, daughter of King Baldwin II, on 2 June 1129. Fulk was closely associated with the Knights Templar.*

THE FIRST FIVE KINGS OF JERUSALEM

Godfrey of Bouillon is regarded as the first king of Jerusalem although he was known as Defender of the Holy Sepulchre. Godfrey was succeeded in 1100 by his brother, Baldwin of Boulogne, who ruled as Baldwin I until he died in 1118. Baldwin's cousin, Baldwin of Le Bourg, then Count of Edessa, became Baldwin II of Jerusalem. He died in 1131 and was succeeded by his son-in-law, Fulk of Anjou, who ruled as King Fulk of Jerusalem. He died in 1143 following a hunting accident while on holiday in Acre, and was succeeded by his

▲ *Baldwin III, King of Jerusalem at the time of the disastrous Second Crusade.*

wife Melisende (Baldwin II's daughter) and his eldest son, who ruled as Baldwin III of Jerusalem until 1162.

nothing of using weapons and understood only the business of buying and selling'. They had to rely on mercenaries to man the walls, and their numbers were dwindling because Archbishop Hugh was a miser who hoarded the city's great wealth rather than put it to sensible use in paying for the defence of the walls.

On Christmas Eve 1144, Zengi's mining operations were complete and he gave the command to set fire to the wooden posts that supported the tunnels beneath the walls near the Gate of the Hours. The tunnels collapsed, the walls fell down, and Zengi's troops poured into the city.

THE ENEMY OF LATIN CHRISTIANS

Thousands were killed in the taking of Edessa before Zengi intervened, ordering his men to stop the slaughter. He made it very clear that his war was only against the Latin Christians or Franks: and he went on to execute all the Latin Christians who had been taken prisoner, but spared all the other Christians, whom he allowed to live on in the city as before. He appointed one of his commanders, Zayn ad-Din Ali Kutchuk, as the city's governor and allowed the Armenian bishop, Basil, to continue in his position. He destroyed the Latin Christian church buildings, but allowed the remainder to stand.

Subsequently Zengi captured Saruj (now Suruç in Turkey) but then retreated to Mosul when the army of Jerusalem at last arrived. He did not attempt to consolidate his power in the County of Edessa nor to attack Antioch, as many had feared. But his capture of Edessa sent shockwaves through Christendom and led to the calling of the Second Crusade. Zengi himself died in 1146, when he was stabbed to death by his eunuch slave during a siege at Qalat Jabar. He was remembered by Muslims as 'the great, the just, the helper of God ... the pillar of religion, destroyer of infidels, rebels and atheists'.

SOLDIERS OF ISLAM
WEAPONS AND TACTICS

Many of the Muslim armies faced by the crusaders in the late 11th and 12th centuries were enormously large and contained a wide range of troops, including untrained, poorly armed peasants alongside professional soldiers with the finest equipment. The core of the armies was made up of crack Turkish troops.

The Turks were famous for their cavalry. They were quick and lightly armed. They wore lighter chain mail than the crusaders and conical helmets that were often inscribed with inspirational words from the Koran. They carried small, round shields that were much less burdensome than the elongated kite-shaped shields used by the crusaders.

They fought with clubs, swords and lances, but their principal weapon was the bow and arrow. They were highly skilled and trained horsemen who had entirely mastered the art of shooting from the saddle – they could fire off arrows while

▼ *Two Turkish cavalrymen practise the use of sword and lance while on horseback. Both also carry a bow and a sheath of arrows. Wearing light armour, they were generally no match for the crusaders in close fighting.*

riding at full speed, and could even fire over their shoulders as they rode away, a version of the famous Parthian shot. The arrows they loosed were not highly penetrative, but they were fired in such numbers that they caused panic and disarray among the Christian armies – various accounts of battle liken the arrows to a plague of locusts, a storm of rain or a thick cloud that blocked out the sun.

SPEED AND MOBILITY

The use of long-range weapons, such as the bow and arrow, and the mobility of the cavalry were the key to the Turkish tactics. Typically they attacked in the rear and the flank of the crusader army. According to contemporary accounts, the Turkish horses were quicker and lighter than the crusader's animals; their speed and movement were a constant threat.

They tried to avoid encountering the European knights' mounted charge, since they were not heavily enough armed to fight on these terms; however, they saw that once the crusader knights had charged the line they tended to dissolve in disarray, leaving them vulnerable to counter-attack and leaving the European

JIHAD

The Islamic faith places a religious obligation on Muslims to spread their faith by waging jihad (which means 'battle'). Mainstream Islam teaches that jihad is intended to be carried out by fighting against sin. Traditionally there are four types of jihad: in the heart, with the tongue, by hand and using the sword. Jihad in the heart is interpreted as meaning fighting evil in one's inner self, jihad by tongue and hand are usually said to mean avoiding wickedness and promoting righteousness. Jihad by the sword involves waging war against enemies of Islam. A key idea behind jihad is that the world is divided into two, one that belongs to Allah, and the other subject to chaos; it is the Muslim's duty to combat the rule of chaos by extending submission to Allah's will, within the self but also in the wider world.

infantry open to assault. A favourite stratagem, used effectively again and again, was to pretend to retreat, leading the European knights on and encouraging them to charge. The Muslim cavalry would then either draw the crusaders on into an ambush or turn quickly to launch a devastating counter-attack.

The heavily armoured and armed crusaders were stronger than the Muslims in close combat, so the Muslim tactics tended to avoid hand-to-hand fighting if they could by holding off and using the lightning cavalry attacks and bombardment with arrows to punish the Europeans; they would only commit to close-quarters combat when they could be confident of success. Eyewitness accounts of the Battle of Dorylaeum in 1097, during the First Crusade, reveal that the crusaders' long chain mail body armour provided a very

▲ *The crusaders were feared for their cavalry assault, but the Muslim warriors, on light and fast horses, were often able to outmanoeuvre them and drive them back.*

effective defence against the light swords carried by the Seljuks – and also against their arrows, unless these were fired from straight ahead when they were able to pierce the armour. If the crusaders were able to draw any of the attackers into close combat, they found they could usually get the upper hand.

FIGHTING IN GOD'S NAME

The Muslim armies were fighting to spread Islam through jihad, or holy war, just as the Christians had gone to war in the name of Christ. Eyewitness accounts of the Battle of the Field of Blood in 1119 reveal that prior to the battle the ra'is, or mayor, of Aleppo, Abu al-Fadi ibn al-Khashshab, rode out before Ilghazi's army and delivered a stirring speech, urging the soldiers to fight jihad without fear. His words reduced hardened soldiers to tears. Meanwhile, Prince Roger addressed his men as 'soldiers of Christ' and urged them to fight to the death if that were God's will.

Likewise, Norman eyewitness accounts of the earlier Battle of Dorylaeum in 1097 report that Seljuk Turks shouted as they came forward, 'calling in great voices in their own language a devilish word that I could not understand'. We know from Radulph of Caen, biographer of Tancred, that this word was 'Allachibar!' – far from devilish, it was a form of the Muslim holy words *Allah Akhbar* (God is Great). For their part, again according to eyewitness accounts, the crusaders were calling out 'God wills it!' 'God wills it!' as they fought.

◄ *The Turkish cavalrymen were renowned for their ability to fire arrows as they rode at full speed in battle. Feigning retreat, they often lured crusaders into rash charges.*

CALL TO A SECOND CRUSADE
BERNARD OF CLAIRVAUX APPEALS TO THE RULERS OF THE WEST

On 1 December 1145 Pope Eugenius III responded to the news that Turkish general Imad ed-Din Zengi had captured Edessa by calling a new crusade.

THE LOSS OF EDESSA

The first news of Edessa's fall had been brought back by pilgrims and then had been confirmed by Bishop Hugh of the Syrian town of Jabala, who was sent as part of an official embassy to Rome by Raymond of Antioch. In Italy, Bishop Hugh had an audience with the pope; he also informed the historian Otto of Friesling that a Christian king of India was ready to come to the aid of the crusader states – this was the first documented appearance of the enduring medieval myth of Prester John (*see* box).

▼ *'I opened my mouth; I preached; and the crusaders have multiplied beyond counting!' Peerless orator Bernard of Clairvaux casts his spell over a vast crowd at Vézelay.*

A CALL TO ARMS

Eugenius issued his rallying call in a bull, or papal letter, known as *Quantum praedecessores* and addressed to King Louis VII of France and his people. (Papal bulls were untitled and are named from their first words. In this case, *Quantum praedecessores nostri Romani pontifices* is the beginning of a phrase that translates 'The extent to which our predecessors the pontiffs of Rome did work to free the Eastern Church, we have learned from the accounts of older writers and by studying their deeds.') The bull recalled the heroic achievements of the crusaders of 1096–99 and offered remission (forgiveness) of sins for those who took the cross together with church protection of their possessions and relatives while they were away on crusade.

In France, King Louis was already planning a crusade, or perhaps a pilgrimage, and announced his plans at his court at Bourges at Christmas 1145, probably before hearing of Eugenius's bull. He encountered opposition at home, but after liaising with French preacher Abbot Bernard of Clairvaux, who referred him to the pope, Louis received Eugenius's enthusiastic blessing on the enterprise. The papal bull was reissued on 1 March 1146 and Bernard was authorized by the papacy to preach the crusade through Europe.

BERNARD PREACHES THE CRUSADE

On Easter Day 1146 Bernard preached before a vast crowd at Vézelay in central France. He was a great orator and he succeeded in whipping the crowd up into an absolute frenzy of enthusiasm. At the conclusion of his sermon, they leapt up almost to a man, shouting 'Crosses! Give us crosses!' Bernard had these prepared in advance, but even so he ran out – and reputedly then tore off his own clothing to make more crosses for the eager knights and infantrymen.

▲ *Frederick, Duke of Swabia, seen here being crowned emperor in 1155, took the cross at Spires in south-west Germany.*

Louis VII and his nobles were among those who took the cross: Louis received a cloth cross blessed by the pope, and people also flocked to the cause. Bernard wrote to the pope: 'I opened my mouth; I preached; and the crusaders have multiplied beyond counting. The countryside is deserted. You will hardly find one man for every seven womenfolk. In every place you will find widows whose husbands are far from dead.'

He continued the tour, preaching in Switzerland and Germany. Conrad III of Germany was initially unmoved by Bernard's pleas, but on Christmas Day at the Diet of Spires the abbot preached a second sermon to the German king, in which he took the part of Christ himself and asked Conrad directly: 'O Man, what should I have done for you that I have not

▼ *Louis VII, depicted here on his royal seal, was another head of state persuaded by Bernard of Clairvaux to take the cross.*

PRESTER JOHN

Legends of Prester John, a priest-king ruling over a Christian realm somewhere in the Orient, were popular from the 1100s until the 17th century.

The first mention of the king is found in the *Chronicon* of 1145 by Bishop Otto of Friesling, who reported that he had heard of the king from Bishop Hugh of Jaballa at the papal court in Viterbo, Italy, in that year. According to this version, the priest-king was a descendant of the Three Wise Men, or Magi, and after defeating the Muslim rulers of Persia had intended to free Jerusalem but had been waylaid by trouble crossing the River Tigris. The origin of the legend may have been in reports of successes against Muslim Persia by Central Asian Mongol rulers, one of whose queens and many of whose subjects were Christians.

The king soon became the subject of colourful legends that placed him in 'the three Indies' as ruler of a peaceful realm, sometimes said to contain the Fountain of Youth and to be adjacent to the Garden of Eden. One 12th-century document identified him as guardian of a

▲ *Prester John was still a legend around 1550 when he appeared as one of the wonders of the Orient on this mariners' chart of the Indian Ocean.*

shrine to the biblical apostle St Thomas at Mylapore, India. Later versions of the legend located Prester John's realm in Ethiopia. The goal of finding Prester John's kingdom inspired generations of eastbound adventurers, including the 13th-century Venetian, Marco Polo.

done?' Conrad was so deeply moved that he burst into tears: he and several of his noblemen, including Frederick, Duke of Swabia (later Emperor Frederick I Barbarossa), took the cross on the spot. Many ordinary Germans also joined up for the expedition.

As at the time of the First Crusade, the crusade sermons provoked anti-Jewish rioting in Germany. They were particularly inspired by an anti-Semitic monk named Rudolf who whipped up popular feeling by declaring that the Jews were not making any contribution to the rescue of the Holy Land. Abbot Bernard was eventually able to bring this outburst of violence to an end, persuading many of the rioters to join the official crusade, and ordering Rudolf to return to his monastery.

THE KINGS' CRUSADE

The departure date for the crusade was set for the summer of 1147. Bernard had recruited an impressive cast of Europe's royalty and nobility. In addition to two kings, Louis VII of France and Conrad III of Germany, Louis's wife, the celebrated Eleanor of Aquitaine and his brother Robert I of Dreux travelled on the crusade; other leading figures were William II, Count of Nevers; William of Warennes, 3rd Earl of Surrey; and Hugh VII 'the Brown' of Lusignan.

Another notable participant on the Second Crusade was Alfonso Jordan, a son of Raymond of Toulouse; Alfonso was born in Tripoli in 1103 but returned to Europe with his mother at the age of five and became Count of Toulouse.

CRUSADERS SET OUT

FROM EUROPE TO CONSTANTINOPLE

The armies of the Second Crusade set out in three waves in May and June 1147. The first departure in mid-May was from England and consisted of Norman, English, Scottish, Flemish and a few German crusaders. They were followed later the same month by a larger, mainly German army under Conrad III and then in June by a French force led by King Louis, containing armies from Aquitaine, Brittany, Burgundy and Lorraine.

EUROPEAN CRUSADES

In addition to its main theatre in the Holy Land, the Second Crusade had two European fronts, for Pope Eugenius also authorized holy wars in Germanic territories against the pagan Wends and in Spain against Muslims. He promised the knights

▼ *The first part of this itinerary to Jerusalem guides a prospective crusader from London to Dover. On the Second Crusade, many English knights travelled no farther than Lisbon in Portugal.*

and infantrymen who fought in these wars the same crusading indulgences he had offered for the war in the Holy Land.

The first wave of crusaders left England by sea, sailing around Brittany and the Iberian Peninsula, and were driven by bad weather to make landfall in June in Porto, where the local bishop persuaded them to make a diversion to Lisbon. There they backed King Alfonso I of Portugal in a four-month siege of the city, and looted it raucously after it fell on 24 October. Thereafter, some elected to remain in Portugal, and an English priest named Gilbert of Hastings was named the first Bishop of Lisbon, but most of the crusaders travelled on by sea to the Holy Land, departing in February 1148.

VIEW FROM THE EAST

In the Byzantine Empire memories of the First Crusade 50 years earlier were naturally still strong. When the new crusade was being planned, Emperor Manuel I Comnenus had given permission for its armies to pass through the empire, but he did not trust them – fearing that they had designs on his territories. He broke off a war against the Seljuk sultanate of Rum in spring 1147, signing a peace treaty with Sultan Mesud I, so that he could give his full attention to defending his lands against the crusaders.

The Muslim scholar and writer Ibn al-Qalanisi, mayor and chronicler of Damascus, described the sense of mounting fear in Syria as news filtered through that another wave of crusaders was about to break in the Holy Land. He wrote: 'The news was coming in from Constantinople, from the lands of the Franks and from neighbouring countries, too, that the kings of the Franks were travelling from their homeland to attack the land of Islam. They had left their own lands empty, without defenders, and brought with them great wealth.'

▲ *Manuel I Comnenus managed the Second Crusade's passage through his lands very successfully. He was reputedly a great jouster and fearsome warrior.*

THE PROGRESS OF THE GERMANS

The German army travelled by land through Hungary without much incident. Alongside Conrad in the royal party were his nephew, the haughty Frederick, Duke of Swabia, and the kings of Poland and Bohemia. Some contemporary accounts reported excitedly that this force numbered as many as one million, but in truth it was probably only about 20,000 strong. Before passing into Bulgaria, then part of the Byzantine Empire, Conrad swore an oath of loyalty to Byzantine emperor Manuel I Comnenus, pledging that he would do nothing likely to harm the emperor or his territory.

The army was given a Byzantine military escort, but this did not prevent it pillaging and looting as it went. At Philippopolis (modern Plovdiv, Bulgaria) a riot erupted after crusaders accused a local of witchcraft, and the outer part of

▲ *Kneeling humbly, King Louis VII receives a pilgrim's staff from Pope Eugenius III in the abbey church of St Denis in June 1147.*

the town was burned to the ground; then at Adrianople (modern Edirne, western Turkey), local robbers killed a German noble outside a monastery and Frederick of Swabia launched murderous reprisals, burning down the monastery and killing all the monks. Conrad then ignored the emperor's request to pass into Anatolia by the Dardanelles, and instead marched the ill-disciplined troop to Constantinople, where they arrived in mid-September.

KING LOUIS THE PILGRIM

On 8 June 1147 King Louis VII formally handed control of France to Abbot Suger of St Denis in a candle-lit service at the abbey church attended by the pope. Dressed as a pilgrim in a black tunic with red cross, Louis received the pope's blessing and, before a cheering congregation, was handed a pilgrim's staff and wallet. Leaving from Metz, the French army marched in the wake of Conrad's German

force across Hungary, with the contingent from Lorraine marching ahead of the main force. The Provençal army under Alfonso of Toulouse waited behind, having decided to depart in August and go by sea.

In early October the French army arrived at Constantinople. There was some trouble at first, when the contingent from Lorraine clashed with the rear of Conrad's army outside the walls of Constantinople. But the Germans were already in the process of moving on, at the emperor's insistence, into Anatolia. In addition, some of the French wanted to attack the city on the grounds that the emperor had made a truce with the Seljuks, but the papal legates restored peace. King Louis was royally welcomed and entertained within the city. Manuel prevailed on him to swear an oath under which the crusaders would return to the Byzantine Empire any lands they captured on the crusade.

Troops from Savoy, Montferrat and Auvergne joined up with Louis at Constantinople. They had come overland through Italy, then by sea from Brindisi to Byzantine territory. Thus bolstered, the

French army travelled across the Bosphorus into Anatolia. Unlike his grandfather Alexius at the time of the First Crusade, Manuel did not provide the crusaders with an army. The French marched on, accompanied only by a few Byzantine scouts, to meet their fate.

▼ *Abbot Suger acted as co-regent during the reign of Louis VII, when the king was absent on the Second Crusade.*

DISASTER AT DORYLAEUM
AND THE CRUSADERS' DIFFICULT PROGRESS TO ATTALIA

At Dorylaeum, the scene of the European armies' first victory in 1097 during the First Crusade, the bulk of the German army suffered a devastating defeat at the hands of the Seljuks, led by Kilij Arslan II, the son of the Seljuk ruler defeated there in 1097.

▼ Warrior of the cross. Conrad survived defeat at Dorylaeum and a serious illness to take part in the final stages of the crusade.

DIVIDED AND DEFEATED

When the German army reached Nicaea, Conrad decided to split it in two. He sent the largely non-combatant contingent of pilgrims led by Bishop Otto of Friesing, along a safer, but longer, route through Byzantine territory, while he and his army headed straight across Anatolia towards the Seljuk realm. Meanwhile, Seljuk scouts were keeping close tabs on the German progress. The main German army stopped to rest at Dorylaeum after a gruelling march and were ill-prepared for the Seljuk attack when it came out of the blue.

In the battle, the Europeans were out-thought and outmanoeuvred. The Seljuks once again tricked the European warriors by feigning retreat, luring the German knights into what they thought was a triumphant charge – only to be surrounded and utterly defeated by the Seljuks. The German army was virtually wiped out at a stroke. Conrad, Frederick and a few survivors, at most a tenth of the original army, began the retreat to Constantinople.

FRENCH PROGRESS

At Nicaea the German survivors joined up with the French army under Louis. They then marched along the western, largely coastal route already followed by Bishop Otto of Friesing as far as Ephesus. Conrad fell badly ill and was forced to return to Constantinople to convalesce; he was cared for there under the personal supervision of Manuel.

The French force marched on and succeeded in defeating a Turkish army in a minor skirmish outside Ephesus. As they pressed on through difficult winter conditions, under constant harassment by the Turks, discipline became ragged and morale very low.

In the region of Laodicea (near modern Denizli, in south-western Turkey) on 8 January 1148 the French army suffered a heavy defeat at the hands of the Turks. This setback came just a few days after a similarly damaging defeat nearby for the pilgrim contingent under Bishop Otto von Friesing.

RAYMOND OF ANTIOCH

Raymond of Poitiers took power as Prince of Antioch in 1136 on his marriage to the 10-year-old Constance, daughter of and heir to Bohemond II of Antioch, and was co-ruler with Constance. Raymond was the second son of William IX, Duke of Aquitaine and Count of Poitou, the French nobleman celebrated as the first troubadour poet, and was uncle to Duke William's granddaughter, Eleanor of Aquitaine. His rule in Antioch was not successful, for he was twice forced to pay homage to the Byzantine emperor and was unable to contain the threat of Nur ed-Din. Moreover he failed to divert the Second Crusade towards an attack on Nur ed-Din's powerbase at Aleppo.

Raymond was, however, one of the greatest courtly noblemen of his time. William of Tyre described him as being 'of noble descent, tall and stylish in figure, the finest-looking of earthly princes, a man of great charm and wit, generous and magnificent beyond measure.' Raymond was also a patron of literature – he was responsible for funding the composition of the crusade poem the *Chanson des chétifs*. He was a most generous host when Louis VII and Eleanor of Aquitaine made their visit during the Second Crusade – to the extent that rumours ran rife that he was Eleanor's lover. William of Tyre rehearsed this story, but modern historians tend to discount it as being unfounded.

BY SEA FROM ATTALIA

Louis and the survivors pressed doggedly on until they reached the port of Attalia (modern Antalya), close to where Byzantine territory gave way to Seljuk lands. Food was short, the army starving and desperate. The plan had been for the whole army to embark by sea from Attalia for Syria, but the fleet supplied by Emperor Manuel was far too small.

Louis took the available ships for himself, his household and the leading knights and essentially abandoned the remainder of the army to its fate. Although he left money with the Governor of Attalia to feed them, the soldiers and pilgrims had little alternative but to press on by land largely unprotected by knights through dangerous Seljuk territory to Tarsus. Most of the army's remnant was killed before reaching Tarsus.

Meanwhile Louis and his elite corps reached St Simeon, and were received with lavish hospitality by Raymond of Antioch. Escorted by Raymond, they arrived – exhausted and weary of both battles and voyaging – at the capital of the principality on 19 March.

▼ *King Louis, Conrad and the leading lords of Outremer arrive in Antioch. Here they took time to recover from the hardships of campaign, and debate the crusade's future.*

IN ANTIOCH

Louis considered what to do next. Raymond was keen to divert what force remained in the crusade against the rising power of Nur ed-Din, the Zengid ruler of Aleppo in Syria. Joscelin of Edessa, meanwhile, urged Louis to make the reconquest of Edessa his primary goal, arguing that the fall of Edessa had precipitated the crusade and therefore its recovery should be the expedition's primary goal. Louis

▲ *The main part of the French army had to make its own way, without king or knights, to Tarsus, travelling through country that had been the ruin of many before them.*

himself was preoccupied by his pilgrim's vows and wanted to press on to Jerusalem.

For a while the French lords and their ladies enjoyed the comforts of court life. Louis's wife, the intelligent and fiercely independent Eleanor of Aquitaine, was a keen advocate of her uncle Raymond's policy; in later years it was alleged that she was having an incestuous love affair in Antioch at this time with Raymond. But Louis was not minded to listen to her and when Fulk, the Patriarch of Jerusalem, arrived with an invitation from Queen Melisende and King Baldwin III, urging Louis's presence in Jerusalem, the French king began to make preparations for his departure. The royal couple argued – Eleanor stating that she would remain behind in Antioch and ask for a divorce. Louis reportedly dragged Eleanor forcibly out of the palace and made her come with him to Acre. Eleanor was not the only one who was angry – Raymond refused to take any part in the remainder of the crusade.

THE COUNCIL OF ACRE
AND THE HUMILIATING SIEGE OF DAMASCUS

When King Louis VII and Eleanor arrived in Acre, a great council was convened there on St John's Day (24 June) 1148 to discuss the future direction of the crusade. At this council the assembled lords agreed to attack Damascus, and the abject failure of this expedition was to bring the Second Crusade to an end.

CRUSADERS IN JERUSALEM

By the time Louis reached Acre, the remnants of the German pilgrim contingent under Bishop Otto had reached Jerusalem. Also in the Holy City was their king, Conrad III, who had recovered in Constantinople from his sickness and sailed directly as far as Tyre before travelling on to Jerusalem.

Other crusader groups had also made it to the Holy Land. Those who remained of the first wave of crusaders who had fought in the siege of Lisbon had arrived by sea, and the Provençal army that had

▼ *On three thrones, Louis VII of France, Conrad III of Germany and Baldwin III of Jerusalem hold court at the Council of Acre.*

▲ *This illustration from William of Tyre's History of Outremer (c.1280) shows the three kings at Acre and, below, the siege of Damascus that they decided to attempt.*

departed under Alfonso Jordan, Count of Toulouse, had landed. Alfonso almost immediately met his end, reputedly poisoned while at Caesarea by Raymond II, Count of Tripoli, who was fearful that Alfonso had come to claim the lands in Tripoli he had held in his infancy as the legitimate son of Raymond of Toulouse. (Count Raymond II was, in fact, Raymond

of Toulouse's great-grandson, descended through an illegitimate brother of Alfonso Jordan named Bertrand of Toulouse. This made him Alfonso Jordan's great-nephew.)

The council in Acre was officially a meeting of the High Court of the Kingdom of Jerusalem. In attendance were: Queen Melisende and her son King Baldwin III of Jerusalem; Manasses of Hierges, the constable of Jerusalem; Patriarch Fulk of Jerusalem; Louis VII; Conrad III; Bishop Otto of Freising; Duke Frederick of Swabia; and Henry II, Margrave of Austria. In addition, the masters of the military orders were there – Robert of Craon, master of the Knights Templar, and Raymond du Puy of Provence, master of the Knights Hospitaller. Other leading nobles of Outremer at the council included Walter Grenier, lord of Caesarea, Philip of Milly, lord of Nablus and Humphrey II, lord of Toron; but none of the lords of Antioch, Tripoli or Edessa were in attendance.

King Baldwin and the Knights Templar urged an attack on Damascus. Several local lords argued against this line of action, particularly on the grounds that

Mu'in ad-Din Unur, emir of Damascus, was an ally of the Christians against the Zengid lords of Syria – including the increasingly formidable Nur ed-Din of Aleppo. King Louis and King Conrad, however, were persuaded to back the attack on Damascus; the European lords, unversed in local politics and diplomacy, could not readily accept arguments in favour of making alliances with Muslim rulers and wanted principally to pursue a holy war against 'the infidel'. Moreover, while Aleppo meant nothing to them, Damascus was a city they knew from the Bible. An army was raised and in July assembled at Tiberias.

THE ORCHARDS OF DAMASCUS

The crusader lords decided to attack Damascus from the west, where a thick band of orchards would provide them with a steady food supply. They arrived there on 23 July, with the troops of the Kingdom of Jerusalem leading the way, followed by Louis and the French and then Conrad and the remainder of the German contingent in the rear. Emir Unur was warned of their approach, and had poisoned water sources, taken steps to strengthen his fortifications and sent out appeals for help to rival Muslim lords.

Taking the orchards was the crusaders' first task, but it was not an easy one: according to William of Tyre, they stretched for more than five miles 'like a dense, gloomy forest', the trees growing close together and accessible only by way of narrow footpaths between mud walls; in addition, there were defensive towers set at regular intervals. The crusaders poured into this difficult terrain, losing many men to arrow shots from the towers or to sudden attacks with spears from the darkness between the trees. They also had to face the city defenders who poured out of Damascus across the Barada river.

Both sides fought fiercely – according to a contemporary account, Conrad III made himself the talk of the entire army by dealing an overwhelming blow to a Turkish warrior that sliced through his

entire body, cutting off his head, neck and left shoulder. By the end of July 24 the crusaders had prevailed, taking control of the orchards and driving the Damascene defenders back behind their city walls.

Within the city, the people began to build barricades in the streets, fearing that they would be overrun. But at this point the crusaders paid the price for not encircling the city, for a relief army began to arrive from Aleppo in response to Emir Unur's cry for help – and this force, approaching from the north, was able to march right up to the city and enter through its North Gate. They began to launch counter-attacks on the Christian position in the orchards.

EASTERN APPROACHES

On 27 July the crusader lords took the fateful decision to move the army around the city to its open east side. Here they thought they might better be able to defend their camp. But – as they discovered the moment they arrived – there was

▲ *The crusader armies fought bravely at Damascus, but were undone by their leaders' bad tactical and strategic decisions.*

little or no food or water available there, and the eastern section of the city wall was very heavily fortified.

The crusaders and their leaders must have looked about in dismay. They could not return to the orchards, for by this stage Nur ed-Din himself had arrived and encamped his army there. In the burning heat of July, with insufficient water and the city strongly reinforced, their chances of taking Damascus had melted away; their position became untenable.

At dawn on 28 July, the Christian army began to abandon the siege, retreating in despair and disarray, harried all the way by the Turks. They lost many more men and horses during this humiliating retreat, and according to local chroniclers the human and animal corpses that lined the road sent up a stench powerful enough to make birds fall from the sky.

DESPAIR AND RECRIMINATIONS
THE AFTERMATH OF THE SECOND CRUSADE'S FAILURE

The crusaders' shambolic retreat from Damascus spelled the end of the Second Crusade, which fell apart in bitter recriminations. The failure of this enterprise had important and enduring consequences for the crusader states of Outremer and for their relations with the kingdoms of Europe.

In the immediate aftermath of Damascus, unity among the Christian forces was destroyed. Conrad took his troops to Ascalon, with the plan of taking that important port, but when none of the other parts of the army came to his aid he had to make another retreat. He headed home in September, but broke his journey to spend Christmas 1148 as a guest of Emperor Manuel in Constantinople. Louis, meanwhile, returned to Jerusalem. He did not embark for Europe until June 1149, then stopped on the way with King Roger of Sicily in Calabria, and with Pope Eugenius in Rome, before arriving back in Paris on 11 November.

THE FAULT OF OUTREMER LORDS

The crusaders felt bitterness towards both the native lords of Outremer and the Greeks of the Byzantine Empire. They asked how it was that the army had abandoned its hard-won position of strength in the orchards of Damascus, with the city almost at their mercy, to occupy an exposed and badly supplied position on the city's east side. They blamed the decision on bad advice from local lords, and began to circulate allegations that these lords had deliberately thrown away the military advantage.

One theory was that the lords had been outraged on discovering that the crusaders planned to grant the city to Count Thierry of Flanders and had secretly plotted to scupper the attack for this reason; another was that the lords were in league with Emir Unur of Damascus and had received payment for their part in making the siege

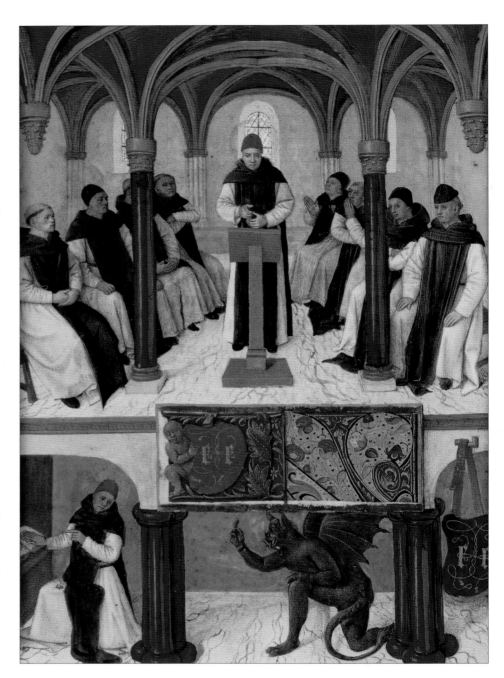

▲ *St Bernard of Clairvaux was a great teacher and inspiring preacher, but his reputation was ultimately damaged by the failure of the enterprise that he had done so much to instigate.*

fail. A third theory was that the lords had been plotting with Raymond of Antioch, who was still fuming at Louis's decision not to help him against Aleppo.

One of the central complaints of the crusaders was that both the lords of Outremer and the Byzantines had entered into alliances with Muslim rulers – in the case of Jerusalem with Emir Unur of Damascus, in the case of the Byzantine Empire with the Seljuk sultan Mesud I. This was inexplicable to the crusaders, fired as they were by the rhetoric of Bernard of Clairvaux.

BYZANTINE TREACHERY

The crusaders also had a string of complaints against Emperor Manuel and the Greeks of the Byzantine Empire. Some claimed that Byzantine scouts had deliberately led the German army into a Seljuk ambush at Dorylaeum – they asked whether perhaps Emperor Manuel had agreed this deal as part of the treaty he signed with Seljuks in 1147. In addition, they bemoaned the lack of support from Constantinople during the march of the French army across Anatolia and the fact that the fleet sent to King Louis in the port of Attalia was too small even for the much reduced army that had made it that far. Odo of Deuil, Louis VII's chaplain on the crusade, claimed that Manuel had betrayed the crusaders because Louis was an ally of Manuel's enemy Roger of Sicily.

CRITICISM IN EUROPE

In Europe Bernard of Clairvaux was at a loss fully to explain how the enterprise he had promoted as being devised and blessed in heaven could end in such abject failure. He attempted to blame the treachery of the Byzantines, but also said that the failure must have occurred because the sins of the crusaders had caused God to withdraw his support. Bernard participated in an attempt, driven by Abbot Suger of St Denis, to start a new crusade; at a meeting in Chartres in 1150, Bernard himself was elected leader of the enterprise. However, it came to nothing. Bernard was by now around 60 years old and having undergone many severe austerities as part of his spiritual life was far too frail to become a warrior monk.

Wider attempts to understand the crusade's failure led to criticism of almost all its aspects in Europe. There was denunciation of those, including Bernard, who had preached the enterprise. The anonymous Annalist of Wurzburg in Germany declared that the crusade preachers were 'witnesses of anti-Christ' who had misled good Christian folk. Other critics blamed the crusade leaders or the greed of Frankish lords in Outremer.

One idea with important consequences was that the considerable number of non-combatant pilgrims who had accompanied the crusade had been a major hindrance. The preaching of later crusades was focused more narrowly on mobilizing knights and infantry and avoided stirring up the passions of the people; indeed, after this crusade attempts were made to prevent pilgrims who could not fight or support themselves from travelling with armies to the East.

A WEAKENED OUTREMER

In the wake of the crusade's failure, the Kingdom of Jerusalem was in a far weaker position. The attack on Damascus had destroyed a valuable alliance, boosted Muslim morale and greatly strengthened the position of Nur ed-Din.

Moreover, the souring of relations between the crusader kingdoms and Europe meant that the leading knights among the European nobility were far less willing than previously to come to the aid of Outremer. Crusading and making a pilgrimage to the Holy Land suffered a severe decline in popularity. The success of the First Crusade had give the idea glamour and force, but these were dissipated by the failure of the Second. William of Tyre commented that after the Second Crusade Europeans 'looked askance at our leaders' ways' and 'showed complete indifference about the business of the kingdom'; this attitude spread – 'their influence caused others who had not been there to loosen their love for the kingdom' and so 'fewer folk, and those less committed in spirit, made the pilgrimage after this time'.

A QUARREL WITH CONSEQUENCES

The violent quarrel between Louis VII and his wife, Eleanor of Aquitaine, in Antioch during the Second Crusade had consequences that were still being felt in Europe in the 15th century. Eleanor tried but failed to get Pope Eugenius to grant a divorce on the couple's way home, but in March 1152 an annulment was granted on the basis of consanguinity (they were third cousins, once removed, as common descendants of Robert II of France). Just six weeks later, Eleanor married Henry, Count of Anjou and Duke of Normandy, who would become King Henry II of England in 1154. Because under Aquitaine law women would inherit property and her father's will had specified that the duchy should remain in the hands of her heirs, Eleanor brought vast and wealthy possessions in south-western France into the hands of the English crown.

▶ Louis VII was both learned and devout. His wife, Eleanor, is said to have declared that she had thought she was marrying a king but found she had married a monk.

Disputes over this land between England and France led to centuries of conflict, running right down to the Hundred Years War of 1337–1453. The royal couple had certainly begun to be estranged before travelling on the Second Crusade, but the quarrel in Antioch appears to have been a decisive moment, marking a split from which they did not recover.

NUR ED-DIN AND A UNIFIED SYRIA
MUSLIMS UNITE IN JIHAD

Buoyed by the abject failure of the Second Crusade, Nur ed-Din, whose personal reputation was enhanced by his part in driving back the crusaders at Damascus, prepared a new attack on the Principality of Antioch. His ultimate goal, however, was to capture Damascus and so unite Syria.

THE RISE OF NUR ED-DIN
Nur ed-Din was born in 1118, the second son of the great Turkish Muslim general Imad ed-Din Zengi, ruler of Aleppo and Mosul in Syria. On his father's death in 1146, Nur ed-Din took power in Aleppo while his brother Saif ed-Din became the ruler of Mosul. Nur ed-Din was already establishing himself as a scourge of the crusader lords, capturing a number of castles in the Principality of Antioch and also in November 1146 defeating an attempt by Joscelin of Courtenay, the ousted count of Edessa, to recapture his capital. In 1147 he formed an alliance with Emir Unur of

▼ *Knights ride out to battle in Syria. Nur ed-Din plotted his rise to power carefully, using diplomacy as much as warfare.*

Damascus as part of an attempt to create a united Muslim front against the advancing crusaders, but the two leaders were suspicious of each other's motives. Nevertheless, in 1148, as we have seen, Nur ed-Din came to Emir Unur's rescue when he brought his army to relieve the ill-conceived siege of Damascus that had been mounted by the crusader lords.

In the wake of the events at Damascus, Nur ed-Din's name was trumpeted far and wide. It was proclaimed that the crusaders had fled at the approach of his army. The victory of the city's defenders was recorded and celebrated as a triumph of jihad.

VICTORY IN ANTIOCH
In 1149, with help from Emir Unur of Damascus, he moved against Antioch, attacking the crusader castle of Inab in the Principality. Raymond, Prince of Antioch, rode out with an army to defend the citadel and was heavily defeated on 29 June 1149. Raymond was killed during the battle; afterward his head was cut off by Nur ed-Din's general Shirkuh and despatched by Nur ed-Din in a silver casket to the Abbasid caliph of Baghdad.

▲ *A wall painting depicts Templar Hugh IX the Brown of Lusignan, who died at Damietta on the Fifth Crusade. Nur ed-Din's campaigns had strengthened the Muslim defence for 40 years after his death.*

This victory put much of the territory of the principality in Nur ed-Din's hands and he marked his triumph by marching as far as the sea and having a celebratory swim in the Mediterranean. He did not move against the city of Antioch itself, however. He possessed the Principality east of the Orontes River and seemingly was happy for the capital of the state to remain in crusader hands: perhaps he did not want to get drawn into conflict over its possession with the Byzantine Empire, for Emperor Manuel Comnenus claimed it as his possession.

In 1149 Nur ed-Din's brother Saif ed-Din died and was succeeded as ruler of Mosul by another brother, Qutb ed-Din. The new ruler recognized Nur ed-Din as overlord of Mosul. Nur ed-Din's main concern was now to take control of Damascus and so create a united Muslim Syria.

TRIUMPH IN DAMASCUS

He besieged Damascus four times in 1150–54 without launching an assault on the city. By this time, Mu'in ad-Din Unur had died and been succeeded by a weaker ruler, Mujir ad-Din, who agreed to pay tribute to the king of Jerusalem. Finally, in 1154, the people and the garrison turned against their ruler, who they felt had betrayed Islam by making a demeaning treaty with the Christians, and opened the city gates to Nur ed-Din.

For once, the end of a siege was not marked by rioting and bloodshed. Nur ed-Din promised the leading citizens that he would protect their livelihoods; he provided food for the poor. He even cut taxes, and began a public building programme.

Nur ed-Din proceeded with caution. He did not march on Jerusalem, in fact he reaffirmed the treaty that had caused controversy and continued to pay tribute. He went on chipping away at the crusaders, in 1157 besieging the Knights Hospitaller at the Castle of Banias and trouncing a

▲ *Nur ed-Din beseiged the formidable walls of Damascus four times. A map from 1620 shows what a challenge this was.*

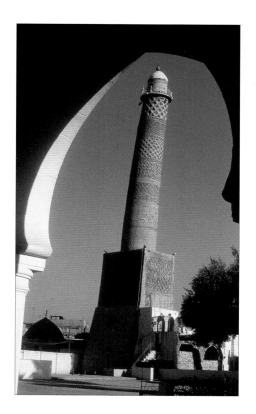

▼ *The leaning minaret, 170ft (52m) high, is all that remains of the mosque of Nur ed-Din at Mosul in Syria.*

relief army despatched from Jerusalem. In 1160 he captured Reynald of Châtillon, Prince of Antioch, who he kept in prison for 16 years. He also became involved in conflicts to the north, in 1159 agreeing an alliance with the Byzantine emperor Manuel Comnenus against the Seljuk Turks and the same year mounting an attack on the Seljuk sultan Kilij Arslan II.

THE RULE OF NUR ED-DIN

Nur ed-Din was celebrated for his piety and his just rule. A staunch follower of Sunni Islam, he did not make personal use of the wealth he generated through conquest, but poured it into the building of mosques, madrasas (religious schools), hospitals, public baths and caravansaries (lodges for Islamic travellers). He established fairer taxation and an effective civil service and justice system. He also built a network of khanqas, centres for Sufis, followers of a mystical branch of Islam. And he improved communication by introducing the use of carrier pigeons.

SUFISM

This branch of Islam outlines a path to God through self-purification, inner exploration and mystical experience. It probably developed at some time under the Umayyad caliphate in AD660–750, although all Sufi traditions trace their history right back to the time of the Prophet Muhammad (c.AD570-632); teachings were reputedly passed down the generations from master to pupil. Early Sufis were careful to stress their path as a complementary way to God alongside the Shariah (religious law), but from the late 12th century onwards Sufism and Shariah began to separate. Sufism is known for its magnificent collections of religious love poetry.

THE BATTLE FOR EGYPT
SYRIA LOOKS TO EXTEND MUSLIM POWER

In 1162, with Syria secure against intervention from the crusader lords, Nur ed-Din went on pilgrimage to Mecca. He had achieved his ambition of uniting Syria. His eyes – and those of his nominal masters, the Abbasid caliphs of Baghdad – began to turn to Egypt, and to view the possibility of overthrowing the Shi'ite Fatimid caliphate there and establishing a united Sunni Muslim state of Syria and Egypt. The same year, a new king mounted the throne in Jerusalem – Amalric I, brother of Baldwin III.

POWER STRUGGLE IN CAIRO
In Egypt, although rule was nominally by the religious leader or caliph, real power lay in the hands of the chief administrator, or vizier. In 1163, at a time when the caliph was the inexperienced 14-year-old al-Adid, the vizier Shawar was ousted and replaced by Dirgham. King Amalric of Jerusalem, seeing an opportunity,

mounted an expedition into Egypt claiming that the Fatimids were not paying tribute that had been pledged during the reign of Baldwin III. This campaign failed and he was forced to withdraw to Jerusalem. Meanwhile, Shawar visited the court of Nur ed-Din begging for military help to restore himself to power, and offering lavish rewards.

In 1164 Nur ed-Din sent an army under his leading general Asad ed-Din Shirkuh bin Shadhi to Egypt. Shirkuh had risen from relatively humble origins by dint of his energy, leadership qualities and military excellence. His name, of Kurdish-Iranian origin, meant 'Mountain Lion'. William of Tyre described him as a short and 'very stout' man, and already in the early 1160s 'advanced in years', with a cataract in one eye; he presented him as a formidable leader, experienced in military affairs, possessed of 'great endurance in the face of hardships' and beloved of his

men because of his profound generosity. With him to Egypt rode his nephew, Salah ed-Din Yusuf (later known as Saladin).

Shirkuh did his job: Dirgham was killed and Shawar reinstated. But at once Shawar reneged on his promises and entered an alliance with Amalric against the Syrians. Amalric invaded Egypt once more and with Shawar's troops besieged Shirkuh in the fortress of Bilbeis.

CRUSADERS HUMILIATED IN ANTIOCH
In response, Nur ed-Din launched an attack on the Principality of Antioch, where he besieged the castle of Harim and won a crushing victory against the crusader armies of Tripoli and Antioch. He

▼ *Qalaat ar-Rahba in Syria was one of the strongholds of the 'Mountain Lion' Asad ed-Din Shirkuh, general in the service of Nur ed-Din and uncle of the great Saladin.*

captured a roll-call of crusader lords: Bohemond III, Prince of Antioch; Raymond III, Count of Tripoli; Joscelin III, Count of Edessa; and French nobleman Hugh VIII of Lusignan, who had recently arrived on pilgrimage. Nur ed-Din had them all led in chains into Aleppo and cast into jail there. As many as 10,000 were killed in the crusader army, according to the Arab historian Ibn al-Athir.

But Nur ed-Din did not capture Antioch itself; it remained officially a Byzantine possession and he did not want to provoke Emperor Manuel Comnenus, with whom he had lately agreed a treaty. He did, however, capture Banias, and then kept up a constant harrying of the crusader states for the following two years. Meanwhile in Egypt, Amalric and Shirkuh made terms, agreeing to lift the siege and return home.

EGYPTIAN BATTLES

But in 1167 Shirkuh and Saladin invaded Egypt again. They were followed by Amalric's army in 1167. Initially there was a stand-off between the Christians and Shirkuh's army at Cairo. Shirkuh offered Shawar the chance to make a deal and unite against the crusaders, but he turned it down and instead renewed his alliance with Amalric. Shirkuh then led his men south, followed by the crusader army. The

▲ View of Cairo and the valley of the River Nile from the citadel constructed in the city by Saladin after he became vizier of Egypt.

two sides fought without clear result: Shirkuh occupied Alexandria, where he was welcomed by the largely Sunni Muslim population, but was then besieged by the crusader army.

Shirkuh broke out of the city in the hope that the crusader troops would follow him and engage in battle. But they sat tight, and Saladin was left in control of a starving population within the besieged city. Finally the standoff was broken not by a battle, but a truce; Saladin played no small part in brokering a deal under which both leaders took their armies home.

THE TAKING OF CAIRO

In 1168 Amalric entered an alliance with the Byzantine Empire and invaded Egypt once more. He captured Bilbeis, massacred the inhabitants and then besieged Cairo. Shawar changed sides once more, turning to Nur ed-Din and the great Shirkuh for help. Shirkuh and Saladin responded with all speed to the summons, marching south with an army containing 8,000 cavalry. The crusader army, badly outnumbered, withdrew once more and Shirkuh entered Cairo in triumph on 9 January 1169.

THE KURDS

Originally a pastoral people living in the mountains to the north and north east of what is now Iraq, the Kurds were subjects of the Abbasid Empire who established independent warrior principalities when the power of Baghdad waned in the 11th century. These states were overwhelmed by the invasion of the Seljuk Turks, but in the 12th century the Kurds rose to prominence again as soldiers of fortune in the pay of the Syrian rulers Imad ed-Din Zengi and Nur ed-Din. The brothers Najm ed-Din Ayub and Asad ed-Din Shirkuh made their names under Nur ed-Din: Ayub was governor of Damascus while Shirkuh was Nur ed-Din's leading general. Saladin was Ayub's son.

▼ Kurdish mounted warriors battle against Arab counterparts.

At first Shirkuh dealt amicably with Shawar, but then, ten days later, Shawar was killed after Saladin and his associates dragged him from his horse and had him beheaded – notionally on the orders of the caliph. Shirkuh then became vizier of Egypt. But within thee months Shirkuh had died, reportedly from overeating, and Saladin was in power in his place.

THE CHIVALROUS INFIDEL
SALADIN

Saladin was undoubtedly the leading Muslim figure of the entire crusading era. He inspired fear and awestruck admiration among the Westerners he repeatedly defeated in battle, while his magnanimous behaviour in victory won him a reputation as a chivalrous infidel, a seeming contradiction in contemporary Christian terms. He rose from relatively humble origins to become ruler of Egypt and Syria, and won undying fame in the Muslim world as the man who recaptured the Holy City of Jerusalem from the crusaders.

SALADIN'S YOUTH AND RISE TO PROMINENCE

The son of Najm ed-Din Ayub, governor of Damascus, Saladin lived as a young man at the splendid court of Nur ed-Din in that city, studying Islamic law, rhetoric and Arabic grammar, and developing a reputation as a brilliant all-rounder. He was a refined courtier who was skilled in debate, elegant in conversation, well versed in the traditions and military achievements of the Arab tribes, knowledgeable about the genealogies of the finest Arabian horses and a superb player of polo. This game was the equivalent at

▼ *Saladin was reputed to be equally at home pursuing learned discussion at court as he was directing armies in battle and making strategic decisions on campaign.*

Muslim courts of the chivalric tournament in Europe, a proving ground for young lords and a way of making a reputation among the political–military elite: Saladin achieved the distinction of being invited to join Nur ed-Din's own polo team.

He served his military apprenticeship in the service of his uncle Shirkuh, already established as Nur ed-Din's foremost general. Alongside Shirkuh he invaded Egypt three times, in 1164, 1167 and 1168–69. On the second of these occasions, Saladin was in command of the city of Alexandria while it was besieged by the crusader army – he later recalled: 'I endured many hardships at Alexandria that I can never forget.' Subsequently he took a leading role in the negotiations that brought the siege to an end and allowed both the Syrian and the crusader armies to go home with heads held high.

During these negotiations, Saladin's skill and nobility of character greatly impressed the crusader lords; he spent some time in the crusader camp after the siege was lifted, and according to some accounts was knighted by Humphrey II of Toron, Constable of the Kingdom of Jerusalem. The enduring myth of Saladin the infidel knight was born at this time.

VIZIER OF EGYPT

During the invasion of 1168–69, Saladin killed the vizier of Egypt, Shawar, and General Shirkuh became vizier in his place. When Shirkuh died on 22 March 1169 Saladin triumphed in politics within the Syrian army and took power for himself.

Saladin had triumphed in Egypt as a soldier of Syrian ruler Nur ed-Din, but his relationship with his nominal overlord became increasingly strained as it grew clear that Saladin was determined to rule in Cairo on his own terms, independently of influence from Damascus. In particular, he refrained from immediately removing the Shi'ite Fatimid caliph, while Nur ed-

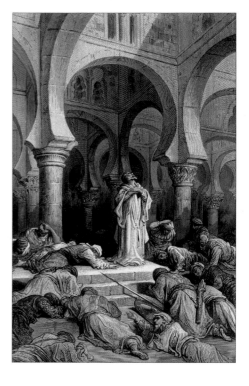

▲ *Saladin gives thanks to Allah after his conquest of Jerusalem returned the city to Muslim control.*

Din was impatient for Sunni Islam to be imposed on Egypt. Finally, in September 1171, when the Fatimid caliph al-Adid died, Saladin abolished the Fatimid caliphate and proclaimed the name of the Abbasid caliph of Baghdad, Al-Mustadi.

Saladin's barely concealed ambition was to unite Egypt and Syria in an Islamic empire. He had been joined in Egypt by his father, a trusted intimate of Nur ed-Din, and on his advice did not make open moves against Syria and publicly behaved as if he were no more than Nur ed-Din's servant. But Nur ed-Din was not fooled and his anger with Saladin grew, especially when Saladin twice retreated from invasions of the crusader Kingdom of Jerusalem that his overlord had ordered. In 1174, Nur ed-Din was preparing to invade Egypt when he died of a fever resulting from a throat infection.

The heir to Damascus was Nur ed-Din's

ten-year-old son, al-Salih, and Syrian emirs began a scramble for power. Saladin marched on Damascus, according to some accounts following an invitation from local lords. His reputation went before him: when he arrived in October 1174, he was welcomed into the city by the people. He bolstered his position by marrying Nur ed-Din's widow and reinforced his popularity among his devoutly Muslim populace by vigorously promoting himself as a committed leader of jihad against the crusaders. Initially he did not have authority over Syria's other leading centres of power, but he imposed his authority on Aleppo in 1176 and on Mosul in 1186. By this stage he was close to his ultimate victory over the Kingdom of Jerusalem.

CONFLICT WITH JERUSALEM

Saladin had been reluctant to attack the Kingdom of Jerusalem while Nur ed-Din was alive: he was well aware that if he attacked from Egypt in the south while Nur ed-Din invaded from Syria, their combined force could wipe the crusader state off the map – but the outcome would then have been that Nur ed-Din, officially still Saladin's overlord, would have become

immeasurably more powerful. But after Nur ed-Din's death, any victory over Jerusalem was only going to boost Saladin's own power base; moreover, he had committed himself to attack the crusaders by public proclamations of his enthusiasm for jihad.

In November 1177 he marched north from Egypt against the Kingdom of Jerusalem. The new king of Jerusalem, Baldwin IV, who had succeeded his father Amalric I in 1174, had installed himself with 375 knights at Ascalon expecting a siege; but Saladin bypassed the city, sending a force to surround it, and moved on towards Jerusalem itself. Baldwin bravely broke out through the surrounding army and rode with a force of about 80 Knights Templar and a few thousand infantry to intersect Saladin's progress.

DEFEAT AT MONTGISARD

The Christian knights took Saladin's much larger army entirely by surprise near the fortress of Montgisard on 25 November and inflicted a devastating defeat on them that was celebrated for years; the Old French translation of William of Tyre's chronicle said that the Christians found St

George riding into battle at their side. Saladin lost his entire bodyguard and only just escaped with his life – according to contemporary accounts, because he was mounted on a racing camel and was able to outrun his pursuers. Only around 3,000 Muslim troops from an army of 30,000 or more limped back to Egypt.

Two years later Saladin had revenge of sorts. In a show of defiance, Baldwin had begun constructing a great castle at Jacob's Ford at the only crossing of the Jordan on the route from Damascus towards the Kingdom of Jerusalem. The king's men managed to complete the castle's outer walls, which stood 32ft (10m) in height, before Saladin marshalled his resources to attack. When the onslaught began Baldwin was in Tiberias: Saladin managed to breach the walls and killed 800 members of the castle's vast garrison, captured another 700 crusader soldiers and poisoned the water sources.

▼ *With an inferior force Baldwin surprised and defeated Saladin at Montgisard. The king fought left-handed since his leprosy had affected his right arm.*

CRUSADERS DESTROYED
SALADIN'S VICTORY AT THE HORNS OF HATTIN

In July 1187 Saladin moved again against the Kingdom of Jerusalem. On 4 July he annihilated the crusader army at the Battle of the Horns of Hattin, on one day destroying the Kingdom's united military capability and making inevitable his triumphant capture of Jerusalem later in the same year.

THE PROVOCATION OF REYNALD OF CHÂTILLON

Following Saladin's defeat at the Battle of Montgisard in 1177 and his revenge at Jacob's Ford in 1179, conflict between Saladin and the crusaders continued throughout the 1180s. A constant provocation was Reynald of Châtillon, a highly controversial figure in his own lifetime and beyond, the former Prince of Antioch (1153–60) who had spent 16 years in jail in Aleppo after being captured by Nur

▼ *Guy of Lusignan was crowned King of Jerusalem in 1180. He came to the throne as consort of Sibylla, daughter of Amalric I and sister of the leper-king Baldwin IV.*

ed-Din in 1160. Following the death of his wife, Reynald had made a powerful second marriage in 1183 when he wed Stephanie of Milly, heiress of the lordship of Oultrejordain, which included the powerful fortress of Montreal. From here, Reynald repeatedly attacked Muslim trade and pilgrim caravans, provoking Saladin to besiege the castle without success in 1183 and 1184. Reynald briefly practised restraint, but he was soon back to his old ways, attacking a caravan of pilgrims making the *hajj* (pilgrimage) to Mecca in 1185. (According to the 13th-century Old French *Continuation of the Chronicle of William of Tyre*, in this attack Reynald captured no less a figure than the sister of Saladin, but this is probably an invention since it is not confirmed in any of the contemporary accounts.) In May 1187 he attacked again, sweeping down from Montreal to attack a Muslim trade caravan from Cairo headed for Damascus. Saladin decided to act. He reputedly swore then that if he were ever to capture Reynald, he would kill him with his own hand.

THE SUCCESSION DISPUTE IN JERUSALEM

Saladin was also encouraged to attack by the weakness of the regime in Jerusalem, which had been undermined by a succession dispute. The dispute had begun in the reign of Amalric I's son, Baldwin IV, who, although a great military commander, was also a leper and was often too ill to govern and was unable to leave an heir. Two factions fought over the succession: on one side was Baldwin's eldest sister Sibylla and her ambitious husband Guy of Lusignan, supported by (among others) Reynald of Châtillon; on the other side was Raymond of Tripoli and the powerful Ibelin family, who backed the cause of Baldwin and Sibylla's half-sister Isabella, whose mother, Maria Comnena (widow of Amalric I), had married Balian of Ibelin.

▲ *Guy of Lusignan was banished from France by the future King Richard I of England. Guy arrived in the Holy Land some time after 1174, and can be seen here at his coronation as King of Jerusalem.*

Baldwin IV had Sibylla's young son Baldwin V crowned as co-ruler and heir in 1183 and when Baldwin IV died in spring 1185 the boy became king at the age of 8, with Raymond of Tripoli as regent. Baldwin V lasted less than 18 months: he died in summer 1186, and in the aftermath, Sibylla and Guy won the power struggle and Sibylla was crowned Queen with Guy as her consort.

A RECKLESS ADVANCE

Saladin gathered his army in May–June 1187 and on July 2 attacked Tiberias. The Christians gathered their forces at Sephoria under the leadership of Guy of Jerusalem (as Guy of Lusignan was known following the coronation of his wife Sibylla as Queen of Jerusalem). The army numbered around 1,200 knights and perhaps 20,000 infantry, representing the entire military strength of the Kingdom of Jerusalem. In attendance was the Bishop of Acre carrying a piece of the True Cross, the Kingdom's most sacred relic.

The position at Sephoria was a strong one, but Saladin was hoping that by his attack on Tiberias he could lure the crusaders out into open country. He got his way. Guy ignored advice from Raymond of Tripoli who counselled him not to risk a pitched battle against Saladin, and – urged on by the hot-headed Reynald of Châtillon – advanced towards Tiberias on 3 July. This was desert country, and the crusaders marched for hours without food or water, being harassed by Saladin's advance troops, until in the evening they encamped just to the south of the twin-peaked hill known as the Horns of Hattin.

SURROUNDED IN THE DESERT

In the morning they found that they were surrounded. Ahead of them, within sight, was a green valley and a lake, but Saladin's army barred the way. Saladin's men set fire to the dry grass around the crusaders, increasing the searing heat. Thirst maddened the crusaders, smoke billowed around them and arrows rained down on them from the sky. Saladin's secretary and chronicler Imad ed-din al-Isfahani later

▼ *Knights of the Kingdom of Jerusalem lie dead on the battlefield following the defeat at Hattin. By tradition, a heavenly light shone over them for three nights.*

▲ *The crusaders were overrun and all but wiped out by Saladin's army at the Battle of the Horns of Hattin. Fires set by Saladin's men swept smoke across the battlefield.*

recalled that: 'the people of the Trinity were eaten up by a worldly fire of three kinds, each irresistible and overwhelming: the fire of racing flames, the fire of raging thirst and the fire of whistling arrows.'

The crusaders tried to drive back the advancing army of Saladin, but without success. Only one sortie succeeded: Raymond of Tripoli, Reynald of Sidon and Balian of Ibelin broke out but were then unable to rejoin the battle; they rode away, knowing that Guy's rashness had brought the Kingdom to the brink of extinction.

Back in the heat of battle, the crusader army was driven up the hill towards the tent of King Guy, visible on the summit. To the despair of all, while fighting, the Bishop of Acre was robbed of the relic of the True Cross. Templars and Hospitallers fought bravely but they could not prevent the inevitable and eventually King Guy's tent fell and the battle was over.

HONOUR AND REVENGE

Guy and Reynald of Châtillon were still alive and were brought to Saladin's tent. Saladin gave the thirst-maddened Guy a drink of iced rosewater and the king

handed it to Reynald. Saladin grew angry, and made it clear that he had not offered the drink to his enemy Reynald – for by the Muslim warriors' code of war if a prisoner were offered food or drink by his captor his life had to be spared. Saladin did spare Guy, but slew Reynald by his own hand. 'Kings do not kill kings,' he said to Guy, but looking at Reynald added, 'that man's insolence went beyond what can be tolerated.'

On the following day Saladin ordered the execution of the surviving warriors among the Knights Templar and the Knights Hospitaller. Muslim holy men and Sufi mystics, who had joined the army in answer to the call to take part in jihad, begged to be allowed to perform the deed. Saladin seated himself on a mounted platform and watched, with his assembled soldiers, as the Christian warriors were put to death agonizingly slowly by these inexperienced swordsmen.

JERUSALEM RECAPTURED

SALADIN TAKES THE HOLY CITY

On 2 October 1187 Saladin and his army recaptured Jerusalem, ending almost 90 years of Christian rule.

CONTROL OF THE KINGDOM

Defeat at the Horns of Hattin had wiped out the crusader states' military strength and Saladin proceeded through the Kingdom virtually unopposed. Acre surrendered within days of the battle, and shortly afterwards Saladin's brother Al-Adil captured Jaffa. Nazareth, Caesarea and Haifa were taken and on 4 September Saladin captured Ascalon. Darkness fell by day because there was an eclipse of the sun; Christians who had heard of the eclipse of the moon witnessed before the capture of Jerusalem in 1099 may have seen this as an omen – and shuddered.

On 20 September 1187 Saladin began a siege of Jerusalem. The city's defence was

In triumph the Muslim army was highly disciplined. Saladin had his enemies at his mercy but treated them respectfully. There was no repeat of the lawlessness of 1099.

the responsibility of Balian of Ibelin, one of the knights who had broken out of the Muslim encirclement at the Horns of Hattin; he had returned to the city in order to rescue his wife Maria Comnena (the city's former queen and widow of Amalric I). He did not have sufficient manpower to mount an effective defence of the city walls – according to one contemporary account, there were only two other knights and a limited number of men-at-arms. Nevertheless, he inspired the defenders to hold out for nine days.

TERMS OF SURRENDER

On 30 September, after the Muslim siege equipment had made a breach in the wall near the Gate of the Column, Balian rode out to Saladin's camp to discuss terms under which the city might be given up. At first Saladin did not want to negotiate. He reminded Balian of the terrible behaviour of the Christian knights in taking Jerusalem in 1099. He wanted nothing less then unconditional surrender.

Balian responded by threatening that if they could not agree a truce and ransom, he would order the Christians within the city to slaughter the 5,000-odd Muslim slaves and prisoners, then to kill their own wives and children, destroy their valuable

▲ Within Jerusalem, Balian of Ibelin led a few knights in desperate resistance to the siege, but they were vastly outnumbered. The Holy City passed into Saladin's hands.

possessions, attack the Muslim holy places and then fight to the death on the city walls. The city would be a bloodbath, loot would be destroyed, sacred places desecrated, and many of Saladin's soldiers would be killed unnecessarily in taking the city by force.

Saladin wanted to capture the city intact and did not want to cause the deaths of his fellow Muslims, so he agreed a ransom deal with Balian: ten dinars for each man, five for each woman and one for each child, with a lump sum of 30,000 dinars payable for 7,000 of the population who were too poor to pay their own ransom, the remainder of the unransomable poor were to be sold into slavery.

THE REOCCUPATION OF JERUSALEM

On 2 October 1187 Saladin and his disciplined army took the city peacefully. He was true to his word and the Franks were allowed to leave unmolested. Saladin sent groups of armed soldiers into the city to ensure that there was no looting or

SALADIN'S CHARACTER

Saladin was celebrated for his lively mind and sense of honour. Crusaders praised him for his generosity in victory and his wit in negotiation. His Muslim biographer Baha ed-Din ibn Shaddad wrote of him that he was a mine of fascinating information in conversation, a caring leader who would always ask after friends, and attempt to raise people's spirits. He would not allow fellow Muslims to be criticized in his presence, wanting to hear of people's good qualities instead. When he encountered orphans he always made sure that they were helped. Baha ed-Din ibn Shaddad recounted the story of how a distraught crusader woman demanded to see Saladin after her daughter had been stolen by Muslim soldiers: Saladin not only saw her and listened to her, but also sent men to scour the markets to see if they could find the girl; they did and he reunited her with her mother.

▼ *A monument to Saladin in Damascus.*

▲ *An illustration of c.1400 looks back to the fight for Jerusalem in 1187. The besieging Islamic army has been reimagined as a conventional European force.*

to pilgrims. The manner in which they reoccupied Jerusalem was a great and lasting credit to Saladin and his men, and should have shamed the Christian knights of 1099 had they been alive to see it.

Saladin's reputation for magnanimity and piety were enhanced by his treatment of the ransomed prisoners. Forty days were allowed for the Christians to raise the necessary ransoms. Throughout, Saladin behaved with the utmost generosity: when his brother, growing distressed at the vast numbers of captives, asked for some to be spared, Saladin freed 1,000; he gave another 700 their freedom in response to a request by the Patriarch of Jerusalem; and set another 500 free as a tribute to Balian. He then went even further, freeing the elderly and the infirm and all the husbands of women already freed.

MUSLIM JOY

According to Imad ed-din al-Isfahani, Saladin held a joyful court in the days after his retaking of Jerusalem, and was visited by many leading Muslims who 'covered his carpet with kisses'. He maintained a sober and dignified bearing, but his face was 'bright with joy' and 'his expression shone'; the great triumph he had achieved, Imad ed-din wrote, appeared to give him a halo of moonlight.

CHRISTIAN DESPAIR

The Kingdom of Jerusalem appeared to be close to extinction. In the two years following the Battle of the Horns of Hattin, Saladin captured more than 50 crusader strongholds. He did not move against Tripoli or Antioch and Tyre remained in Christian hands, but the taking of Jerusalem was a great propaganda victory that suggested there was no future for the Christians in Palestine.

News of the defeat at the Horns of Hattin and the loss of Jerusalem reached Europe in the autumn of 1187 and Pope Urban III is reported to have died of grief. Writers and preachers lamented the terrible turn of events. One declared: '... on that day, October 2, 1187, the queen among all the cities in the world was cast into slavery.' It was an end, but also a beginning – within weeks, Urban's successor Pope Gregory VIII issued a call for a fresh military expedition to the Holy Land and a new crusade began.

rampage. He then set about cleaning up the city, restoring the al Aqsa mosque and the Dome of the Rock to sacred use for Muslims. Although he was urged by his compatriots to destroy the Church of the Holy Sepulchre, he merely ordered it to be closed for three days, then reopened

THE THIRD CRUSADE

The kings, princes and knights who conducted the Third Crusade of 1189-92 were inspired by tales of the heroic deeds of Christian warriors on the First and Second Crusades (1095-99 and 1145-49). In particular they were driven by a desire to repeat the extraordinary achievement of the knights of the First Crusade, who succeeded against all odds in capturing Jerusalem for Christ and for the leader of the Latin or Catholic Church to which they belonged. They had little political or economic motive in fighting in the East — they were inspired principally by religious motives. The outcome of the crusade was shaped decisively by the character and generalship of one man, the English warrior-king Richard I, who as a general, was always a practical realist. After inflicting a famous defeat on Kurdish Muslim general Saladin in the Battle of Arsuf, Richard was urged to attempt the capture of Jerusalem, but he chose not to, seeing that he clearly lacked the military strength to hold the city even if he managed to take it. Instead he elected to open peace negotiations.

▲ *Frederick Barbarossa, Emperor of Germany, and his crusading army*
begin their journey during the Third Crusade.

▶ *The gruelling siege of Acre had stagnated for months with both defenders and attackers dying in*
large numbers from dysentery and disease. It was finally ended when Richard the Lionheart arrived and
supervised fresh assaults on the city, which were at last successful. Here Kings Philip II and Richard I
oversee the surrender of the city's garrison.

THE KINGS ON CRUSADE

The origins of the Third Crusade were notably different from those of the first two crusades, since it was called by the will of secular rulers as much as by that of the pope. Richard's participation – along with King Philip II of France and Emperor Frederick I of Germany – made the 'Kings' Crusade' one of the greatest and most glamorous of the wars of the cross – but, equally, the involvement of these monarchs was its undoing, for they were unable to put aside their fierce rivalries. These kings were larger than life characters whose reputations as warriors was already established. Other charismatic and powerful lords were also involved, men like Conrad of Montferrat, who gambled with the life of his hostage father, and Tancred, Count of Lecce causing trouble in Sicily by kidnapping King Richard's sister. With feuds between kings, diversions for personal gain and various delays, it was almost four years after Pope Gregory's call to arms that Richard arrived at the place he was sorely needed; Acre. The siege of the city had begun in the summer of 1189, and by the time Richard finally arrived with his reinforcements in on 8 June 1191 the beseiging crusaders had endured months of terrible suffering and hardship.

▲ *Frederick Barbarossa, King of Germany, invades Italy by sea in 1157.*

◄ *According to* jongleur *Ambroise, an eyewitness of the Battle of Arsuf, Richard was like a crossbow bolt fired against the enemy, who cut down his foes like a farmer harvesting wheat.*

ONCE MORE TO JERUSALEM

A THIRD CRUSADE IS CALLED

On 29 October 1187, in Ferrara, Pope Gregory VIII issued a crusading bull known to historians from its first words in Latin, *Audita tremendi* (the first part of a Latin phrase that translates as 'On hearing of the dreadful and profound judgement inflicted on the land of Jerusalem by the divine hand'). The papal bull was issued in response to the defeat at the Battle of the Horns of Hattin in July, before news of the fall of Jerusalem had reached Europe.

The bull called the defeat at Hattin and the loss of the relic of the True Cross in the battle 'a terrible judgement inflicted by the Lord on the land of Jerusalem' and declared that the news – which had reputedly ended Pope Urban III's life, by bringing on a heart attack – had thrown his successor as pope and other church leaders into confusion and left them battered by 'such a deep horror and resounding grief that it was not apparent what we should do'. But it called for all to maintain their faith and to believe that God 'once softened by our repentance' would bring 'gladness after grief'; Christian warriors should see this as 'a chance to repent and do a good deed', offering themselves and their wealth for recovery of 'the land where Truth itself was born from the earth in order to bring about our salvation'.

Those who made the journey with 'humble and contrite heart' or who died 'in repentance of their wrongdoing and in the right faith' would earn a plenary indulgence and eternal life 'by the mercy of God Himself, on the authority of the apostles Peter and Paul' and that of the papacy. As in previous crusades, the property of those who took the cross would be protected by the Church and those who incurred debts making the journey should be free of the requirement to pay interest. The bull also urged those travelling to avoid ostentation and aim for simplicity – not to take dogs,

▲ *When elected to the papacy Alberto di Morra took the name Gregory in honour of Pope Gregory VII (r.1073-85), pictured here, a key establisher of papal primacy.*

hawks and expensive clothes but to have plain robes and equipment, to make clear that they are travelling in penitence rather than indulging idle vanity.

CRUSADE SERMONS

A Church campaign to preach the new crusade was put in train. In the British Isles, the Archbishop of Canterbury, Baldwin of Exeter, made a tour of Wales in 1188 to preach the cross. Baldwin's journey was described by the colourful Norman–Welsh churchman and chronicler Giraldus Cambrensis, or 'Gerald of Wales', in his *Itinerarium Cambriae*, written in 1191.

According to Giraldus Cambrensis Baldwin convinced 3,000 men-at-arms to take the cross. The sermons were delivered in Latin and French, sometimes with a Welsh interpreter, but even when the crowd could not have understood the words, knights and men-at-arms still rushed forward to take the cross. According to Gerald, a miracle occurred that showed God's blessing on the enterprise and the holiness of Archbishop Baldwin – in the area near Haverfordwest,

an old lady who had been blind for many years was cured when she rubbed her face with earth upon which the archbishop had stood when giving the sermon.

SALADIN TRIUMPHANT

In Outremer in July 1187, in the immediate aftermath of Saladin's victory at the Battle of the Horns of Hattin, the Muslim general's armies marched virtually unchallenged and imposed his will where they went. City after city passed out of crusader control. But the important port of Tyre was saved at the last moment following quick thinking by the charismatic European lord Conrad of Montferrat.

Conrad had sailed from Italy for Jerusalem in 1185 in order to join his father, William V of Montferrat, but he had been waylaid in Constantinople, where he had married Princess Theodora, sister of Byzantine emperor Isaac II Angelus. In July 1187 Conrad set out for the Kingdom of Jerusalem, probably fearing reprisals after he killed a rebel general named Alexios Branas when putting down a rebellion on behalf of Isaac. He set sail on board a Genoese merchant ship.

When Conrad arrived by sea at Acre on 14 July he found the place eerily quiet and cautiously dropped anchor offshore; then he and his companions saw Saladin's standards above the walls – the town had just fallen to the Muslim general. When messengers from the port approached by ship, Conrad pretended to be a merchant ally of Saladin; he promised to bring his goods ashore the next morning. But in the night he lifted anchor and inched away, setting sail for Tyre.

TYRE SAVED FROM SALADIN

There are differing versions of precisely what happened next. According to the 13th-century Old French *Continuation of the Chronicle of William of Tyre*, Conrad arrived in Tyre just as the port, which was

▲ *At Tyre, Saladin and his apparently invincible army were defeated for the first time since the Battle of the Horns of Hattin.*

in the hands of crusader lord Reginald of Sidon, was preparing to mark its surrender to Saladin by raising his banners. But Conrad – resolute, determined and charismatic – threw the banners into the city ditch and convinced the people to transfer their allegiance to him; when they did so he led them to a last-gasp defence.

The truth may have been more prosaic. Other accounts suggest that Conrad arrived in advance of Saladin's army while Reginald was absent seeking to fortify his castle of Belfort; Conrad strengthened the town's defences and inspired its merchant community and other residents to put up a stout defence. Whatever truly happened, Saladin's attempt to take the city of Tyre was repulsed and he moved on to take Caesarea, Arsuf and Jaffa.

In November Conrad repulsed another, larger-scale attack on Tyre by Saladin, who

▼ *The victory at Tyre, snatched as it was from seemingly inevitable defeat, was the kind of triumph against all odds that had occurred on the First Crusade and inspired later generations to try to emulate it.*

had blockaded the city by land with his troops and by sea using an Egyptian fleet. Saladin paraded Conrad's aged father, William, who had been captured at the Battle of the Horns of Hattin, before the walls of Tyre and threatened to kill him if Conrad did not surrender; but Conrad was unmoved, declaring that his father had already lived a long life, and even – it is said – aimed a crossbow at the old man. His bluff worked, Saladin backed down and later released William. Again Conrad drove him off, leading an assault on the Egyptian fleet, and then a brave charge out of the city gates that surprised the besiegers and forced them to retreat.

The saving of Tyre was a turning point for the crusaders. This strategically placed port was to be a vital point of access for Western ships bringing supplies and troops in order to make the Third Crusade possible. Saladin's decision not to press home his advantage by taking Tyre was one of the very few strategic mistakes he made in a long and glorious career.

KINGS OF EUROPE TAKE THE CROSS

HENRY II, PHILIP II AND FREDERICK I JOIN THE CRUSADE

At Gisors, north-west of Paris, in January 1188 a crusading sermon by Archbishop Joscius of Tyre convinced two kings, Philip II of France and Henry II of England, to take the cross. According to the account given by the English chronicler Roger of Howden in his *Chronica* (*c.*1191), the sermon was accompanied by a miracle, when the Cross of Christ appeared in the sky above the kings.

Joscius had been sent to the west by Conrad of Montferrat after Conrad had repulsed Saladin's initial assault on Tyre. Joscius sailed in a ship with black sails to spread the news of Saladin's victories and call for urgent help and, according to Arabic accounts, carried with him pictures designed to outrage the Christians in Europe – for example, one of Saladin's army horses urinating in stables he had supposedly set up within the Church of the Holy Sepulchre, and another of a 'Saracen' hitting Christ in the face.

Roger added that the kings, who had been at war, were inspired by Joscius to put aside their enmity and agreed to

▼ *Frederick Barbarossa and his crusaders are called on to liberate the Holy Land, and begin their journey.*

pursue a common goal in the Holy Land – as Roger commented: 'those who were once enemies were persuaded to become friends on that day, through his preaching and the help of God'. At their meeting the kings also agreed on distinctive crosses to be worn by their armies to help tell them apart on campaign: the English army would wear a white cross, while the French would wear a red one. The troops of Philip, Count of Flanders, who also took the cross on this day, would wear a green cross.

DECISIONS AT LE MANS

In a meeting at Le Mans in February, Henry and Philip discussed ways to finance the crusade and decided on a tax of 10 per cent on income and property for an entire year to be applied to both Church and laity. This tax became known as the 'Saladin tithe' because it was imposed to raise money for a campaign against the Muslim general. It was administered by the Church rather than by lay authorities; clerics and knights who took the cross were exempt from the tax, but those who refused either to go on crusade or to pay the tax were excommunicated. The tax was extremely unpopular, and sparked fears that it was not a one-off but the beginning of a permanent taxation of the people; Philip II was faced with such opposition that he had to issue a proclamation in summer 1189 to the effect that the tax was an extraordinary measure and would not be perpetuated.

The kings also agreed on a sober code of conduct for the crusading armies. In order to generate a penitent and suitably sombre mood, furs and other fine clothes, games of dice and swearing were all outlawed; in addition, no knight or yeoman was permitted to bring a woman with him – 'save possibly a washerwoman on foot, to be beyond suspicion'. Anyone who died on crusade would be required to give up

▲ *Clockwise from top left: King Henry II, 1133–89, Richard I, 1157–99, John, 1167–1216, Henry III, 1207–72, from Matthew Paris',* Historia Anglorum, *1250.*

the money he carried with him: it would be divided to meet immediate needs, such as maintaining his bondmen, helping the land of Jerusalem or feeding the poor.

FREDERICK TAKES THE CROSS

At Pentecost – the church festival celebrating the descent of the Holy Spirit on early Christians – in 1188, Emperor Frederick I of Germany took the cross at a special 'Court of Jesus Christ' convened in Mainz. By now in his mid-sixties, Frederick was a veteran of the Second Crusade on which he had travelled, as Duke of Swabia, in the company of his uncle, Emperor Conrad III. He had called the court the previous December, when, according to contemporary reports, he was visibly moved by a sermon at Strassburg (modern Strasbourg, now in France) that

▲ A stained-glass window in St Stephen's Cathedral, Vienna, represents Holy Roman Emperor Frederick I taking the cross.

cast Christ in the role of a feudal lord wronged by his enemies and left unsupported by his liegemen.

On that day of Pentecost, around 13,000 princes, bishops, dukes, margraves, counts, nobles as well as many lesser knights took the cross alongside Frederick and his son Frederick, Duke of Swabia. According to the author of the anonymous *Historia de Expeditione Frederici* (Narrative of Frederick's Expedition), many men were in tears as they listened to a reading of Pope Gregory's encyclical, and a sermon from Bishop Godfrey of Würzburg. Frederick put himself forward as leader and standard-bearer for the crusade. No warlike man in Germany ignored the call, said the chronicler, and those who took the cross: 'burned with a great passion for fighting. For them, life was in Christ and death was a prize to be gained.' They set the departure for St George's Day (23 April) 1189.

WAR OF WORDS

Frederick traced his descent from Charlemagne himself and in 1165 had brought about the elevation to sainthood of that great leader, the creator of a Christian empire. Frederick had also, since 1157, used the term *Sacrum Imperium* (Holy Empire) to describe his own territories; and he believed it was the necessary and rightful task of a leader of a Christian empire to come to the aid of the faithful in the East against their 'infidel' opponents. He had even in 1165 considered launching a crusade on his own initiative.

Now, according to the crusade history called the *Itinerarium Regis Ricardi* (The Voyage of King Richard), he sent a proud missive to Saladin, demanding his retreat from the Holy Land and threatening a 'trial by battle' on 1 November 1189, 'by the merit of the life-giving Cross of Christ'. He claimed that Saladin would be shocked by the ferocity and strength of the warriors of the German empire: the untamed warriors of the Rhine, young soldiers from the Danube who would never flee, the towering Bavarians and canny Swabians, Saxons expert with the sword, circumspect Franconians, Bohemians unafraid of death, men from Bologna wilder even than their own beasts. And he said that he himself could still enforce his imperial will with a sword, for his arm was not wearied by age.

The *Itinerarium* also gave details of Saladin's equally proud response, in which he boasted that only three cities – those of Tyre, Tripoli and Antioch – remained in Christian hands in all the lands of Outremer and that 'these will inevitably be captured'. He also said that he was quite happy to undergo a trial by battle but that peace was a possible outcome if the three cities were handed over; in which case, he would allow Christian pilgrims to come and go freely.

▼ Passions run high at Mainz on Pentecost 1188 when Frederick I accepted the call to take up the cross once more, together with many great men of the empire.

BARBAROSSA'S CRUSADE

THE CAMPAIGN LED BY FREDERICK I OF GERMANY

The German army under Frederick I was the first crusading force to depart, leaving on 11 May 1189. Contemporary reports claim that his army was 100,000 or even 150,000 in number – easily the largest ever to set off on crusade – and took three days to march past an observer.

DISCIPLINE AND BELIEF

Frederick, now 67, must have had a good amount of grey in the red beard that gave him his nickname 'Barbarossa', but he still cut an imposing figure at the head of his vast force. He attempted to maintain strict discipline, reportedly turning away a group of 500 small-time criminals at Vienna and accepting into the army only those who could prove their capacity to support themselves. He had absolute confidence in his ability to regain Jerusalem and the Holy Land for Christianity: in common with the soldiers of the First Crusade, he believed that the Last Days

▲ Frederick and his vast army survived a long overland journey, with many difficulties, and then boarded ships in Constantinople to sail across the Hellespont to Anatolia.

▼ An idealized portrait from the 19th century of Frederick I Barbarossa, Holy Roman Emperor.

as described in the Bible were upon humankind, and that when the emperor laid his sceptre down in Jerusalem the final act would begin with a reign by the Anti-Christ prior to the triumphant Second Coming of Jesus.

BY LAND ACROSS EUROPE

The German army departed from Ratisbon (modern Regensburg, in Bavaria, Germany) and followed the overland route to Constantinople taken by the soldiers of the First Crusade almost a hundred years earlier. Frederick led the way through Hungary and Serbia into Byzantine territory. Frederick had planned ahead, and conducted prolonged negotiations with Byzantine emperor Isaac II Angelus to ensure the crusader army's safe passage across Byzantine territory, but they did not receive the warm welcome they expected. Isaac was in negotiations with Saladin, who wanted Constantinople's troops to

impede the progress of the crusader army in return for support against the Seljuk Turks in Anatolia and his help in ensuring that the church in Palestine would be under Orthodox Christian control. The Byzantine emperor was also suspicious of Frederick's motives – and reports reached him that parts of the army wanted to conquer his empire for Latin Christianity.

CONFLICT WITH BYZANTIUM

In October there were several open clashes between German and Byzantine troops in the Balkans. Frederick reported in a letter to his son Henry (the future Emperor Henry VI) that the crusader army had endured 'plundering' and 'massacre', and

At this point the crusade seemed well-starred. The army had survived a difficult passage from Europe, had won a great victory and appeared to be on the threshold of great deeds in the Holy Land. But in a twist of fate on 10 June, Frederick died when he fell from his horse while crossing the River Saleph (now called the Göksu) and drowned in its icy though shallow waters. In that moment, all the energy and conviction went out of the German wave of the crusade.

Saladin and the other Muslim leaders declared that Frederick's death was the work of Allah, who had acted to deliver them from a great impending threat; to the Christians it appeared that God was not supporting their march on Jerusalem. Many Germans gave up and returned to Europe; some were reportedly so shocked that they renounced Christianity entirely.

Barbarossa's son Frederick of Swabia took control of the army and marched on to join the crusader siege of Acre, where they arrived in October 1190.

▼ *Frederick drowns in the icy River Saleph – like many crusaders before and after, he died in humiliating circumstances far from home, without having achieved the crusading mission he saw as his destiny.*

▲ *After setting out from Germany in a spirit of religious devotion, Frederick had a rude awakening when he encountered what seemed to be attempts by the Byzantine emperor to undermine the crusade.*

that attacks had been 'obviously instigated by none other than the emperor'. They were, he wrote, attacked by bandits, had their way blocked with great rocks and felled trees and even found castles fortified against them. Nevertheless, they progressed and spent the winter of 1189–90 in Philippopolis (modern Plovdiv, Bulgaria).

In the letter Frederick indicated that Isaac 'with little concern for his reputation' had also imprisoned German ambassadors in Constantinople and seized 'upwards of two thousand marks' of their money – and that relations had deteriorated to the extent that Frederick was planning to attack Constantinople. He asked Henry

to gather a fresh force of knights to embark by sea to help in the battle. He instructed him to send more money to Tyre, where he would collect it – and he also asked to be remembered in Henry's prayers and those of the people at home.

In the event, full-scale war between Germans and Byzantines was averted, the German army bypassed Constantinople, and crossed the Hellespont into Anatolia – on board transport ships provided by Isaac – on 28 March 1190. They marched across Anatolia and won a great victory over the Seljuks, capturing the capital of the Sultanate of Rum at Iconium (modern Konya in Turkey) on 17 May. They stayed in the city for almost a week, restocking the army with horses and supplies, before moving on towards Armenian-held Cilicia. They also captured the town of Laranda (modern Karaman) around 60 miles (100km) farther south and just to the north of the Taurus Mountains.

IN SICILY AND CYPRUS
RICHARD I AND PHILIP II STOP EN ROUTE TO THE HOLY LAND

The kings of France and England did not follow the German army to the Holy Land until July 1190. Although in their meeting at Gisors in January 1188 Henry II and Philip II had agreed to put disagreements to one side in the interests of Jerusalem, feuding had resurfaced.

In particular Henry II's eldest surviving son, Richard of Poitou, had allied with Philip II and invaded Henry's territory in Anjou. Henry was defeated, and was broken by this, the latest of a series of rebellions involving his sons, and he died at Chinon on 6 July 1189. He was succeeded by the Count of Poitou, who became King Richard I of England. Richard set about raising money for the crusade: he cancelled the Treaty of Falaise

▼ *On 24 June 1190, Philip II receives the royal standard in the abbey church of St Denis prior to embarking on the crusade.*

of 1174, thus freeing the Scots from their acknowledgment of English overlordship, and in return received a payment of 10,000 marks from King William of Scots.

FROM FRANCE TO SICILY

Richard and Philip II embarked together from southern France, bound initially for Sicily, where, following the death of William II of Sicily, his successor Tancred, Count of Lecce, had imprisoned William's widow, Joan of England (Richard's sister), seized her dowry and stolen a legacy intended for Richard himself.

Arriving in Sicily in September 1190, the crusader armies came into conflict with the locals; but they were given an outlet for their energies when on 4 October Richard captured and sacked the capital city of Messina. The *Itinerarium Regis Ricardi* reported that the attack was so swift and easy that it took less time than

▲ *Leaving on crusade, Richard appointed William of Mandeville, Earl of Essex, and Bishop Hugh of Durham as his regents. But William died and his position was taken by the chancellor, William Longchamp.*

a priest needs to sing the Mass; Richard spared the citizens, but his army seized vast quantities of loot. Tancred backed down, freed Joan and returned the moneys he had taken.

But Philip and Richard quarrelled fiercely about who should take most credit for the victory, with Philip enraged that Richard flew his standard above the walls rather then Philip's banner. In the end, on 8 October they made up and swore an oath to defend one another and each other's armies on the campaign ahead. Nevertheless, the differences between the two kings would dog the entire crusade.

The armies of France and England then spent the winter on the island, while their leaders continued to squabble – principally now over a marriage, for Richard had pledged to wed Philip's sister Alys, but then proposed to renege on that promise in order to marry Princess Berengaria, the daughter of the king of Navarre. According to the *Chronica* of Roger of Howden, Richard took time in Sicily to listen to the prophecies of Joachim, Abbot of the Cistercian monastery at Corazzo, who had visions of St John the Evangelist, and declared to Richard: 'the Lord is to grant you a great victory over his enemies, and will raise your name above that of any other prince on the Earth'.

THE KINGS PART COMPANY

Finally the two kings went their separate ways. Philip left Sicily on 30 March 1191, and landed at Tyre in the middle of May. He moved on towards Acre, and joined the crusader siege of that city on 20 April. Richard made another diversion, for several of his ships – including the one carrying his intended wife Berengaria and his sister – had been caught in a storm and put in to Cyprus. There, the Cypriot ruler, Isaac Dukas Comnenus, had seized a large load of treasure that Richard was carrying and had imprisoned many of Richard's men.

Isaac Comnenus had come to power by treachery and trickery and ruled as a tyrant, so when Richard landed and

▼ *Philip and Richard swore a vow like that of chivalric brothers in arms after their quarrel in Sicily. They promised to protect one another throughout the crusade. But they would soon be at loggerheads again.*

ANTI-SEMITIC RIOTS IN ENGLAND

The Third Crusade was no different to its two predecessors in that the preaching of the cross sparked widespread anti-Jewish rioting. The violence afflicted England particularly, where Richard's coronation was marred by a major anti-Semitic riot in London, sparked when onlookers saw wealthy Jews apparently gaining access to the celebration. The following year violence against the Jews swept the country. The

▲ *Members of the London mob run riot in a Jew's house during Richard I's reign. Crusading rhetoric drove violence at home as well as in the disputed territories of Outremer.*

worst outbreak was in York, where on 16 March around 150 Jews committed suicide by setting fire to the tower in which they had taken refuge rather than face the mob in the streets below.

attacked Limassol the people welcomed him as a bringer of freedom. Isaac agreed to return the treasure and pledged to add 500 troops to the crusading army.

Once he had ensconced himself within his castle of Famagusta, however, Isaac attempted to take a hard line, ordering Richard's departure from the island. At this point, a ship arrived from the crusader camp at Acre, seeking news of Richard; on board were leading members of the Knights Templar, to whom Isaac owed a large amount of money. With their backing and encouragement, Richard led the conquest of the island, which was thereafter to be an important ally of the

crusader states in Palestine. The campaign took 15 days and, according to the *Itinerarium Regis Ricardi,* Richard found extraordinary stores of wealth that had been hoarded by the miserly Isaac – treasure was piled high in the castles of the island: the king and his knights found golden cups, silver jars, gilded saddles, precious spurs, silken cloth and fine scarlet robes, and they took them all, thinking it a gift of God to help finance the crusade.

Also during his stay on Cyprus, on 12 May, Richard married Berengaria at the port of Limassol and made her his queen. Richard finally left Cyprus and arrived at Acre on 8 June 1191.

VICTORIES
AND DEFEAT

On 7 September 1191, during the Third Crusade, King Richard I of England won a stunning victory over the great Saracen general Saladin at the Battle of Arsuf. Richard's battle tactics, which demanded total discipline from his knights in holding back from attacking under enormous provocation, were almost spoiled by a hasty charge led by the Knights Hospitaller, but ultimately were triumphantly vindicated as the Christians swept the Saracens off the battlefield in three unstoppable mounted advances.

The Third Crusade is forever associated with Richard I and his encounters with Saladin. The capture of Acre and the Battle of Arsuf were two of the victories Richard won over Saladin – and they had other memorable diplomatic encounters. In the chivalric literature of chansons and of chronicles, the clash of these great generals shines as an example of chivalry at its finest. Although the reality of this campaign was often starvation, disease and deprivation, there were moments of enduring heroic legend, such as the Hospitaller's charge at Arsuf, and Richard's arrival at Jaffa. Defeating Saladin at the Battle of Arsuf did not lead to Jerusalem, Richard was forced to accept that the Holy City was beyond his reach, but showing admirable kingly qualities he and Saladin managed to reach a peaceful agreement to end hostilities.

▲ *Richard the Lionheart leads a force of Knights Templar and Hospitaller from Acre to Jaffa.*

◀ *A German army, sent by Henry, Duke of Brabant, landed at Acre in September 1197 and briefly occupied Beirut and Sidon.*

A SICK WINTER
CRUSADERS SUFFER DURING THE LONG SIEGE OF ACRE

While King Richard and King Philip were occupied on Sicily in the winter of 1190–91, the crusader forces in the Holy Land were enduring terrible suffering as they doggedly besieged the port of Acre, while they were themselves besieged by the army of Saladin.

THE START OF THE SIEGE

The siege had begun in the summer of 1189. Saladin had imprisoned Guy of Lusignan, former king of Jerusalem, in Damascus, but in 1188 released him on condition that Guy promise to take himself overseas and never again make war against Islam. However, having sworn this oath, Guy disregarded it at once, and set about trying to rebuild his power base. He marched to Tyre, where he attempted to take control of the city but was refused by Conrad of Montferrat, who had saved the city from Saladin and saw the opportunity to establish his own territory. Then Guy, with the help of fleets from Pisa and Sicily, moved on to Acre and began a siege. A fleet of 50 ships arrived, bearing powerful Danish and Frisian warriors to bolster his army. Louis of Thuringia managed to prevail on Conrad of Montferrat to take part in the siege, and bring men from Tyre to further boost the Christian army.

▲ *Crusaders mixed with Saracens outside the walls of Acre and, by holding jousting bouts, tested in sport the fighting skills they would soon use in earnest.*

SALADIN'S ASSAULT

Saladin had considered attacking while Guy was marching south from Tyre, but he held off until the Christian army was encamped before Acre. He arrived at Acre just a few days after the crusaders at the end of August and settled in behind them. There was only desultory fighting between the two armies in September, and an atmosphere akin to that of a European tournament developed. There was even a staged contest between two boys from the Christian army and two from the city garrison; one of the Christian youths was defeated and had to be ransomed by a crusader lord for two dinars.

Battle was joined by Christians and Saracens on 4 October. After an initial success in which the Christians drove back the centre and right wing of Saladin's army, the crusaders threw away their advantage and began looting the Muslim camp; they

▼ *Men and supplies arrived at Acre to strengthen the hand of the besieging army.*

▲ *Hunger was a recurring problem for the crusaders. According to tradition, parts of the German army on the Third Crusade lost hope and flung themselves down in the shape of the cross to await starvation.*

were then themselves forced back by a combined assault from Saladin's besiegers and the garrison of the city, who had broken out to attack. The battle was ultimately indecisive, but was certainly costly. The crusaders lost as many as 7,000 men with many Knights Templar, including their Grand Master, Gerard of Ridefort, killed. Conrad of Montferrat was isolated and had to be saved by Guy of Lusignan.

THE CRUSADERS STARVE
The siege dragged on and on. Trapped between the city walls and Saladin's army, unable to break out and forage in the countryside, the Christian army became desperately short of food. According to the *Itinerarium Regis Ricardi*, the soldiers fought over bread, and those who could afford it would pay 12 shillings for a fowl or a 100 gold pieces for a measure of wheat. They grew so desperate that they killed the finest horses for food.

A SUCCESSION DISPUTE
There were repeated outbreaks of fever and dysentery. During a stalemate in fighting in the summer of 1190, probably on 25 July, Queen Sibylla of Jerusalem died in the camp, and this sparked a succession dispute over the throne of Jerusalem.

Sibylla was the eldest daughter of King Amalric I (by Agnes of Courtenay) and was the wife of Guy of Lusignan, who had held power in the kingdom as her consort; on her death, the crown rightly passed to her half-sister, Isabella, Amalric's daughter with his second wife, Maria Comnena. But Guy refused to concede the crown and demanded to be recognized as king. Conrad of Montferrat launched an attempt to take control by marrying Isabella. At Acre, rumours circulated that Conrad was supplying food only to those in the camp who were his allies and accomplices, and that those who backed Guy of Lusignan's claim were left to starve.

In October 1190 spirits in the crusader camp were raised when the remnant of the German crusade arrived under the command of Duke Frederick of Swabia. These men were bedraggled and severely reduced in numbers, but their arrival was taken as a sign that the European armies were on their way. A little while afterwards, an English contingent arrived under the command of Baldwin, Archbishop of Canterbury. The crusaders launched a fresh assault on the city, and knocked down part of the walls with a pair of battering rams, but the garrison held firm and the attackers made no further progress.

HARD WINTER MONTHS
The winter was very hard on the Christian army. Wells and other water sources became contaminated and disease was rife in the camp. Frederick, Duke of Swabia, Theobald, Count of Blois, Stephen, Count of Sancerre, Archbishop Baldwin of Canterbury and Patriarch Heraclius of Jerusalem all died of sickness. Count Henry II of Jerusalem (the future Henry I of Jerusalem, 1192–97) was very seriously ill for several weeks, but finally recovered.

New hope came with the spring. Duke Leopold V of Austria arrived by sea in March and took control of the army. He brought the news that King Philip II of France and King Richard I of England were on their way.

▼ *A fresh assault following the arrival of Archbishop Baldwin of Canterbury came close to success but Acre's garrison did just enough to drive back the attackers.*

THE CAPTURE OF ACRE

RICHARD I'S ARRIVAL BRINGS LONG SIEGE TO AN END

Philip II arrived at Acre on 20 April 1191 with a Genoese fleet. He was followed on June 8, by Richard I with an English fleet carrying a force of 8,000 men. Within five weeks of Richard's arrival, the city of Acre, which had steadfastly withstood a siege since August 1189, fell to the crusader army.

Richard's reputation had preceded him to Palestine. Saladin knew from his military intelligence that although Philip II was the highest-ranking of the European kings on the crusade, Richard was the leader in terms of battle prowess and charisma, a far more powerful warrior than his rival, driven by a burning desire for warfare. For several weeks before Richard arrived, Saladin and his officers heard boasts from crusader lords in the besieging camp to the effect that when this king of England arrived, the siege of Acre would be swiftly brought to its conclusion. The day of his arrival turned into a

festival. According to the *Itinerarium Regis Ricardi*, trumpets, pipes and drums sounded out 'until the earth shook with the happiness of the Christians'; as darkness fell, people celebrated with carousing and dancing and lit bonfires that burned so brightly that the garrison of Acre thought the land around them was on fire.

SIEGE TIGHTENED

After his arrival in April, Philip II had put in train the construction of several powerful new siege engines, and Richard now personally supervised the erection and use of many more as the crusader army stepped up its attacks on the city. One of his military catapults had sufficient range to hurl great stones far over the walls and into the heart of the city; it reputedly killed 12 men with one shot. Richard fought in the front line: he had his men build a moveable protective shed beneath which the army's foremost crossbowmen

could shelter as they fired; he himself worked a crossbow and killed many of the defenders manning the walls.

The garrison fought back forcefully, using Greek fire to consume the laboriously constructed siege towers and engines, manning the battlements and clearing the ditches, but they were outnumbered and increasingly desperate. On 3 July the crusaders made a substantial breach in the walls. There was intense fighting at close quarters as the crusader army, containing many hastily armed lords, including the Earl of Leicester and the Bishop of Salisbury, tried to enter the city – but the Turks rallied strongly and held them at bay. On 4 July the city's defenders offered their surrender, but Richard was unhappy with the terms: the crusaders were asking for the Kingdom of Jerusalem to be restored to its boundaries prior to the Battle of the Horns of Hattin.

ACRE SURRENDERS

On 7 July the garrison sent a message to Saladin indicating that if he did not come to their aid they would be forced to surrender. Saladin attacked the crusaders once more on 11 July but without driving them off and on 12 July the garrison formally surrendered.

They did so without the agreement of Saladin, who reportedly wept tears of frustration and grief when he heard the news, for he had just received yet more reinforcements and was confident that a final assault might drive the crusaders off and save Acre. The garrison, moreover, had agreed punitive terms on Saladin's behalf, as negotiated by Conrad of Montferrat (or of Tyre, as he was often now known): a vast ransom of 200,000 gold dinars for the lives of the garrison, 3,000 of whom would be held as prisoners; the cherished relic of the True Cross, in Saladin's possession since it had been captured at the Battle of the Horns of Hattin, would be returned, and around 2,000 Christians held prisoner by the Muslim army would be released; the city, all its possessions and the ships in its harbour would be handed over to the crusaders. Despite his anger, Saladin felt honour-bound to accept the terms agreed in his name.

The English army took possession of the city. King Philip II installed himself in the Acre mansion of the Templars, while Richard made himself at home in what had been the royal palace. Almost at once Richard quarrelled openly and fiercely with Duke Leopold of Austria – in a disagreement almost identical to the one that

had followed his capture of Messina. Duke Leopold saw himself as the commander of the German contingent on the crusade, for Frederick Barbarossa had died in Cilicia and his son Frederick, Duke of Swabia, had died during the siege; Leopold, therefore, demanded equal ranking with Philip II and Richard I. He issued an order that his standard should fly alongside that of

▼ Their long months of suffering at an end, the crusaders establish themselves in Acre after the garrison's formal surrender.

▲ Saladin was impressed by the valour of Hubert Walter, Bishop of Salisbury, at Acre and later asked to meet him. On returning from crusade to England, Walter was named Archbishop of Canterbury.

Richard on the city walls; but shortly afterwards the standard was found in the ditch, having been torn down and thrown over the wall. The result was that Leopold and the force at his command abandoned the crusade and set off for home.

KING PHILIP'S DEPARTURE

Philip II also left shortly afterwards. He had been severely ill with dysentery and also needed to settle the succession in Vermandois and Flanders, for the lord of that region, Philip of Alsace, had died in the camp at Acre and left no heirs. Philip left behind in Acre a French army of 10,000 under the command of Duke Hugh III of Burgundy and set sail for Genoa, bound for France. His departure greatly displeased Richard, who declared: 'It is a pity and a shame on my lord to leave this place without having brought to an end the enterprise that brought him here. But if he finds himself in bad health, and in fear perhaps lest he should die here, his will must be done.' His displeasure was no doubt principally caused by the knowledge that his territorial possessions in northern France would be open to interference from Philip while himself was engaged in pursuing the crusade.

ATROCITY AT ACRE?

RICHARD I AND THE MASSACRE OF MUSLIM PRISONERS

On 20 August Richard had 2,700 Muslim prisoners from Acre beheaded on the plain in front of the city, in full view of Saladin's camp. He said that he did it because Saladin was refusing to honour the agreed terms of the surrender.

The prisoners killed included soldiers from the garrison, but also women and children. Many historians have expressed horror at the deed, contrasting it with Saladin's frequent magnanimity in victory. The Muslim army launched an attack in an attempt to stop the killing, but were driven back.

▼ *Kings Philip II and Richard I oversee the surrender of Acre and the taking of the city's garrison and people into captivity.*

It may be that Richard's decision was a justified act of war. It is certainly true that Saladin was dragging out the settlement of the ransom payment. Saladin had made an initial payment of the ransom fee on 11 August but according to the 12–13th-century Muslim historian Baha ad-Din ibn Shaddad, the general had then refused to hand over the next instalment until all the garrison prisoners had been released, and had wanted to provide a new batch of prisoners from his own camp to stand in place of the members of the Acre garrison. His motive was probably to make the settlement of the agreement drag out so long that the campaigning season would end before Richard could succeed in launching an attack on Jerusalem.

A LION IN A HURRY

Richard, on the other hand, was in a hurry. He had seen Philip II set sail for home, and had had time to consider the possible ramifications of the king of France being at large in Europe unchecked by the presence there of the king of England – Richard himself. He wanted to hasten the crusade towards its conclusion, so that he could return to manage his European affairs. He wrote to his justiciar in England from Acre on 6 August describing his victories on campaign, but indicating that he would soon be returning home – 'as soon as we have brought Syria back to its previous position'. He promised to be back in English waters by the following Lent.

▲ Barbarous act or necessary military decision? On Richard's orders, one by one, 2,700 Muslim prisoners are put to death.

He was in any case a decisive man who liked to act swiftly: already on the crusade he had conducted two whirlwind campaigns, one in southern Italy, where he had captured several Byzantine possessions, and one in Cyprus, where he had captured the island in just a fortnight.

He wanted to move on from Acre, and he did not have sufficient manpower to leave an army behind to guard the prisoners. Among the garrison were many crack Turkish soldiers who had fought bravely and with great skill to prolong the siege – he could not allow these men to escape or be released and then rejoin Saladin's army. Some writers have argued that the killing of the prisoners was an act of barbarity, but it can be viewed as a sensible and necessary strategic decision.

ALL THINGS FAIR IN WAR?

Moreover, it would appear from Saladin's later friendly relations with Richard that the Muslim general did not view the killing at Acre as an act of brutality – he did not conceive a contemptuous hatred for Richard as he had done for Reynald of Châtillon. While Saladin was certainly often notable for his clemency in victory, he, too, was capable of acts of great ferocity, such as when he ordered the beheading of the captured Knights Templar and Hospitaller after their defeat at the Battle of the Horns of Hattin. On that occasion, the killing of the knights was made into an amusing spectacle, as the Muslim army jeered and laughed while untrained and unskilled army followers hacked at the knights.

Richard's actions did, however, have consequences that cannot have been good for army morale. The killing of the prisoners naturally brought an end to negotiations. As a result, the 2,000-odd Christian prisoners in the Muslim camp were not released and the sacred relic of the True Cross, captured at the Horns of Hattin and held in Saladin's camp, was not returned to the crusaders. However, the failed attack by the Muslim army left the crusaders in even stronger control of Acre than previously.

FIERCE AND RUTHLESS

Throughout his career, Richard demonstrated ruthlessness and decisiveness and a knack for making correct strategic decisions. In most ways the man known as *Coeur de Lion* was the very type of the chivalric knight – a great leader of men, charismatic, brave, strong, skilful, good-looking, hearty, and not lacking courtly accomplishments as a well-educated lover of poetry and song. But he was not the kind of knight who placed a greater importance on chivalry than on victory.

The massacre at Acre should probably be viewed in this light, seen alongside his treachery towards his father, Henry II of England, or his ruthlessness on European campaigns as another example among many of a clear-eyed desire for victory – a willingness to do whatever is necessary to win. The killing of the prisoners freed the crusader army to move on swiftly from Acre and impressed his ferocity and strength of purpose on his opponents. (Later, Saladin was unable to garrison Ascalon against Richard, for his men were too frightened by reports of Richard's behaviour at Acre to volunteer.) *Coeur de Lion's* heart was not only brave and strong, but also ferocious – and dangerous.

▼ Ruthless in victory, Richard does away with the prisoners. He saw them as a threat that had to be eliminated.

RICHARD'S MARCH TO JAFFA
AND A GREAT VICTORY AT THE BATTLE OF ARSUF

Richard set out from Acre on 22 August with the intention of moving swiftly on to Jerusalem. He led his army southwards along the coast to Jaffa (modern Tel Aviv-Jafo), accompanied at sea by a fleet carrying supplies and water. But Saladin's troops shadowed them all the way and launched wave after wave of skirmishing attacks. In a pitched battle at Arsuf on September 7, the crusaders drove off their persecutors, winning a resounding victory over the Muslim force.

THE MARCH
Richard imposed absolute discipline on his army. He knew that over-enthusiasm and a lack of respect for the harshness of climate and terrain had led to disaster at the Horns of Hattin: for this reason, he decreed that the army would march no more than 4–5 miles (6–8km) per day, moving only in the cooler hours of the morning and making camp each afternoon by a source of water.

On the march Richard insisted that his men kept in a tight formation, with the infantry on the landward side to fend off attacks by the Muslim army and protect the mounted knights riding in the centre of the column. The infantrymen carried large crusader shields and wore heavy armour over thick felt jerkins. According to Muslim historian Baha ed-Din, the arrows of the Turkish archers could make little impression on them: 'I saw,' he wrote, 'warriors with no fewer than ten arrows stuck in their back armour, marching on unperturbed without breaking rank.' Periodically, the infantrymen on the landward side were replaced by fresher men who had been marching on the seaward side, where there were no attacks.

In the centre of the main column was the royal standard, mounted in a wagon and guarded by an elite reserve. In front of this rode the Knights Templar and behind it the Knights Hospitaller. The rear of the army had to cope with repeated attacks, and take care not to fall behind. The Muslim force harried the column, hoping to force the crusaders to break rank, but they failed. King Richard was constantly vigilant, barking out orders, tirelessly riding out to meet attacks with his great sword shining in the harsh sun.

▼ *Richard's troops make their way in searing heat and through bare desert from Acre to Jaffa, his men under strict orders not to respond to attacks by Saladin's army.*

▲ *The crusaders fought fiercely, but it was Richard's ability to make instant tactical decisions that triumphed at Arsuf. When the Hospitallers broke rank it was a potential disaster, but with a swift general charge Richard won the day.*

There was no great crowd of camp-followers as there had been on previous crusades – only this strictly disciplined column. Baha ed-Din described the Muslims' frustration at being unable to break the self-control of the Christians: 'You could not help but admire the patience of these soldiers, who put up with the most extreme difficulties.' Richard would not allow women to accompany the army, save for a corps of washer-women who were responsible for cleaning the soldiers' linen, washing their hair and delousing them.

THE ATTACK AT CAESAREA
The crusader army reached Caesarea on 30 August. A major Muslim attack succeeded briefly in isolating the rear of the crusader column under Hugh III, Duke of Burgundy, but with the help of Richard himself they managed to drive off the attack and reunite the column. As they fought the crusaders called out 'Help us, Holy Sepulchre!'

THE BATTLE OF ARSUF

On 7 September Saladin unleashed a full-scale onslaught on the crusader army at Arsuf. His plan was to draw the Christian knights out into a series of charges, and then attack and overpower them once they were split up into small groups.

The first attack came at nine in the morning, accompanied by a fearful noise of gongs, cymbals and trumpets and by the Muslim soldiers screaming. A second attack concentrated on the Hospitallers in the rear of the army column. Each attack came in waves: first Nubian and Bedouin soldiers unleashed a storm of arrows and javelins, and then moved aside to allow a follow-up onslaught from the Turkish mounted archers who rode swiftly forward before wheeling away in the hope of drawing out a charge. Here and there along the columns were pockets of fierce hand-to-hand fighting.

All this time the crusaders continued to march forwards towards Arsuf. Richard's plan was to hold the line and keep his

▼ *Richard was everywhere at Arsuf, leading his men by personal example and trying to ensure that they kept their discipline.*

knights back for one overwhelming charge. This demanded extraordinary discipline, for the Christians were under extreme pressure and the natural response of many of the knights in the army was to break out and charge.

In mid-afternoon, the vanguard of the Christian army marched into Arsuf just as the Hospitallers in the rear came under very severe attack. The Hospitaller general, Garnier of Nablus, begged Richard for the order to charge but the king commanded him to hold the line. But at this point discipline snapped: the Hospitallers charged, with a great shout of 'St George!' They were followed by the French knights who were just ahead of them in the line.

Richard acted decisively, making the best of what had happened by ordering a Templar-led charge right along the line. Saladin's army was driven back, but regrouped; Richard managed to gather his knights for a second charge and the Muslim force scattered. According to the *Itinerarium Regis Ricardi*, Richard led by example: the author likened Richard's sword to a sickle, harvesting a crop of warriors: he claimed that Richard covered the battlefield with Muslim corpses.

▲ *Saladin's attack was carefully planned at Arsuf. He thought he had Richard trapped, but the crusaders turned the tables on him.*

The crusaders still had to weather one more storm, for Saladin's nephew Taqi al-Din led an attack on the left flank, but Richard managed to regroup his knights for a third charge. This time Saladin's army fled in disarray into the hills. Richard's knights mounted his standard on the hill where Saladin's had flown and looted the abandoned Muslim camp. Since darkness was now falling Richard ordered his men to abandon the chase.

A GREAT BUT NOT DECISIVE VICTORY

The Battle of Arsuf was a major victory. It blew a hole in Saladin's reputation for invincibility and demonstrated Richard's superb generalship and personal bravery. But it was not a victory on the scale of the Horns of Hattin, for it wasn't a decisive blow against Saladin's military strength. The Muslim general prepared to block the route to Jerusalem: Richard's triumph at Arsuf did not leave the way open to the Holy City as Saladin's victory at the Horns of Hattin had done. In the short term, instead of marching on Jerusalem Richard occupied and refortified Jaffa.

AN UNCERTAIN FUTURE
RICHARD'S NEGOTIATIONS WITH SALADIN, AND THE JERUSALEM SUCCESSION

After the immense demands of the siege of Acre, the difficult march down the coast and heroic victory in the bruising Battle of Arsuf, Richard and his army recuperated in Jaffa. Saladin went to Ascalon and broke down the fortification to prevent Richard taking it and using it as a stronghold. In October Richard opened negotiations with Saladin in search of a diplomatic solution to bring the war to an end.

With the year drawing to a close, Richard saw the difficulty of mounting a swift campaign to capture Jerusalem, given Saladin's surviving military strength and the fact that elements of Richard's own army had drifted back to Acre. He also saw that lack of manpower would make it virtually impossible to defend the Holy City even if he succeeded in capturing it, especially because many in his army were crusader-pilgrims and could be expected to return to Europe having entered Jerusalem and worshipped in the Church of the Holy Sepulchre. On 1 October 1191 Richard wrote to the abbot of Clairvaux, describing his successes at Arsuf and reoccupation of Jaffa, and look-

▼ *Richard and Saladin were exemplars of chivalry throughout the medieval period. These tiles representing the adversaries date from the 13th century.*

ing hopefully forward to future conquests. Richard indicated that he and his men were exhausted and that the land of Palestine needed reinforcement, for if they captured more territory they would need men to hold it: he asked the abbot to inspire more European lords and yeomen to travel to the Holy Land.

NEGOTIATIONS AT JAFFA
Meanwhile, Saladin sent his brother al-Adil to Jaffa to carry out the negotiations. Richard was negotiating from a position of relative strength, and initially made a remarkably bold demand: the handover of Jerusalem together with all the territory between the coast and the River Jordan, and the return of the sacred relic of the True Cross, which was still in Saladin's possession following the breakdown of negotiations after the slaughter of prisoners at Acre. Saladin returned a cautious response, noting that Jerusalem was as much a Muslim as a Christian city, that the wider territory in Palestine had been in the possession of the crusaders for only a century or so and that he was willing to hand over the True Cross if he received something of equal value in return.

Then Richard made a shockingly original suggestion to al-Adil. He proposed that al-Adil marry Richard's sister, Joan of England, who, since the death of William

II of Sicily, had been the Dowager Queen of Sicily. Richard would give them possession of Acre and Jaffa and Saladin, should he agree, would give them the remainder of Palestine: then together they would rule the entire country from Jerusalem. Richard would return to England; the war would be over. The only problem he could see, Richard said, was that the pope would not agree: in which case, Richard suggested, one of his nieces could take the place of Joan.

Saladin, remarkably enough, agreed to this proposal – although according to Baha ed-Din, only because he knew it was a practical joke. But Joan of England refused to marry a Muslim; and Richard's suggestion to al-Adil that he convert to Christianity was also rejected. The negotiations ended amicably but without lasting results.

MARCH ON JERUSALEM
Richard then marched to Ascalon and began to rebuild the fortifications that Saladin had dismantled. In the winter, when Saladin had largely disbanded his army, Richard marched the crusader force towards Jerusalem. He got within 12 miles (20km) of the Holy City in January 1192, but in terrible weather that made rivers of the roads he decided not to risk an assault; the waterlogged, mountainous terrain did not play to the strengths of the crusader cavalry and instead favoured the mobile Turkish horsemen and archers. He returned to Ascalon.

Negotiations continued. Richard felt an increasingly urgent need to return to Europe to safeguard his possessions, for he was receiving reports that his brother John was seeking to seize power in England while Philip II was eyeing Normandy. At the end of March a workable compromise seemed to have been reached: the crusaders would retain Acre, Jaffa and Ascalon and would have the relic

◀ Richard's decision to pull back from an assault on Jerusalem in 1191–92 may be a sign of his willingness to compromise.

Isabella's consort from 1192 to 1197, although for unknown reasons he was never crowned.

Rumours soon began to circulate as to who had been behind Conrad's murder, with some claiming that Richard had hired the Assassins to do the deed. But it seems unlikely, given that he did not try to force Guy of Lusignan on the kingdom but accepted the elevation of the kingship to Henry of Champagne. More likely the cause lay in conflict between Genoese merchants who had Conrad's backing and their rivals from Pisa who would have been excluded by a Genoese monopoly had Conrad succeeded, but under Henry won important concessions in Acre.

of the True Cross returned; in addition, they would have the right to visit Jerusalem as pilgrims and maintain priests there. On Palm Sunday, 29 March, Richard knighted al-Adil in a splendid ceremony.

THE JERUSALEM SUCCESSION

In April the long-running succession dispute between Guy of Lusignan (also known as Guy of Jerusalem), the husband of the deceased Queen Sibylla, and Conrad of Tyre (also known as Conrad of Montferrat), husband of Sibylla's younger sister Isabella, was decided in Conrad's favour at a meeting of a council of Jerusalem's leading knights and barons. Richard had backed Guy but Guy received no votes at all in council. Richard subsequently arranged for him to buy the Kingdom of Cyprus. But then, on April 28, before he could be crowned, Conrad was killed in the streets of Tyre by two Assassins (*see* box).

Within a week of Conrad's death Henry II, Count of Champagne, nephew to both Richard I of England and Philip II of France, had married Conrad's wife Isabella and been acclaimed King of Jerusalem. He ruled as king on account of being Queen

THE ASSASSINS

The Assassins who killed Conrad were members of a militant Shi'ite Muslim sect, founded in 1094 in opposition to the new Shi'ite Fatimid caliph in Cairo and in support of his deposed brother Nisar. They believed in terrorist murder as a sacred duty, and were known as *hashshashin* in Arabic, from their reported practice of smoking hashish before embarking on suicide murder missions. The English word 'assassin' comes from *hashshashin*.

The Assassins carried out deadly missions against Sunni and certain Shi'ite Muslims whom they considered religious enemies as well as against crusaders. Their first leader, Hasan-e Sabbah, oversaw the establishment of a string of castle strongholds in Iran and Iraq from which terrorist killers emerged on missions. In the 12th century they captured several fortresses in Syria,

▶ The fortress that became the Assassins' castle at Masyaf in Syria was originally built by the Byzantines.

including the celebrated castle of Masyaf, from which their Syrian chief Rashid ad-Din as-Sinan and his successors sent men out on a series of murder missions. Sinan and his successors were called *shaykh al-jabal* (mountain chieftain in Arabic), which the crusaders rendered into English as the 'Old Man of the Mountain'.

THE TREATY OF JAFFA
LAST BATTLES AND FINAL TREATY OF THE THIRD CRUSADE

In May–June 1192, when Richard and his troops came within striking distance of Jerusalem for the second time in just six months, Richard elected not to launch an assault. Subsequently, back on the coast, he won two astonishing victories over Saladin before agreeing the terms of the Treaty of Jaffa, which brought the crusade to an end.

SECOND APPROACH TO JERUSALEM
In May 1992 Richard marched southwards down the coast from Ascalon and captured the fortress of Darum. Then he marched inland towards Jerusalem and encamped in the hills about 12 miles

▼ *In war and diplomacy Richard and Saladin treated each other with respect, each aware of the other's prowess. Chivalric authors and storytellers ever since have imagined encounters between the two men.*

(20km) from the city. Two events occurred in the hills before Richard ordered a surprising retreat to the coast.

The first was that he attacked a trade caravan heading from Egypt to Jerusalem and seized rich booty, including several hundred camels and horses – according to Saladin's secretary, Imad ed-din al-Isfahani, Richard disguised himself as an Arab in order to reconnoitre the landscape as the caravan approached. On another occasion, while pursuing some Turks in the hills he looked up and saw the Holy City in the distance. This was to be the only time he saw Jerusalem – and because he had made a vow that he would look on the city only as its conqueror, he raised his shield in front of his eyes to block off the view and rode away.

After the attack on the caravan, Saladin expected an assault on Jerusalem and prepared for a siege by poisoning water sources around the city and calling his

military advisers to a council of war. But on 5 July he received reports from his scouts that the crusaders had broken their camp in the hills nearby and were marching away from Jerusalem, back to the coast. Saladin rode out to watch the retreat. Many in the crusader army were puzzled and angered by Richard's decision. It would appear that he again decided that it would be pointless to launch a major assault against a target that he could not hope to hold even if he won it.

THE BATTLES OF JAFFA
Richard retired to Acre, expecting the stand-off to continue, but Saladin launched a heavy attack on Jaffa. Here, for once, the great Muslim general lost control of his men, who ran amok looting and plundering in defiance of Saladin's orders to allow the Christians to leave the city peacefully with their possessions. Some contemporary reports suggest that Saladin urgently communicated with the Christian garrison, encouraging them to take refuge in the citadel while he struggled to impose order on his troops.

Richard meanwhile gathered a small force and sailed along the coast from Acre to Jaffa. Arriving on 31 July he anchored off the city: a priest from the garrison, seeing the royal standard, swam bravely out to the ships to let Richard know that, although the city was in Saracen hands, the garrison was holding out in the citadel and negotiating terms of surrender.

What followed was truly the stuff of chivalric legend. Richard leapt immediately from the boat and swam ashore, loyally followed by his knights. This force of just the king and 54 others succeeded against all odds in driving the Saracen forces back. Richard and his knights camped outside the city, for inside it was in ruins following its earlier sacking and the stench of corpses in the streets made it uninhabitable. At dawn on 5 August

Saladin launched an attack with 7,000 cavalry; Richard and his knights had just 15 horses between them but – supported by around 2,000 Italian crossbowmen – they went resolutely forward to defend the edge of their camp, which was marked by a line of sharpened tent pegs. That day the crusaders won another extraordinary victory, holding the camp and the city against the Saracen attack. Saladin abandoned the campaign and retreated to Jerusalem.

Richard and Saladin were both exhausted, and both fell ill in the days after the extraordinary battles of Jaffa.

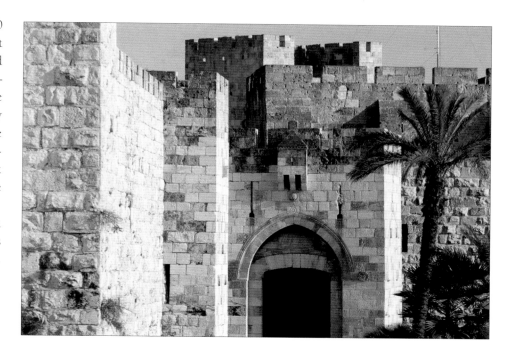

▼ *Richard's heroic assault on Jaffa with just 54 knights really was an occasion when history matched the brave feats of legend.*

▲ *These stones, in the gateway to the Old City at Jaffa, witnessed the clash of armies and the great deeds of kings and knights.*

With typical chivalry, Saladin sent fruit and mountain snow to Richard to speed his recovery.

PEACE AT LAST

Negotiations for a peace settlement were reopened and the two leaders reached agreement and signed the Treaty of Jaffa on 2 September. Under its terms, there would be a three-year truce between the two sides. The Christians agreed to demolish Ascalon and not rebuild it in those three years; they were to keep the coastal lands from Acre down to Jaffa, as well as the Principality of Antioch and the County of Tripoli; they would be allowed access as pilgrims to the churches and shrines of Jerusalem; and Roman priests would be able to celebrate services in the city.

In the weeks following the agreement, hundreds of crusaders made their way to Jerusalem to fulfil their vows. But Richard refused, declaring that he could not enter the city since God had denied him the chance to do so as conqueror. He was in any case very keen to return to Europe to look after his possessions there. He set sail on 9 October.

AFTER THE THIRD CRUSADE

THE AFTERMATH AND LEGACY OF THE 1189–92 CAMPAIGN

The Third Crusade ended in 1192 without the capture of Jerusalem. The crusade did not have a dramatic conclusion, and although it succeeded in preventing the complete destruction of the Latin Kingdom of Jerusalem, there remained in many quarters a sense of unfinished business. Just three years later, in 1195, another crusade was being organized by Pope Celestine III (ruled 1191–98) and German emperor Henry VI.

▼ *Coeur de Lion's martial prowess counts for nothing as he is fatally injured by a crossbow bolt from Chalus-Chabrol castle.*

RICHARD LEAVES PALESTINE

Richard I's homeward journey from the Holy Land was a disaster. Shipwrecked in the Adriatic, he attempted to cross the lands of the Holy Roman Empire in disguise, well aware that he could not expect a hospitable welcome from either Duke Leopold of Austria (with whom he had quarrelled violently at Acre) or German emperor Henry VI (angry that Richard had recognized Tancred as King of Sicily). By rights, these lords should have offered Richard immunity from attack because he was returning from the crusades, but both were keen to punish and to profit by him.

Richard was betrayed to Leopold who passed him on to Henry. Richard languished in prison for months before being ransomed for 150,000 silver marks.

His great opponent, Saladin, died after morning prayers on 4 March 1193 in Damascus, just five months after Richard's departure from Acre. Baha ed-Din ibn Shaddad declared that the Islamic world was filled with a grief so profound that only Allah himself could plumb its depths. Famed for his generosity, Saladin died bankrupt – at his death his treasury contained a gold coin and 47 pieces of silver – not enough to pay for his funeral.

Saladin's death presented an opportunity for the crusaders at an extremely inopportune moment. The great general's army was dispersed, and his power evaporated in family squabbles as one of his sons, al-Afdal Nureddin, marched on Damascus, while a second son, al-Aziz Uthman, was besieged in Cairo by Saladin's brother, al-Adil. Had Richard I waited in the Holy Land just six months longer, he would almost certainly have been able to capitalize on Saladin's death by capturing Jerusalem and re-establishing it as a Christian city. In the event, it took al-Adil ten years to reunite Saladin's territorial possessions.

Richard was never to return to the Holy Land. He spent most of the remainder of his life fighting over his French possessions with Philip II and died in April 1199 aged 41 after being shot in the neck by an archer during a siege of the unimportant castle of Chalus-Chabrol in the Limousin.

THE 'CRUSADE' OF 1195

On 25 July 1195 Pope Celestine III issued a call to arms for a fresh crusade. His letter, as reported by English chronicler Ralph of Diceto, declared that although the most recent crusade had not entirely succeeded in its aims, Christian folk should be strong in faith that God would 'exalt in his miracles' and 'instruct their hands in battle and their fingers in fighting'. As his predecessors had done before him, Celestine promised a plenary indulgence for the crusaders' sins 'and afterwards eternal life'.

German Emperor Henry VI, the son of Frederick I Barbarossa, responded to the call. Between October 1195 and March 1196 a great throng of Germans took the cross; they departed from southern Italy for the Holy Land in spring 1197. The army, sent by Henry, Duke of Brabant, landed at Acre in September 1197 and occupied Beirut and Sidon. But Henry died of malaria in September 1197 in Messina while campaigning in Sicily; and the German crusaders, as their predecessors had in 1189, simply melted away when they heard the news of the emperor's untimely death. The crusade of 1195 ended in a hurried truce.

LEGACY OF THE THIRD CRUSADE

The Third Crusade did not succeed in achieving one of its principal targets, capturing Jerusalem, but in many ways it was a success. At the outset in 1187 Saladin appeared to be invincible and it seemed only a matter of time before the greatest of Muslim generals drove the Latin settlers out of Palestine altogether. Yet Richard I managed to inflict stunning defeats on this towering figure at Acre, Arsuf and Jaffa and in the process re-established the Kingdom of Jerusalem on a relatively secure footing. Moreover, the island of Cyprus, which Richard captured in 1191, proved to be a very valuable conquest,

▼ *Saladin died in Damascus, where he was buried close to the Umayyad Mosque.*

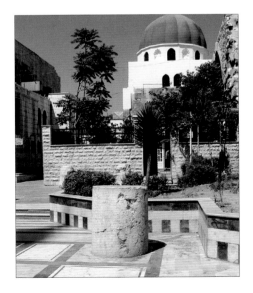

▲ *German crusaders capture Beirut in 1197, but the victory was to be short lived.*

since it provided a vital long-term partner for the Latin states in the Holy Land.

The Third Crusade set the pattern for future crusades to the Holy Land. After the campaign of 1189–92, crusaders no longer made their way to Palestine by way of Constantinople and Anatolia, but by sea directly to the ports of Acre or Tyre. In the first two crusades the European soldiers had chosen violence over diplomacy in every impasse, but after the use by Richard of truces and negotiated settlements with Saladin, relations between the crusaders and the Muslims were transformed. Moreover, just as the crusade had failed to capture Jerusalem, but still achieved certain valuable goals in consolidating the Latin presence in Palestine, so in future crusades the focus shifted away from the earlier narrow focus on liberating Jerusalem to a more general focus on aiding the Christian settlers in the Holy Land.

In 1198 a young, power-hungry pope, Innocent III, began to organize another crusade. The fruit of his labours would be the Fourth Crusade of 1202–04.

THE CATHOLIC EXPANSION

The sense of glorious achievement felt by the Christian world after the success of the First Crusade was never to be repeated. Later crusades in the Holy Land and Europe were more complex and often severely compromised by mixed or deliberately duplicitous motives. The Fourth Crusade spiralled out of control amid political machinations and ended in the sacking and looting of Constantinople. In Europe, the crusading model was applied both to the fight against Muslim power in the Iberian peninsula and to campaigns waged against enemies both religious and political. The religious exaltation felt in 1100 did not accompany these events.

THE FOURTH CRUSADE

The Fourth Crusade was called by Pope Innocent III in August 1198. Its forces, which took some time to gather, departed from Venice in October 1202, bound initially for the former Venetian colony of Zara, which had become part of Hungary in 1186. (Today the city, on the Adriatic coast of Croatia, is called Zadar.) The crusade was vastly in debt to the city of Venice after negotiating an extravagant deal to supply a crusade fleet, and paid off part of the money owed by attacking and capturing Zara; from this point on they lost papal backing, for Zara was under the protection of a Roman Catholic monarch, King Emeric of Hungary, and Pope Innocent III had outlawed attacks on Christian cities. Some crusaders wanted no more to do with the enterprise and sailed directly from Zara to the Holy Land, but the bulk of this now badly flawed expedition became embroiled in the attempt by exiled Byzantine prince Alexius Angelus to oust Emperor Alexius III and claim the throne for himself.

Promised great wealth – nominally to help fund the recapture of Jerusalem – the crusaders left Zara on Easter Monday 1203 and arrived at Constantinople on 24 June that year. They landed on the far side of the Bosphorus but on 5 July crossed in transports and began a siege of the city. They took the Byzantine capital on 17 July, but then were forced to wait in their encampment for several months while the former Prince Alexius (now Emperor Alexius IV) raised the money he had promised them. Before he could do so, Alexius was deposed and a courtier named Alexius Doukas took power as Alexius V. A new siege began. The crusaders captured the city on 13 April 1204 and looted it wildly over three days. They established the Latin Empire of Constantinople; Count Baldwin of Flanders was elected Emperor Baldwin I. The crusade did not move on to the Holy Land.

RECONQUISTA

The *Reconquista* (Reconquest) of the Iberian Peninsula from its Muslim rulers was regularly promoted as a crusade from the 1090s onwards. The war against Islam in what became Spain and Portugal had

▼ *The papacy lost control of the Fourth Crusade, an enterprise in which religious crusading rhetoric was used to mask nakedly political motives. After the capture of the Byzantine imperial city, and the establishment of the Latin Empire of Constantinople, a large part of southern Greece was captured in winter 1204–05.*

The Reconquista in Spain
- Christian-Muslim border 1050
- Christian-Muslim border 1100
- Christian-Muslim border 1157
- Christian-Muslim border 1224
- Christian-Muslim border 1275
- Christian territory in 1275
- Muslim territory in 1275
- Castle
- Battle

▲ *The final war waged by Ferdinand and Isabella was explicitly a Christian crusade, and their army – as well as being equipped with the latest artillery – was reinforced by Christian troops from around Europe.*

actually begun almost 400 years earlier, not long after Arabs and north African Berbers seized most of the Christian kingdom of the Visigoths in AD711–716. Catalonia was recaptured in the late 8th century and became known as the 'Spanish March'. By the late 9th century Christian territory extended right across the north of the Iberian Peninsula; the remainder of what is now Spain and Portugal was ruled by a Muslim caliph from Córdoba.

After the Caliphate of Córdoba collapsed in 1002, the 30 or so independent Muslim kingdoms that succeeded it proved vulnerable to Christian advance: King Alfonso VI of Léon took Toledo in 1085 and looked set to recapture the entire peninsula but was defeated by the Almoravids of north-west Africa in the Battle of Sagrajas in 1086. They made southern Spain and Portugal part of the Almoravid Empire, but this too collapsed after 1140 and was succeeded by the Almohad Caliphate, which held roughly the southern third of the country. The Muslims were pushed farther and farther south by the expansion of Christian Castile, Aragon and Portugal – until by the last quarter of the 13th century the Muslims held only the small Kingdom of Granada in the far south. This territory survived for 200 years until it was finally

conquered by King Ferdinand and Queen Isabella of a united Castile and Aragon in 1482–92. With the capture of the city of Granada on 2 January 1492 the monarchs of the fledgling Spain ended 750 years of reconquest.

CATHAR CRUSADES

The first major battle of the decades-long Albigensian Crusade against the Cathar heretics of southern France was at Béziers on 21 July 1209: around 20,000 were killed. Carcasonne surrendered the next month. A Cathar fightback, supported by Peter II of Aragon, was defeated at Muret near Toulouse in September 1213. After 1216 the Cathars under Raymond VI of Toulouse and his son, Raymond VII, did win back a good deal of territory.

The war ended in 1229 but the fight against heresy continued through the often brutal activities of the Dominican Inquisition. The final Cathar strongholds in the hills and mountains east of Perpignan were captured in 1240–55.

▼ *The Cathars were especially numerous in what is now western Mediterranean France, then part of the Kingdom of Aragon. Although Cathar ideas did not originate in Languedoc, one of the most urbanized and populated areas of Europe at the time, it was there that their theology found its most spectacular success.*

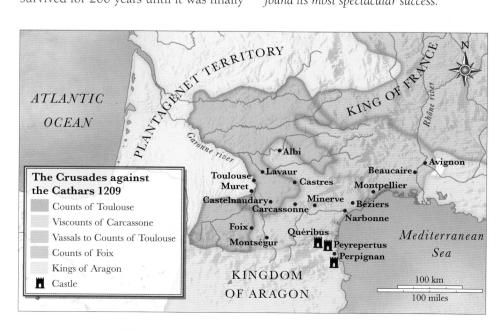

The Crusades against the Cathars 1209
- Counts of Toulouse
- Viscounts of Carcassone
- Vassals to Counts of Toulouse
- Counts of Foix
- Kings of Aragon
- Castle

INDEX

▲ *Tancred (right).*

▼ *A knight at communion.*

▼ *The Crusade of 1101.*

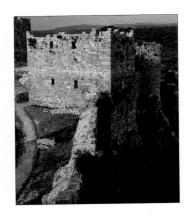

▲ *The keep of Saladin's castle.*

▼ *The siege of Damascus.*

▲ *King Louis VII takes the cross.*